Shaping Knitting

A Designer's Guide to Understanding Stitches

Alison Ellen

Shaping Knitting

A Designer's Guide to Understanding Stitches

Alison Ellen

THE CROWOOD PRESS

First published in 2023 by
The Crowood Press Ltd
Ramsbury, Marlborough
Wiltshire SN8 2HR

enquiries@crowood.com
www.crowood.com

British Library Cataloguing-in-Publication Data
A catalogue record for this book is available from the British Library.

ISBN 978 0 7198 4135 4

Cover design: Maggie Mellett
Photography by Colin Mills (unless stated otherwise)

Typeset by Chennai Publishing Services
Printed and bound in India by Parksons Graphics

CONTENTS

Introduction   6

INTRODUCTION

'Knitting can be solace, inspiration, adventure.'

Elizabeth Zimmerman

Knitting is a wonderful technique for 'building' a fabric or textile with minimal equipment. Not only can you make a piece of cloth, but you can also make a whole garment or item without seams, and you don't need to be tied to a machine or a desk – it's portable. Comparing knitting with other constructive textile techniques such as weaving, it has enormous freedom. In weaving, you are restricted by the need to have warp threads stretched under tension on a loom in order to weave a straight strip of cloth – so, to make clothing, the cloth must be cut. In knitting, any shape can be designed and made with no waste; the fabric and the garment are created in one process, and made to measure.

Looking at some different constructive textile techniques such as lacemaking, tatting, and even other single-thread relations of knitting such as crochet, Tunisian crochet and *nålbinding*, knitting has one unique characteristic: its stretchiness. Formed using two needles and a single thread, the rows of stitches drop from the needle down in columns, one above the other, in a way that enables them to stretch out, particularly sideways, so the finished piece can form itself comfortably around the body.

In many ways crochet and knitting are very similar, and they are indeed closely connected, but looking at crochet from the point of view of a knitter, although it also uses a single thread, it's actually formed from continuous 'casting off' (binding off) stitch; each stitch is locked over its neighbour, which prevents the stitches from stretching out sideways, thus creating a firmer fabric than knitting. Tunisian crochet incorporates rows of both

knitting and crochet, with the crochet again firming it up and restricting stretch.

The reason to look so closely at how knitting works is that if we can understand it and go with its natural strengths, it illustrates the design advantages, and reveals what knitting can achieve. This book will look in detail at what happens to the stitches (or combination of stitches) in each pattern, as the more completely you understand, and the more quickly you can see what is happening in the structure, the better placed you are to make design decisions and see opportunities, or spot an error. If there is a mistake, the sooner you see it and understand where it originated, the better, so you can find an efficient way to go back and correct it – or maybe learn something from it so that a 'mistake' turns into a new design opportunity. When you become familiar with stitches, you can recognize the way an increase or decrease makes a particular mark and how it sets all the stitches off in a different direction; then you can choose the most appropriate increase or decrease for your pattern. The more you experiment, the more you learn, so although there will be more trial, there should be less error.

As this book is mainly concerned with the structure of knitting, it won't go into every aspect of designing and pattern-making as surface decoration or visual impact, but will be looking particularly at how different stitches affect the thickness, drape, length and width of the fabric produced.

There are some characteristics and quirks of knitting that can be seen as downsides and disadvantages, and some restrictions in the action of knitting itself, but can we turn these to our advantage? If we look at the best-known knitted stitch, stocking stitch (or stockinette stitch in the US), this is made by knitting one row plain and one row purl. In other words, pushing all the loops to one side of the fabric, leaving a smooth vertical-faced texture on one side, usually referred to as the right side, and a bumpier, horizontal-textured reverse side where the tops of the loops lie. You get the same result by knitting in the round in knit stitch only: all loops fall to the back. Something happens to this stocking stitch fabric. It behaves in a way that can be very irritating: it wants to roll and curl; the sides curl away towards the purl side, and the top and bottom edges do the opposite, rolling forwards towards the knit side, and we need to examine this tendency. It poses the question 'Why?' and 'How do we make it lie flat?'. The next chapter looks more closely at this, but perhaps this curling tendency shouldn't be a problem but rather something to work with – an advantage of the technique itself for the designer to examine and use in a design.

This may sound simplistic, but why not make things as simple as possible? This is the approach we'll be taking in this book: knitting by hand is a slow process, so any tricks or short cuts to simplify the process are welcome. On the other hand, there is no denying the freedom of knitting, which also gives the opportunity to be as complicated, ornate and intricate as you want. It can not only create its own designs, but imitate other techniques as well. Knitting can play with and reproduce coloured patterns in the same way as embroidery, weaving or many other techniques. Anything is possible. Thinking of each stitch as a dot, patterns and pictures can be built with great freedom, as can be seen in knitting patterns and designs through the twentieth century and before: not just geometric patterns, but any picture can be translated into knitting. However, this book is more concerned with understanding how the structure of knitting works best and letting it guide our designs, rather than imposing designs on the fabric which could be made equally well in a variety of ways. So, even though a picture can be produced or copied in textiles in weaving, embroidery or knitting, what can knitting do that other techniques can't? And why not find the easiest or most logical way to carry out an idea for a design? For instance, if you want a pattern with vertical stripes in different colours, of course you can knit this. You could knit in a Fair Isle technique using two colours in a row, one for each stripe, carrying or weaving the unknitted colour behind. You could use the intarsia method, with a separate yarn for each stripe, each travelling within its own area. But isn't the simplest way of making stripes to knit them across the row, change colour every few rows and make them horizontal? So

how about knitting the design in this logical way, rather than trying to produce a vertical stripe: when you turn it on its side, the stripes fall vertically when finished. Again, this might be a bit unsophisticated and may not fit your requirements of drape and thickness: knitting does hang differently when used sideways, but it's worth considering and searching for the easiest and most suitable option. Other changes to the fabric occur with different techniques in colour knitting and these need to be considered: we're not just looking at surface decoration. Some methods will give a warmer, thicker, less stretchy result, so there are several factors involved as well as the visual impact of stripes or pattern running horizontally or vertically.

Another character of the knitted stitch is the grid formation of the structure; if you think of representing each stitch on a chart, there are then obvious limitations in creating curves in a coloured design, in the same way as curves might be difficult to represent in cross stitch embroidery or weaving. Again, there are ways of working round this by looking at how you can adapt the stitches to fit your ideas, such as using knitted stitches that curve and flow naturally, and incorporating these to produce a more elegant, smoother design with the curves created by the stitches. When you understand what the knitting is inclined to do and how the stitches naturally lie, you can use their 'abilities' to design for, or with you.

Most of the samples or ideas illustrated are concerned with how the stitches affect the knitted fabric, so the edges are not masked for the photographs but shown with all their idiosyncrasies, and often pieces are worked with borders of plain stocking stitch or garter stitch knitting to compare the width and length. Without a 'live' piece of knitting to handle, the thickness and weight and amount the stitch pulls up or inwards must be imagined, so the photographs and text aim to describe this as much as possible. They are mostly knitted in strong 4-ply-weight wool[1], and unless the text discusses the yarn, any good-quality wool will behave like the illustration, as the main influence here is the stitch itself, not the yarn. However, some stitches relying on a lively yarn will be affected by yarns of different character: flatter, softer or more 'drapey' yarns will behave differently, producing texture but not so much stretch, and this will be described in the text.

This book begins with a chapter looking at different ways of constructing a sweater or garment, using the different directions to influence the design, and following chapters will explore different types of stitches and ways of using them to shape the fabric or garment. Hopefully, you will be inspired to explore, experiment and discover new and wonderful ways of using this versatile technique.

CHAPTER 1

CONSTRUCTION AND DIRECTION

'All things are possible in knitting. Women knit almost by instinct, men now for pleasure,
though not so long past it provided him with a means of livelihood.'

Mary Thomas's Knitting Book (Hodder & Stoughton, 1938)

Knitting from bottom up

The only equipment you need in order to knit is a pair of hands and knitting needles. This gives great flexibility and freedom for the knitter, who can move around while knitting, and allows freedom in the designing and the knitted fabric. Without being dictated to or limited by a machine, a hand-knitted item can be created in any direction, and although the fabric grows from the bottom up, the starting point could be anywhere on a garment by knitting in different directions. Although we are used to beginning at what becomes the bottom edge, it's worth looking at the pros and cons of this conventional method and whether there are advantages in using any other starting point, including whether to knit in the round or in separate pieces. Having designed and knitted garments in one piece all my life, I would need a strong argument to persuade me to choose to knit pieces separately. Why would you want seams to sew when you can knit something that doesn't need joining? Working in the round is so intuitive and labour saving, and something that is made possible by the natural inclination of yarn. By knitting in different directions (from different starting points), any three-dimensional shape can be knitted, picking up stitches rather than joining top or side edges with a sewing needle, and by invisibly grafting (joining by Kitchener stitch[2]).

All the ideas in this chapter are directed at designing your own knitwear, but if you are planning to follow a knitting pattern designed in separate pieces, you can still adapt many designs for knitting in the round, just by being aware of a few adjustments that might be needed, listed below.

The simplest T-shaped garment

The simplest T-shaped garment knitted as a tube, with shoulders cast off together and sleeves picked up and knitted downwards.

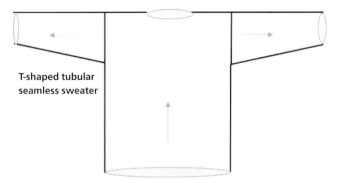

T-shaped tubular
seamless sweater

T-shaped sweater showing the direction of knitting.

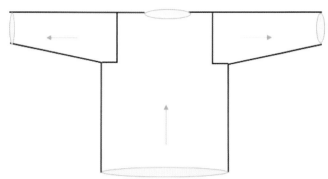

The same construction with set-in sleeves to make a more fitted shoulder seam.

One of the simplest and oldest ways of making a garment is based on the simple T-shape with a tube for the body, and two tubes for the arms. Taking this basic shape (as used in a traditional Guernsey – or gansey) as a model, the body is knitted in the round to the armholes, separated to knit the back and front, travelling back and forth up to the shoulders. These are cast off placing back and front together to join them, and the sleeves picked up round the armhole and knitted downwards, thus closing all the gaps and finishing the garment. Knitting the sleeves from the top down has the practical purpose of making it easy to repair worn-out cuffs as well as doing away with the need for sewn seams. There is another, traditional way of knitting garments in the round to the top, while 'steeking' and cutting the fabric at the end to make the openings, for example, a jacket or cardigan front opening, or sleeve openings. This eliminates the need to purl or work on the wrong side, but it seems somehow counter-intuitive to cut through knitting. Any shape can be knitted with a neat selvedge, enabling a perfectly flat join, whereas cutting necessitates either binding or bonding the edge to make it safe so it can't unravel. There are two things knitting is really good at: first, creating either a flat or a three-dimensional piece of fabric with ready-made finished edges, and secondly, unravelling if the thread is broken. Knitting with selvedges obviously prevents this, and even though traditional steeking also ensures that it won't unravel, it still goes against the grain to cut knitted fabric, which might result in a thick seam instead of a clean edge.

The basic T-shape is not necessarily contoured to the body, but it can be tweaked for more fit by doing a set-in sleeve, raising the sleeve top onto the shoulder rather than the more casual dropped-down sleeve join. The nature of knitted fabric accommodates the fit up to a point, and it can also be shaped with different stitches, as will be explored in later chapters. So, what are the other considerations in knitting in this way?

The downsides of knitting in the round

Style of knitting

Depending how you hold your knitting needles (on top or underneath) and whether you are used to using circular needles, you may find knitting in the round less comfortable, but this is probably to do with unfamiliarity and not a technical problem.

Bulk and weight

Knitting a whole garment can become heavy to handle as it grows larger, and you have the bulk of a garment to keep turning as the knitting progresses. Whether this is too impractical to manage depends on the weight of yarn and size of the garment.

Narrow stripes

As knitting in the round means working in a spiral, there is a danger of a small step in the colour change at the beginning of each round, which is particularly visible in a thick yarn. However, there are ways to overcome this. One option is when you change colour; knit one round then when you get back to the colour change, slip the first stitch in the new colour. Now carry on knitting round, and you will see that the little step or 'hitch' has been smoothed out. There will be one less row in your stripe at this point, but it will be a smoother join. There is more information on this and some neat ideas at Helical knitting tutorials, 'different ways of knitting a spiral with no hitch'.[3]

Uneven textured knitting

If you find you have a different tension with your knit and purl stitches, a stocking-stitch garment would show a difference between an area knitted in the round (where only knit stitch is used), and the area above the armholes knitted back and forth with alternating knit and purl rows, so a difference to the texture would then show up. It should be possible to eliminate this by knitting (or purling) more firmly: the needle should dictate the size of the stitch unless the knitting is loose.

Intarsia

In intarsia knitting, each colour has its own yarn working in a particular area, linking with its neighbouring colour, and producing a colourful pattern or design which has the thickness of a single thread, unlike Fair Isle knitting where yarns are carried along the full length of the row or round. However, knitting round always in the same direction means each yarn is left at the 'wrong' end of its area of colour, so when you get round to the beginning again, you can't reach the yarn you want. Each intarsia area has to be knitted back and forth, but you can still work the whole piece in the round. There are some useful YouTube demonstrations with clever solutions for this problem.[3]

Translating a knitting pattern written for back-and-forth knitting

If you are working from written instructions for knitting back and forth and decide to knit without seams, the most basic point to remember is that any stitch pattern involving knits and purls will have to be rewritten or rethought for knitting in the round, as you are never working on the wrong side, but always from the front. If your pattern is written for separate pieces knitted back and forth, the 'wrong' side rows won't work: the knits and purls have to reverse on alternate rows. The instructions will have been written to be worked

the opposite way on the wrong side. Following a stitch chart would solve this problem, as it illustrates the stitch pattern visually and you can follow each row from either direction, but any shaping instructions would need to be rethought if knitting in the round.

This may sound confusing if you are not used to working in the round, but if you step back and remember every round is a right-side 'row', it makes sense.

The upsides of working in the round

- There is no sewing or joining!
- The satisfaction of casting off the last stitch and holding a complete finished garment.
- It does not have to be a sweater: a long circular needle still works for cardigans and jackets that are knitted back and forth but otherwise all in one piece as for a jumper: no side seams are needed.

Although this is a longer list of downsides to seamless knitting, some of them are surmountable, and the advantages are many, especially if you make your own designs; knitting in the round or at least on a circular needle makes perfect sense.

Simple shapes versus tailored knitting

Having described knitting as being the ultimate flexible way of creating a garment, we need to look at shaping. I can hear one distinct argument against the simple T-shape – what about style and shaping? Back in time, 'simple' shapes meant traditional clothing or basic workwear. Instructions for traditional, simple-shaped garments were probably passed on verbally and by demonstration. Written knitting patterns and books came about when knitted clothing became more popular and the shaping was based very much on pattern cutting for dressmaking. Woven fabric has no stretch, so it is essential for a fitted garment to have shaping around the sleeve and under the arm to allow for movement and give. There is a huge amount of stress on the fabric around these areas, and when fashions dictate close-fitted clothing, this must be allowed for. Historically, working clothes fall into a different category, worn by a different class or section of society. The first knitted clothing was worked in a simple T-shape, but as it began life as undershirts, it was not always visible. Then, once knitted garments became fashionable and achieved the visibility of outerwear, it was expected and presumed it should be in a 'tailored' style, such as a cut-and-sewn garment. Later into the twentieth century, working clothes gradually reached fashion status, and simple shapes returned along with blue jeans, dungarees, artists' smocks, and Guernsey and Aran sweaters. Fashions come and go, and the technique of knitting is so flexible and versatile, that it's perfectly possible to create either simple shapes or to imitate fully fashioned shapes with all the detailing of under-arm shaping made by decreasing, increasing and so on. Where there is perhaps a gap in our thinking, is that most written patterns approach shaping knitting around the edges such as a cut fabric, and there is so much more that can be done by using stitches creatively to shape the fabric *within*, inside the structure, instead of, or as well as, at the edges. So the approach of this book is to look at and rethink the use of simple, basic shapes: an approach led by the technique itself, and its capabilities.

Advantages of the T-shape

The main advantage is simplicity, both in the knitting, and in simplicity of style. It can have a more casual look, related to traditional knitting and to workwear, but simplicity can also be stylish and chic. As we shall see in later chapters, the shape can either be made to fit with use of different stitches, or to be more complicated in structure.

Disadvantages of a T-shaped garment

Sleeve top shaping
You might think the T-shaped garment with sleeves knitted downwards is not really suited to styling a sleeve. What about fully-fashioned sleeves, sleeves with full tops, puffed sleeves, or anything other than a straight-topped sleeve? It is still possible to shape the top of a sleeve, even when picking up stitches at the armhole. One way is to begin with short rows (this could also be a set-in sleeve, as mentioned above). Pick up the stitches all around the armhole, then begin shaping, using 'short row shaping'.

Rather than knitting round all the stitches at once, start with a few at the top of the sleeve and while working back and forth, knit up a few more at the end of every row, until you have joined them in all the way round the armhole. By this time, enough will have been knitted on the top of

the shoulder to angle the sleeve downwards and to give it fullness, rather than it emerging at right angles from the body. You would need to knit samples to work out how many more stitches to knit up each row, as this influences the steepness of the sleeve angle and the fullness at the top. Another approach would be to decrease the sleeve along the top of the arm rather than underneath, so the shaping runs centrally down the top of the sleeve. This could be a decorative part of the design, and again, this slopes the sleeve down at a more natural angle, with less bulk under the arm.

A jacket with an exaggerated set-in sleeve as part of the design.

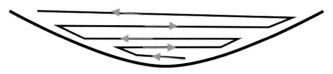

Sleeve top, shaping with short rows

Sleeve top picked up at the armhole and shaped by knitting short rows to give fullness and set the sleeve at a lower angle than the T-shape.

Sloping shoulders
You may not want a completely straight, square shoulder join, but this is easily remedied: work the shoulders in short rows to step them up towards the neck, but leave all the stitches on

Short row shaping for shoulders

Suppose you have 30 stitches on the needle for the shoulder:

Beginning at the armhole edge, work to the neck edge.

Next row: : *work back but leave the last 10 sts on the needle and turn*.

Work back to neck edge, then work twice more from * to * leaving 10 more sts behind each time, and you will have knitted 6 extra rows at the neck edge, creating a sloping shoulder.

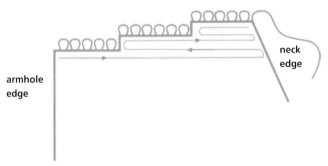

Sloping the shoulder with short rows, with stitches held on needle for joining the back and front by grafting or casting off together.

the needle. These can then be cast off as before, putting front shoulder stitches and back shoulder stitches together and casting off through both. This method leaves a strong 'ridge' on the outside of the knitting, which can be decorative, or it could be made on the inside if you don't like the look of the ridge; or another option would be to invisibly graft (Kitchener stitch[2]) the front and back together.

Designing and sizing

How do you begin to work out a design for a sweater from scratch? There are a few basic common-sense guidelines that are relevant to whatever design or pattern you choose, but the preparation time cannot be avoided. This is where designing your own knitting requires a different mindset from following instructions; it needs more time before beginning the project, but involves the fun bit – experimenting and deciding on your chosen stitch and pattern, as opposed to picking up ready-made instructions, being told needle size and yarn

and getting straight into production. It means spending time playing and exploring and using precious yarn in the process, but it also enables and develops a much greater understanding of how knitting works, and is much more creative and satisfying (and the yarn could be undone and re-used).

It may seem daunting, but if you have already experimented with altering a given design, you are on the way there: anyone can invent their own design, at whatever level of knitting skill, as simple or complicated as you like. There may be a decorative stitch you like and want to use, or you may have been inspired by something you have seen to create a design in certain colours or patterns. When you reach this stage, you are ready to work out the detail of how to begin. The main thing is to experiment: try some stitches, patterns, colours and ideas. This bit is essential, especially to achieve the correct size for the project. Knit a sample in your final selected design/stitch, in the chosen yarn and needle size.

Having done all this, there is a simple calculation to discover how many stitches you will need for your project, based on your measurements. This is discussed in detail at the beginning of Chapter 8, so that whatever yarn you use, you can either adapt a pattern or begin your own from scratch.

Pattern and direction

Although the rows usually travel round a garment, if you are working in a colour pattern, this may make more of a striped effect than you want, and therefore create an unexpected horizontal emphasis. Patterns worked in one colour and using different stitches to make a texture can create an overall effect not necessarily influenced by the direction of the knitting. Without colour changes it's easy to find stitch patterns with either horizontal or vertical emphasis, or diagonal for that matter: for example, ribs and cables break away from the horizontal nature of knitting to make verticals. But if you are working in coloured patterns, especially Fair Isle technique, changing colours immediately draws the eye to horizontal banding, particularly if you change the colours throughout the design. This doesn't happen in a pattern knitted in only two colours if it stays the same all over, but if you have bands of different motifs or shapes, it can emphasize the horizontal, which is something you may not either want or predict until you see the finished item. Sometimes, it's hard to detect banding if you are working closely at your sampling; it only shows up from a distance. You might be knitting something as simple and regular as small squares or blocks, two colours to a row, but changing every band of blocks. Changing colour immediately takes the eye across the row. A great exercise in tones and values of colours and how they react next to each other is to stand back or pin up your knitting every now and then; look from a distance, and see how some colours leap out at you, perhaps much more than you expected. Does this matter? It may not; that is up to you, the designer, to decide, but it's useful to be aware of how the appearance can change from close to far, and think of other alternatives, or consider another way of constructing the garment if you want to avoid stripes travelling across (*see* below).

Slip stitches (*see* Chapter 5) are useful in this respect, as although worked in two (or more) row stripes of different colours, slipping the stitches to create a pattern pulls them up across the rows, giving a vertical element that breaks up the stripes. If only two colours are used, the striping disappears altogether. If more colours are involved, then there might be some horizontal stress again. Slip stitches are also useful in the surprising freedom they allow in patterning, ranging from detailed textures of dots and small geometric patterns to large-scale designs of diagonals, verticals and more.

One solution to this would be to knit the whole design sideways, across the jumper or jacket, to tilt the emphasis to travelling downwards instead of across.

Knitting from top down

This is such a practical way to knit, but still not very common. It is counter-intuitive, as we are so used to thinking that the cast-on edge is the bottom of the knitting, and that it grows upwards.

The main advantages to top-down knitting are how easy it is to adjust the length by trying on the top part and deciding on the length as you go, and any decisions about the kind of edging or welt you want are also much easier once you can see the rest of the garment.

Practical uses

From a practical point of view, knitting from the top down means the bottom could be lengthened if required – for example for a child's garment – and making a repair is easier too. We have already looked at lengthening or repairing sleeves if they are knitted downwards in the original model of the T-shaped garment, and a top-down construction of the body allows this at the bottom as well as the sleeves.

We are hopefully leaving behind a protracted time of throw-away fashion, and making things by hand gives us the perfect opportunity to make something to last, to imagine it being worn, repaired, and worn to the end of its life. This way of thinking was normal until mass production took over in the twentieth century; before that, repairing was actually a part of the life of a piece of clothing. Mending used to be a regular activity for everyone (although with clothing this probably meant women), and perhaps it can be again now that we need to think hard about the life of each garment, how it is produced, and what will happen to it when worn out. Aside from green issues, we probably all know people

Two ways of beginning a sweater from the top down: increasing at regular intervals to make a circular yoke (right) and increasing at 4 points to separate the body from the sleeves for a square yoke (left).

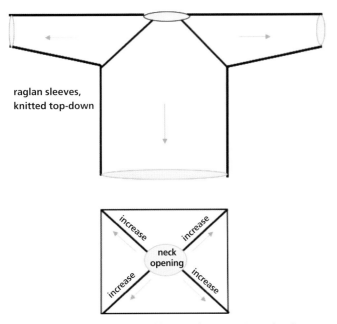

raglan sleeves, knitted top-down

increase · increase · increase · increase

neck opening

Square yoke sweater sample knitted from top down, creating raglan sleeves by increasing twice at four points.

Top-down raglan sweater sample.

Knitting 'over the top', beginning from the bottom up, continuing over the shoulders, and down the other side, leaving sides to be joined.

who love a particular jumper and want it to go on forever, so a method of knitting that is easy to unravel and reknit edges or completely restyle them, would be useful. Mending has also become a new art form, with the repairs being a kind of decoration: and why not, if it prolongs the life of the garment?

Apart from the cuffs, another part of a jumper that is prone to wearing out and needing repairs is the neck, so a variation of the top-down jumper would be to cast on below the final neck edging, and pick up and knit the neck at the end, thus making it easy to unravel and repair.

The recent fashion for Scandinavian and Icelandic sweaters has resulted in huge popularity for circular yokes knitted top down, but square yokes with raglan sleeve lines can work as well, working in a square or rectangle and increasing (double-increases) at each corner for the sleeves. You would need to work out the widths for the back, front and sleeve tops before beginning, and the rate of increase. The simplest way to begin a sweater in this way would give a neck the same height all round, which usually means the back of the neck is too low; but if you needed it higher at the back, this could be achieved with a collar or neckband knitted later, giving height and warmth at the back of the neck, and short-row shaping could be used to build the back of the neck higher than the front.

Knitting up and over

Another idea for knitting with minimum seaming is to knit from the bottom up one side, and continue over the shoulders and knit down the other side, with no shoulder join. With this construction, the side seams will need to be sewn at the

The start of the raglan square yoke sweater sample shown earlier, beginning with the neck and increasing between the body and sleeves, showing how the increases 'hitch' the stripe.

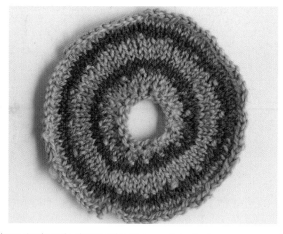

Top-down circular yoke showing the marks made by the increases, exposed by the coloured stripes. Here the increases are knitted into the front and back of a stitch: different increases would make different marks.

end. Two points to watch for here are firstly the fact that the bottom edge is being cast on on one side, and cast off on the other side. This may not matter, but cast-on and cast-off edges look different and are discussed more below. The other point is the small detail of the stitches being upside down on one side: the difference shows up particularly in a colour pattern. There are subtle differences to the look of knitting when it travels upside down. Knitted stitches have a definite shape, a top and a bottom, and in stocking stitch this looks like a V. So, in a geometric pattern such as triangles or zigzags of colour, it's easy to get a clean sharp point at the bottom of the motif where the bottom of the V points down, but the top of the shape will have less of a clear outline. Consequently, if coloured patterns and motifs are used, it's easy to tell which way up the knitting travels. This may not be important or matter very much, but this book is taking a magnifying glass to how knitting works, and the difference is certainly visible if you search. This traditional sweater from the Norsk Folkemuseum in Norway also shows this effect of the pattern being upside down[4].

The back of a coat knitted from the top down with regular increases either side of a slip stitch, spreading the shape until it is cast off at the bottom edge. The structure of the increases fits into and becomes part of the overall design. (Photo: Abb Nazari)

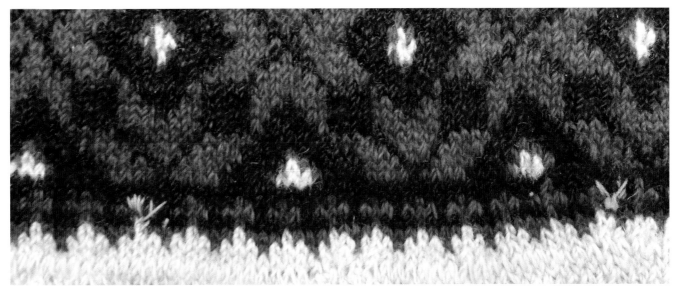

A (well-worn) traditional sweater from Norway knitted downwards, with the colour pattern showing the upside down stitches. (Photo: Author)

Detail of a colour pattern comparing how stitches look different going up one way and down the other, with each stitch showing either ^ or v: knitted up on the right, down on the left.

Increases and decreases

If you are knitting top down in one piece with raglan sleeve shaping, you will be increasing at four points as you go round, to separate the sleeves from the body. Another detail to look at is the many different ways to increase, as each makes a different 'mark' in the fabric, as with different types of decreases. Working conventionally from the bottom and decreasing for a raglan-style armhole, you can knit 2 together either with the right or the left stitch on top, dramatically changing the look of the decreasing line; K2tog decreases two into one with the left stitch on top; SSK (or S1, K1, psso) does the opposite, with the right stitch lying on top. Or, working the yoke of the garment in the round, you could decrease 3 stitches into one to make a single line of one travelling stitch by S1, K2tog, psso, which gives a slightly jumbled decrease; or S2 (as if to knit them tog), K1, p2sso, which produces a clear central stitch running up the decrease.

Working downwards and increasing, a 'yarn over' would make a lacy hole, so this would be a clear decorative increase, with a hole either side of a central stitch or two, for example, YO, K2, YO. A 'make 1' (M1) may indicate knitting into front and back of stitch, which makes a definite 'blip' that then needs to be placed carefully: the blip appears following the stitch, so to match it in mirror image, right with left, you need to increase in the previous stitch, then the central stitch. For example, working in the round, there will be four points of increasing to create the raglan sleeve line. To make each increase, you could try M1 (by knitting into the front and back), K1, M1. This will appear as a blip (the increase), then two central knit stitches followed by another blip. This makes a neat line of 2 travelling stitches with the increases on either side (*see* the start of the raglan square yoke sweater sample, pictured), but the first M1 comes before the central travelling stitches.

Another increase, also sometimes written as 'M1' could be made by lifting the bar between the stitches to make a new stitch. This works neatly, but interestingly as we see in the top-down circular yoke sample (pictured), the coloured stripe becomes hitched out of line by the regular increases round the yoke. It's the designer's decision whether this is a problem or an attractive design feature: you must

Note

In this book, *see* individual instructions and charts for which kind of increase is meant.

be sure it looks right or how you want it to look, and if not, use a different increase sympathetic to your stitch and pattern.

Knitting sideways

This is equally possible, but not so common. The main advantage of this structure is if you want a vertical accent to a design that has a horizontal emphasis in the knitting: a simple example being stripes of colour which are easier to knit horizontally in rows, but if the piece is then tipped on its side, the stripes become verticals. As before, there are options about where to make your starting point. If you begin at one front edge, you can knit all the way round a jacket or cardigan, casting off at the second front edge and joining shoulders and knitting the sleeves afterwards: or with a jumper, join or graft the final edge to the cast-on at the end. Alternatively, knit it as a flat piece beginning at a side seam but knitting back and front as one piece, so the rows travel from the base of the back over the shoulder to the base of the front, so eliminating the shoulder join. In this case, cast off at the front edge, and cast on again for the second front. The side and underarm seams would then need joining.

So the visual aspect is the first thing to think about, and whether there is an advantage in making something from

Jacket (sample) knitted sideways; the side seams and underarm seams will be joined at the end.

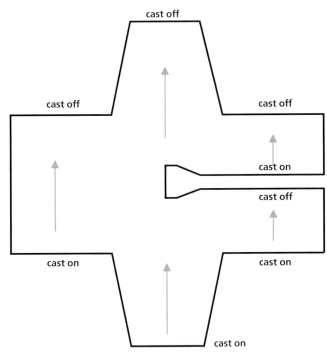

cast off

cast off · cast off

cast on

cast off

cast on · cast on

cast on

Plan of sideways-knitted jacket, beginning at the cuff, increasing up the first sleeve, casting on stitches for the front and back, casting off then on again for front opening, casting off at the second side seam and decreasing down the second sleeve.

side to side, every variation in direction will affect the pattern, and the drape. Another starting point could be the centre, casting on down the centre back and knitting out towards the sleeve and cuff, then mirroring the other side by picking up from the cast-on stitches to knit the second half. If this is a jacket, the cast-on edge could travel from centre back over the shoulder and down the centre front, leaving the front edge open.

The second consideration is the way knitting drapes or hangs. We know knitted fabric is much stretchier sideways across the rows than vertically: this is very helpful for squeezing shoulders through a jumper knitted in the usual bottom to top or top-down way. A sweater knitted sideways would be less stretchy to put on and take off. So, it follows that something knitted plain without textured stitch patterning or colour patterns, but used on its side would have a tendency to drop or droop, especially in a heavy yarn, a yarn without much spin and strength, or a yarn without much bounce and stretch. For example, alpaca, silk, cotton, linen, hemp or other plant fibres that don't have any spring would be more inclined to stretch. There are ways to

counteract and prevent this by using non-stretchy stitches: cables, crossovers, anything with increasing and decreasing within the pattern; Fair Isle or slip stitch colour patterns. All these are firm stitches that keep their shape, and there are many more.

Other knitted items have different stresses and strains compared with garments, but it's always worth thinking about the direction of the knitting and strength of fabric needed. Knitted bags, for example, would have quite different requirements, where firmness is more important than stretch.

Front edges

The edges of a jacket are really important whichever way you knit. Edges can make or break a design if they don't sit comfortably and look right. In any stocking-stitch based pattern, there is a tendency for the edges to curl inwards in vertical knitting, whereas knitting sideways they will curl the other way, curving outwards. As always, this depends on the yarn and stitch, but finding a good edging to help the edge lie flat is another consideration, unless you can use this curling tendency as part of your design.

Options for knitting from side to side:

- Knit from cuff to cuff, all in one piece so it folds over on the shoulders (this works well for batwing designs).
- Knit from cuff to cuff, front and back separately, making it easier to shape the shoulders.
- Knit from one side, round the body, casting off then on again to leave armhole openings, so the sleeves are then picked up and knitted downwards.
- For a jacket, knit from the front edge, all the way round to the other front edge.

A detail to think about here is matching the two front edges. If you knit cuff to cuff, one sleeve and cuff will be knitted 'upwards' and the second 'downwards', so again you need to match the two cuffs, otherwise one will be cast on, and the other cast off, and they look different, and often have different amounts of stretch.

For either cuffs or front edges, you could use a provisional cast on, picking up the stitches later, knitting downwards and casting off to match the opposite edge. Another option would be to use a cast-on stitch that looks identical to casting off, so edges could be matched in this way (*see* Further Resources).

Knitting diagonally

Two main reasons for knitting diagonally would be firstly visual, for design purposes, and secondly for the feel and behaviour of the fabric – the drape.

If your design has a diagonal feel to it, or you want a diagonal emphasis, it might be easier to knit it on the diagonal rather than create a diagonal design within straight knitting. The simple example is, again, stripes: it's much easier to knit these across the rows than knit diagonal, coloured stripes in 'straight' knitting.

As for drape, this direction opens a new door, as any fabric (woven or knitted) used on the diagonal means you have a 'bias' fabric and it can drape and fit wonderfully. This is explored in Chapter 3.

Modular knitting

Modular knitting is a different way of constructing a knitted piece; this is looked at in detail in Chapter 7. Modular knitting means building the fabric in blocks or modules, rather than knitting the full width across the garment. Each module is knitted individually, but with the stitches picked up from the previous module. In the introduction to her book *Domino*

Knitting, Vivian Høxbro explains how this alternative name came about, and the origins of this method of knitting[5]. It is an intriguing way of knitting and opens up a completely new way of thinking and designing. How it works in its simplest form of a square module is by casting on stitches

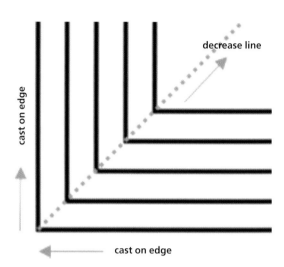

In a mitred corner or in modular knitting, all rows (and stripes of colour) turn a corner at the decrease point.

A sample for a jacket design with a mitred corner, with the cast-on edge travelling along the bottom edge and up the front. The stripes also turn a corner, but are hidden by the welting stitch, which also shapes the jacket by drawing in the front.

Detail of modular knitted jacket, made from blocks or squares without seams, picked up from one square to the next.

Entrelac stitch, where the fabric is made from blocks zigzagging one way then the other, all joined by knitting.

and decreasing in the centre of the row, losing 2 stitches on alternate rows until all the stitches are used up. In effect, this means that the cast-on edge for each block turns a right-angle corner at the point of decrease, becoming two sides of the square: the other two sides are the length of knitting the block. The maths of this action means you knit as many rows as you have stitches and, worked in garter stitch, this forms a square.

This is intriguing, and so different from straight-across full-row knitting. The decrease creates a strong, textural emphasis within each square, varying according to which method you choose, as each way makes notably different marks, all explored further in Chapter 7.

Building shapes in modular knitting can be done in different ways, so that the simple square could be placed to give a straight edge with a diagonal decrease, or tipped up to make diamonds with a vertical decrease. Or, of course, if you build the blocks sideways as diamonds, the decreases will make horizontal lines across. Any design can be built from any starting point – what freedom!

The rows all turn a right-angled corner, so if a coloured stripe is knitted, it immediately forms an L-shape, or a block or small square in the corner. This concept can be expanded as a way of making a whole garment, with one decrease running diagonally through and creating an L-shaped body. The cast-on edge runs down the front edge and along the bottom, with the corner at the edge[6].

Entrelac is another way of building knitting in blocks, but is technically quite different to construct. Here, the blocks are knitted straight across with no decreases, but lie on the diagonal, and the stitches are all held on the needle throughout. Blocks or modules are knitted back and forth sloping one way in one row, with subsequent rows of blocks sloping the opposite way. This is also explored in Chapter 7.

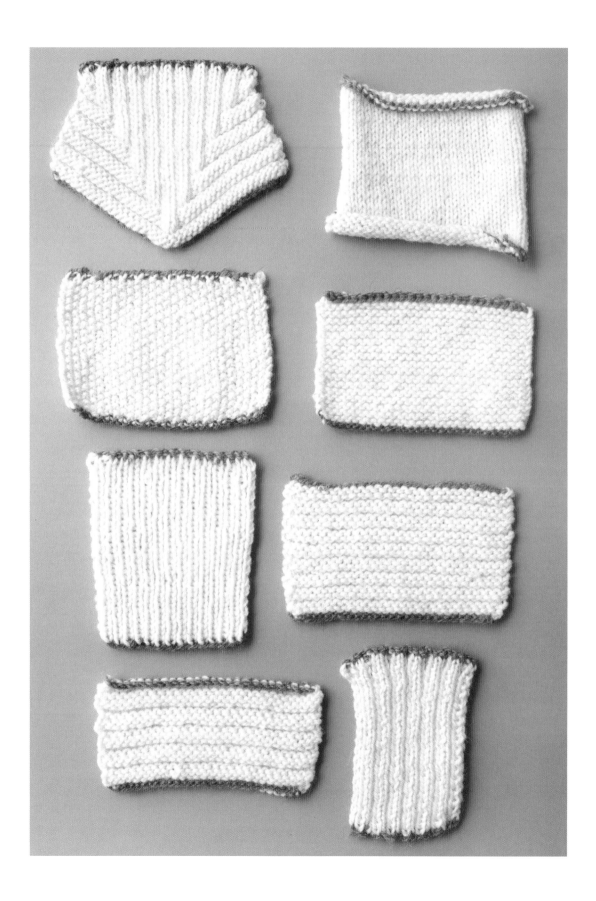

CHAPTER 2

SHAPING WITH SIMPLE STITCHES

'It is here that even the shyest beginner can catch a glimpse of the exhilaration of
creating, by being a creator while at the same time he is checked by
irrevocable laws set by the nature of the material.'

Anni Albers *Black Mountain College Bulletin,* 5 November 1938

How do you shape knitted fabric? The way that first comes to mind may be by increasing and decreasing the numbers of stitches, or the number of rows, which can take place at the edges, making a flat fabric with shaped sides by increasing or decreasing at the side edges, and at the top and bottom, including short-row shaping where only part of the row is knitted. This method evolved when knitting patterns began to be written down, rather than passed on from knitter to knitter. Each separate piece can be shaped like a cut and sewn garment. Shaping doesn't always have to be at the edges. You can also increase, decrease and shape the rows within the fabric, with different results, as these then manipulate all the surrounding stitches, pushing them one way and the other, and sometimes up or down from the surface even into three dimensions.

There is another way of shaping – by using the combinations of the stitches themselves to push and pull the fabric into shorter or longer lengths and widths: in other words, not altering the numbers of stitches or rows, but using the stitches to shape the fabric.

So what do we mean by stitches? It's a term that covers both individual loops and also combinations of stitches. Really there are only two stitches in knitting, but these can be combined in endless different ways. In fact, you could say there is only one stitch, but it can be formed with either the knit side facing, or the purl. This basic stitch is made by inserting the needle to catch a new loop of yarn and pull it through the 'old' stitch, making a new one, either working through the front to form a knit stitch with the loop falling to the back, or bringing the needle through from the back towards the front, so the loop is dropped to the front of the work. These two actions produce stitches that look quite different, with the knit side being smooth, and the purl creating a rougher texture. Forget about colour – endless patterns can be made in textures alone with these two stitches in a plain yarn, and can be seen in historic pieces in museums (several examples are in the V&A collection in London) in traditional Guernsey and gansey sweaters made around the coast of Britain in the nineteenth and early twentieth centuries, and really in any knitting patterns from a time when fancy yarns were not available and knitting was patterned by stitches alone.

We are used to the familiar look of textured stitches, but perhaps less aware of the second thing that happens when you

Opposite page: Shaping with stitches: each piece is knitted on the same-sized needle with the same number of stitches and rows.
Top row: piece shaped by ribs and welts (left); stocking stitch showing its natural curl at the edges (right).
Row 2: Moss stitch (left); Garter stitch (right).
Row 3: K1, P1 rib (left); 2-row welting stitch (right).
Row 4: 3-row welting (left); K2, P2 ribbing (right).

combine knit-face and purl-face stitches, especially when they are in groups, which is a push and pull of movement. Where the knit and purl lie next to each other, a tension occurs between them, which is a great tool for designing. We know that ribbing pulls in widthways, making columns of knit and purl stitches where the knit stitches come forward, and the purl go back, looking the same on both sides of the fabric as the opposite happens on the reverse. This forward-and-back movement can also be achieved across the rows horizontally with two or more rows of knit-face and purl-face stocking stitch, but then the purl rows push forward, with the knit areas falling back. It's the combination of these two effects that becomes interesting for shaping; one pulls in widthways, the second pulls up lengthways.

Later in this book we will explore how else stitches can be manipulated: they can be crossed over each other, knitted at different angles and in different directions, and combined in different colour techniques to alter the fabric; but in this chapter, we are going to look at the basic knit and purl stitches and different effects of combining the two to shape the knitted fabric.

Altering the width

This piece shows four stitches or combinations of knit and purl to compare the width of the fabric. The number of stitches remains the same, and the number of rows in each band is the same.

a) Moss stitch

Row 1: on an uneven number of sts, *K1, P1*, rep to the end, ending K1.
Row 2: as row 1.
This stitch is wider and shorter than stocking st.

b) Stocking st

Row 1: K.
Row 2: P.

c) Ribbing

Row 1: *K1, P1*, rep to the end, ending K1.
Row 2: *P1, K1*, rep to the end, ending P1.

Four different patterns worked on the same number of stitches to compare width:
a) K1, P1 moss st
b) stocking st
c) K1, P1 ribbing
d) K3, P3 ribbing

d) 3 st rib

Row 1: *K3, P3*, rep to last 2 sts, K2.
Row 2: P2, *K3, P3*, rep to end.

Any rib with two or more stitches to each knit or purl pulls in more than K1, P1 rib, although a point will be reached when the groups of stitches become too large to react with each other: some tension will be lost and it will not pull in so much, or only where knit meets purl.

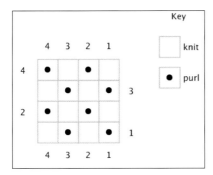

Chart a) K1, P1 moss st.

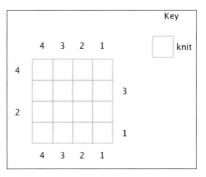

Chart b) stocking st.

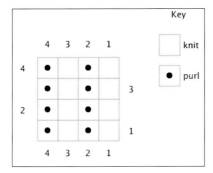

Chart c) K1, P1 ribbing.

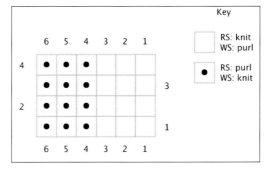

Chart d) K3, P3 ribbing.

Altering the length

In this sample, stitches are compared side by side to show the difference in length.

Cast on 64 sts (16 sts per pattern). The directions are written for each 16 stitches individually so you can see where you are, or put in a stitch marker between each group of 16.

Row 1: K16, (K1, P1) x 8, K16, K16.
Row 2: P16, K16, (P1, K1) x 8, P16.
Row 3: K16, (K1, P1) x 8, K16, K16.
Row 4: K16, K16, (P1, K1) x 8, P16.
Row 5: K16, (K1, P1) x 8, K16, P16.
Row 6: K16, K16, (P1, K1) x 8, P16.

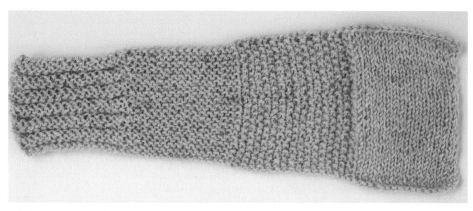

Four different patterns worked on the same number of rows, to compare length. Left to right:
a) welting st (K, P, K, K, P, K)
b) garter st
c) K1, P1 moss st
d) stocking st

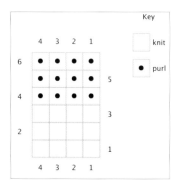

Chart a) welting st.

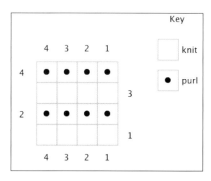

Chart b) garter st.

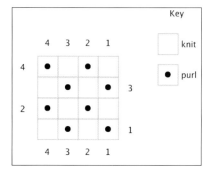

Chart c) K1, P1 moss st.

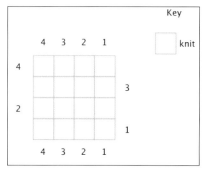

Chart d) stocking st.

Contrasts in width: moss and twice knit

Here are two stitches showing extremes: moss stitch is wide, pushing out further than stocking stitch, and twice-knit stitch is one of the tightest, narrowest stitches. Using the two in bands becomes almost sculptural.

Working on 31 sts, knit 20 rows in moss st, alternating with 6 rows twice-knit stitch.

Moss st

Row 1: K1, P1, rep to end.
Row 2: K1, P1, rep to end.

Twice knit st

Row 1: *K2tog, but only drop 1 st off the needle*, rep to end of row, K last st again (so the second K2tog knits the one remaining on the needle with the next st, and so on). *Don't forget to knit the last stitch again at the end of the row or the number of stitches will decrease!*
Row 2: *P2tog, but only drop 1 st off the needle*, rep to end of row, P last st again.

Comparing the width difference between K1, P1 moss st (a wide fabric) and twice-knit st, which pulls in the width, on the same number of stitches. This sample has been slightly flattened for the photograph.

As this piece comes off the needles, there is great energy in this combination of stitches. (Photo: Author)

The reverse side of these stitches forms a 3D sculptural piece. (Photo: Author)

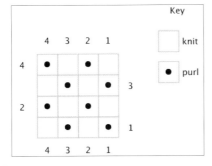

Moss stitch chart.

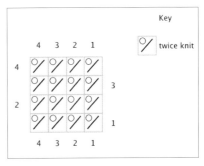

Twice-knit stitch chart.

Rib and welt

Playing with stitches that alter the length and width of the knitting in different combinations is a great way of shaping a garment, using the tendency of particular stitches to do the work of pulling in the waist, widening over the hips, or perhaps making broad shoulders and slim hips, depending on fashion and what body shape you are knitting for. There are two very simple stitches that show this shaping clearly has this pushing and pulling tendency, while staying elastic. If you combine a K2, P2 ribbing with a 3-row welting stitch, suddenly there are many possibilities for textured, stretchy stitches which can combine to sculpt shapes to fit the body, or simply to play with pattern and texture. The width of the ribbed bands could be altered, but as knitted stitches are wider than they are tall, 2 + 2 rib matches well with the 3-row welting.

Cast on an even number of sts. Beginning with welting stitch:
Row 1: K.
Row 2: P.
Row 3: K.
Row 4: K.
Row 5: P.
Row 6: K.
Rep these 6 rows 3 times, then rows 1–3 again.
Change to ribbing.
Row 1: *K2, P2*, rep to end.
Row 2: *K2, P2*, rep to end.
Work for 21 rows, return to welting st and work in alternating bands.

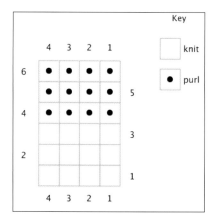

Chart for welting st.

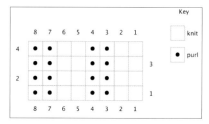

Chart for K2, P2 ribbing.

![Comparing the length and width of two stitches worked with the same number of rows and stitches for each band: 3-row welting and K2, P2 ribbing.]

Comparing the length and width of two stitches worked with the same number of rows and stitches for each band: 3-row welting and K2, P2 ribbing.

Alternate blocks of rib and welt

This is worked (and written) in blocks of 14 sts x 20 rows (*see* chart overleaf).

Cast on 42 sts (the chart shows 2 blocks, so repeat the first 14 sts to make 3).

Row 1: K14, (K2, P2) x 3, K2, K14.
Row 2: P14, (P2, K2) x 3, P2, P14.
Row 3: K14, (K2, P2) x 3, K2, K14.
Row 4: K14, (P2, K2) x 3, P2, K14.
Row 5: P14, (K2, P2) x 3, K2, P14.
Row 6: K14, (P2, K2) x 3, P2, K14.

Rep for 20 rows, so work rows 1-6 x 3, then rows 1 and 2.

New block:
Row 1: (K2, P2) x 3, K2, K14, (K2, P2) x 3, K2.
Row 2: (P2, K2) x 3, P2, P14, (P2, K2) x 3, P2.
Row 3: (K2, P2) x 3, K2, K14, (K2, P2) x 3, K2.
Row 4: (P2, K2) x 3, P2, K14, (P2, K2) x 3, P2.
Row 5: (K2, P2) x 3, K2, P14, (K2, P2) x 3, K2.
Row 6: (P2, K2) x 3, P2, K14, (P2, K2) x 3, P2.

Rep for 20 rows, so work rows 1-6 x 3, then rows 1 and 2. Alternate these two sets of blocks.

The resulting pattern is reversible, but is neater on the even-row side. On this side, each section is outlined with stitches that sink back to make a clear join, so each block is edged with columns of purl vertically, and a couple of rows of knit horizontally.

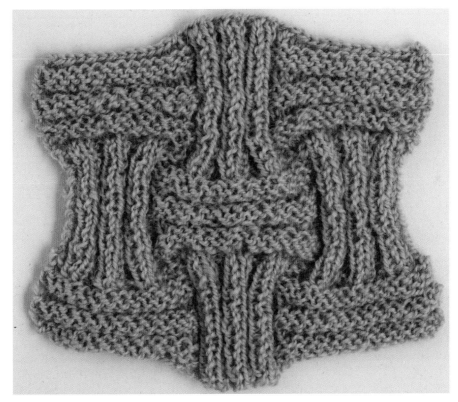

Alternate blocks of 3-row welting and K2, P2 ribbing showing the push and pull of the stitches, again with the same number of stitches and rows for each block.

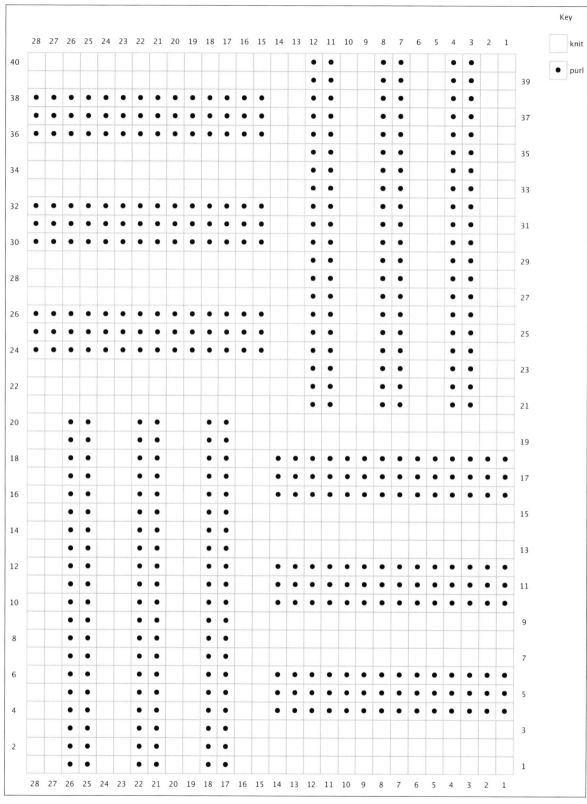

Chart for rib and welting blocks.

A simple square shaped with rib and welt

Rather than jumping directly from a patch of ribbing to a patch of welting, this piece begins with welting stitch, with the ribs introduced gradually from the edges of the row and spreading across, then the bands of ribbing retreat again until you end with welting stitch. The result shows that the knitting is pulled towards the four corners. Either side looks good in this stitch. (*See* chart overleaf.)

Note: in the chart, the stitches are square, so the shape is taller than when knitted.

Cast on 30 sts.
Row 1: K.
Row 2: P.
Row 3: K.
Row 4: P2, K26, P2.

A simple square shaped by ribbing and welting: the ribbing pulls in the shape as it moves in from the sides, with the welting pulling up lengthways at the bottom and top edges.

Row 5: K2, P26, K2.
Row 6: as row 4.
Row 7: K2, P2, K22, P2, K2.
Row 8: P2, K2, P22, K2, P2.
Row 9: as row 7.
Row 10: P2, K2, P2, K18, P2, K2, P2.
Row 11: K2, P2, K2, P18, K2, P2, K2
Row 12: as row 10.
Row 13: (K2, P2) x 2, K14, (P2, K2) x 2.
Row 14: (P2, K2) x 2, P14, (K2, P2) x 2.
Row 15: as row 13.
Row 16: (P2, K2) x 2, P2, K10, P2, (K2, P2) x 2.
Row 17: (K2, P2) x 2, K2, P10, K2, (P2, K2) x 2.
Row 18: as row 16.
Row 19: (K2, P2) x 3, K6, (P2, K2) x 3.
Row 20: (P2, K2) x 3, P6, (K2, P2) x 3.
Row 21: as row 19.
Row 22: (P2, K2) rep to last 2 sts, P2.
Row 23: (K2, P2) rep to last 2 sts, K2.
Row 24: as row 22; now the pattern works backwards:
Row 25: (K2, P2) x 3, K6, (P2, K2) x 3.
Row 26: (P2, K2) x 3, P6, (K2, P2) x 3.
Row 27: as row 25.
Row 28: (P2, K2) x 2, P2, K10, P2, (K2, P2) x 2.
Row 29: (K2, P2) x 2, K2, P10, K2, (P2, K2) x 2.
Row 30: as row 28.
Row 31: (K2, P2) x 2, K14, (P2, K2) x 2.
Row 32: (P2, K2) x 2, P14, (K2, P2) x 2.
Row 33: as row 31.
Row 34: P2, K2, P2, K18, P2, K2, P2.
Row 35: K2, P2, K2, P18, K2, P2, K2.
Row 36: as row 34.
Row 37: K2, P2, K22, P2, K2.
Row 38: P2, K2, P22, K2, P2.
Row 39: as row 37.
Row 40: P2, K26, P2.
Row 41: K2, P26, K2.
Row 42: as row 40.
Row 43: K.
Row 44: P.
Row 45: K.
Cast off.

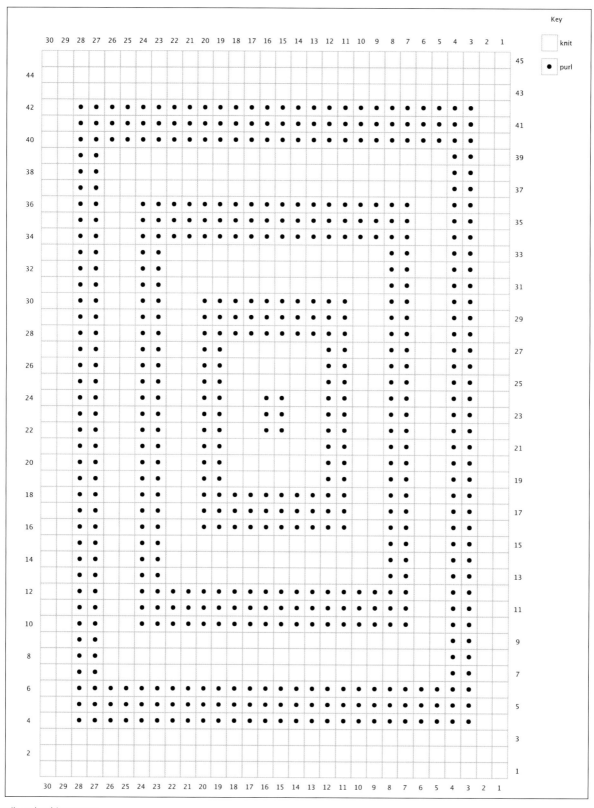

Chart for rib and welting square.

Rib and welt peaks and troughs

You could equally well make a square in the opposite way, beginning with ribbing, and the welting stitch introduced in from the edges towards the centre, then moving back out again. Here, the fabric is pulled towards the centre, with nowhere to go, so it rises into a point. This peaks and troughs sample shows this idea put into repeat, with these two combinations of stitches worked together to create a rising and falling texture. (*See* page 35 for the associated chart.)

Using ribbing and welting squares in repeat to create peaks and troughs, pulling and pushing until it becomes 3D.

This sample shows the groups of ribs and welts gradually widening and narrowing, pulling and pushing the knitting in different directions and creating a heavily textured, stretchy fabric.

Cast on a multiple of 24 sts (2 repeats are shown in the illustration):

Row 1: *K1, (P2, K2) to last 3 sts, P2, K1*, rep.
Row 2: *P1, (K2, P2) to last 3 sts, K2, P1*, rep.
Row 3: as row 1.
Row 4: *K3, (P2, K2) x 4, P2, K3*, rep.
Row 5: *P3, (K2, P2) x 4, K2, P3*, rep.
Row 6: as row 4.
Row 7: *K5, (P2, K2) x 3, P2, K5*, rep.
Row 8: *P5, (K2, P2) x 4, K2, P5*, rep.
Row 9: as row 7.
Row 10: *K7, (P2, K2) x 2, P2, K7*, rep.
Row 11: *P7, (K2, P2) x 2, K2, P7*, rep.
Row 12: as row 10.
Row 13: *K9, P2, K2, P2, K9*, rep.
Row 14: *P9, K2, P2, K2, P9*, rep.
Row 15: as row 13.
Row 16: K11, P2, K11.

Row 17: P11, K2, P11.
Row 18: as row 16.
Row 19: K to end.
Row 20: P to end.
Row 21: K to end. The pattern reverses here, with the ribbing increasing again.
Row 22: as row 16.
Row 23: as row 17.
Row 24: as row 18.
Row 25: as row 13.
Row 26: as row 14.
Row 27: as row 15.
Row 28: as row 10.
Row 29: as row 11.
Row 30: as row 12.
Row 31: as row 7.
Row 32: as row 8.
Row 33: as row 9.
Row 34: as row 4.
Row 35: as row 5.
Row 36: as row 6.

These 36 rows form the pattern; now repeat from row 1.

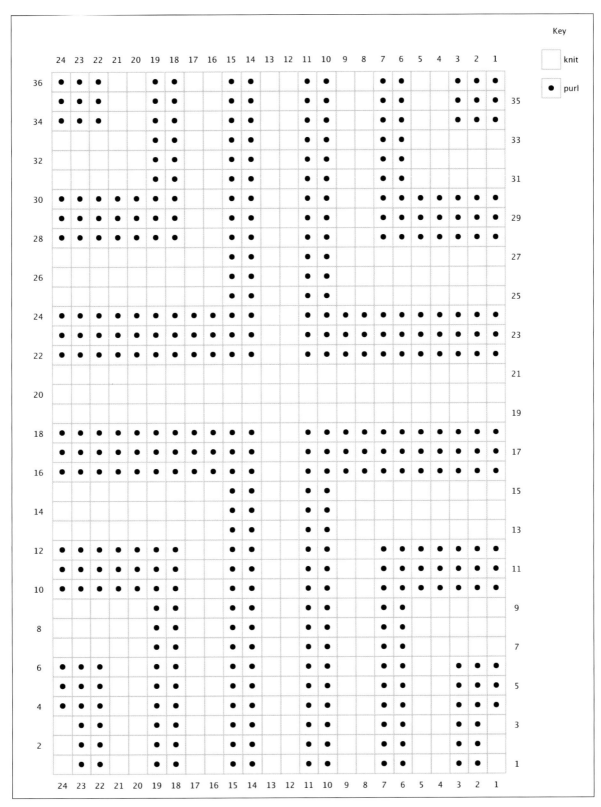

Chart for rib and welt repeated blocks.

Rib and welt 'Greek key' pattern

Another way of combining ribs and welts, worked first as a single piece as shown in the blue sample, the stitches push and pull to draw the shape in and up. This idea can be expanded and developed into a garment with the stitches shaping it to the body at the waist, and growing out to make square shoulders, as shown in the ribbed waistcoat with square shoulders in Pattern 1, Chapter 8.

When put into a repeat, the stitches push and pull to buckle the surface. This piece has a repeat of 32 sts, and is worked on 64 sts to show the pattern in repeat.

Row 1: *K15, P2, K15*, rep to end.
Row 2: *P15, K2, P15* rep to end.
Row 3: as row 1.
Row 4: *K13, P2, K2, P2, K13* rep to end.
Row 5: *P13, K2, P2, K2, P13* rep to end.
Row 6: as row 4.
Row 7: *K11, (P2, K2) x 2, P2, K11* rep to end.
Row 8: *P11, (K2, P2) x 2, K2, P11* rep to end.
Row 9: as row 7.
Row 10: *K9, (P2, K2) x 3, P2, K9* rep to end.
Row 11: *P9, (K2, P2) x 3, K2, P9* rep to end.
Row 12: as row 10.

Row 13: *K7, (P2, K2) x 4, P2, K7* rep to end.
Row 14: *P7, (K2, P2) x 4, K2, P7* rep to end.
Row 15: as row 13.
Row 16: *K5, (P2, K2) x 5, P2, K5* rep to end.
Row 17: *P5, (K2, P2) x 5, K2, P5* rep to end.
Row 18: as row 16.
Row 19: *K3, (P2, K2) x 6, P2, K3* rep to end.
Row 20: *P3, (K2, P2) x 6, K2, P3* rep to end.
Row 21: as row 19.
Row 22: *K1, (P2, K2) to last st, K1* rep to end.
Row 23: *P1, (K2, P2) to last st, P1* rep to end.
Row 24: as row 22.
The pattern changes here:
Row 25: *P1, (K2, P2) x 3, K6, (P2, K2) x 3, P1* rep to end.
Row 26: *K1, (P2, K2) x 3, P6, (K2, P2) x 3, K1* rep to end.
Row 27: as row 25.
Row 28: *K1, (P2, K2) x 2, P2, K10, (P2, K2) x 2, P2, K1* rep to end.
Row 29: *P1, (K2, P2) x 2, K2, P10, (K2, P2) x 2, K2, P1* rep to end.
Row 30: as row 28.
Row 31: *P1, (K2, P2) x 2, K14, (P2, K2) x 2, P1* rep to end.
Row 32: *K1, (P2, K2) x 2, P14, (K2, P2) x 2, K1* rep to end.
Row 33: as row 31.
Row 34: *K1, P2, K2, P2, K18, P2, K2, P2, K1* rep to end.

Rib and welt pattern used to create the suggestion of a body shape: the origin of the design in Pattern 1, Chapter 8.

This shows the blue design put into repeat where it links like a Greek key pattern, forcing the stitches into a 3D texture.

Row 35: *P1, K2, P2, K2, P18, K2, P2, K2, P1* rep to end.

Row 36: as row 34.

Row 37: *P1, K2, P2, K22, P2, K2, P1* rep to end.

Row 38: *K1, P2, K2, P22, K2, P2, K1* rep to end.

Row 39: as row 37.

Row 40: *K1, P2, K26, P2, K1* rep to end.

Row 41: *P1, K2, P26, K2, P1* rep to end.

Row 42: as row 40.

Row 43: K.

Row 44: P.

Row 45: K.

Row 46: K.

Row 47: P.

Row 48: K.

To repeat the pattern, begin again from row 1.

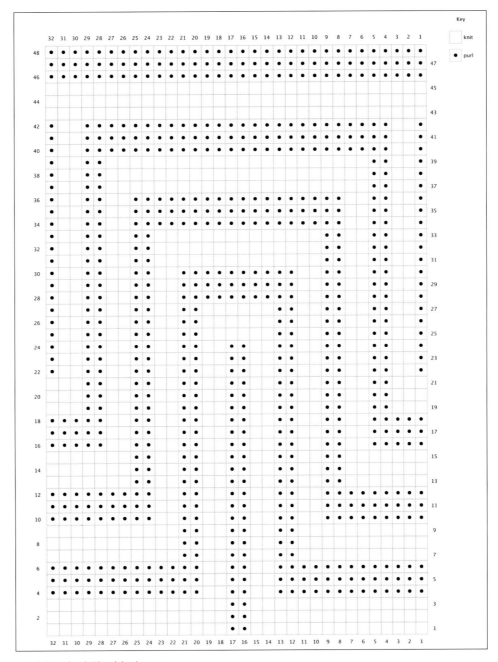

Chart showing one repeat of rib and welt 'Greek key' pattern.

Rib and welt shaped edging

Beginning at the narrow edge, ribbing and welting are repeated in a pattern to shape and push the stitches into a curved shape, as used in the waistcoat Pattern 1, Chapter 8 (which begins at the widest edge).

This idea could be worked as a collar, or a bottom edge (if worked the other way up, moving from welting to ribbing). The effect of the points will increase with a larger stitch repeat (illustrated in the waistcoat of Pattern 1 in Chapter 8, and more designs[2]).

Cast on a multiple of 24 sts.
Row 1: *K1, (P2, K2) x 5, P2, K1* rep to end.
Row 2: *P1, (K2, P2) x 5, K2, P1* rep to end.
Row 3: as row 1.
Row 4: *K3, (P2, K2) x 4, P2, K3* rep to end.
Row 5: *P3, (K2, P2) x 4, K2, P3* rep to end.
Row 6: as row 4.
Row 7: *K5, (P2, K2) x 3, P2, K5* rep to end.
Row 8: *P5, (K2, P2) x 3, K2, P5* rep to end.

Row 9: as row 7.
Row 10: *K7, (P2, K2) x 2, P2, K7* rep to end.
Row 11: *P7, (K2, P2) x 2, K2, P7* rep to end.
Row 12: as row 10.
Row 13: *K9, P2, K2, P2, K9* rep to end.
Row 14: *P9, K2, P2, K2, P9* rep to end.
Row 15: as row 13.
Row 16: *K11, P2, K11 * rep to end.
Row 17: *P11, K2, P11* rep to end.
Row 18: as row 16.
Row 19: K.
Row 20: P.
Row 21: K.
Cast off.

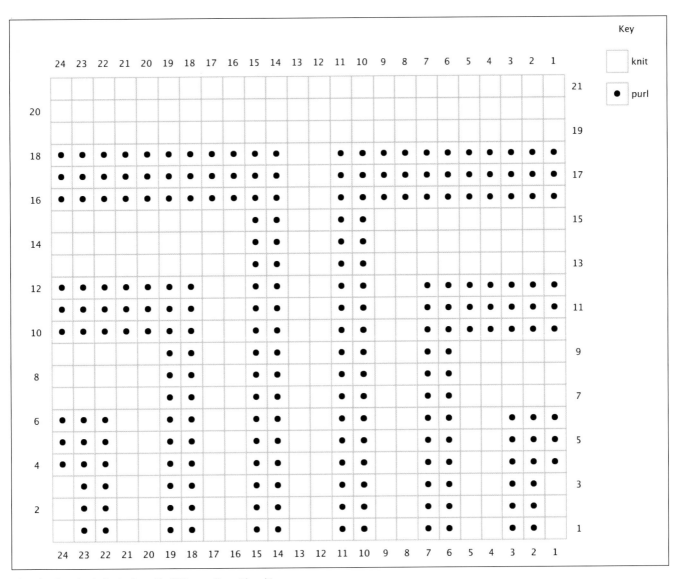

Chart for rib and welt, beginning with ribbing, ending with welting.

CHAPTER 3

KNITTING WITH BIAS

'Bias: a particular tendency, trend, inclination, feeling, or opinion, especially one that is preconceived or unreasoned: an oblique or diagonal line of direction, especially across a woven fabric.'

Online dictionary

The word 'bias' has evolved in English to have meanings ranging from an angle away from vertical or horizontal, causing an incline to one side, to the more abstract meaning of a tendency, a trend or an opinion. In textiles we usually mean that the grain or direction of the fabric travels diagonally, but in knitting, the second meaning is also relevant as what we do to the stitches gives them the inclination and tendency to *push* the fabric to the diagonal.

What difference does this make to the fabric if the stitches travel at a diagonal? As in dressmaking, it changes the character: if woven cloth is cut on the bias, it will have a more flowing fit and drape than 'straight' fabric. Knitting is more elastic than woven cloth so this might not be so much of a priority as it already has flexibility, but it can add to the enjoyment of wearing a garment if you want something either body-hugging or that drapes more.

It's very simple to tilt the grain or direction of the knitting using increases and decreases, either at an edge, or at intervals throughout the row. Placing these shapings at regular intervals every few rows alters the steepness of the slope, with increases and decreases every row producing the most acute angle, but with more plain (unshaped) rows between creating a shallower, more subtle effect.

It also opens up more design opportunities with the knitted rows travelling at an angle rather than straight across, so once again, any pattern with a definite stripe in colour or texture will take on a visual energy with the movement of the rows, whether the whole piece is tilted on one diagonal, or if it zigzags up and down.

Another consideration in designing with bias knitting is that it alters the width of the fabric if the rows are sloping rather than straight, so projects need some planning and experimenting to achieve the intended size.

Sides slope (shaped at edges only)

With an increase at one edge and a decrease at the other, if you hold the base of the knitting horizontal, the sides slope off at an angle while the stitches continue to travel straight up. Of course if you hold the sides vertically, the top and bottom edges and the stitches will then slope. A small sample creates a rhomboid shape rather than a rectangle, so already here is something new to play with. An elongated piece works well for scarves, and the slope can be made in either direction, or both directions within the same piece. If you

Increases at the RH edge and decreases at the LH edge every second row make the fabric lean, but the stitches stay straight.

want the piece of knitting to stay the same width and not actually become wider or narrower, you need to balance each increase with a decrease to keep the number of stitches the same.

Shallower slope

Worked in stripes to highlight the angle of the slope, this piece of stocking stitch increases at the beginning and decreases at the end of alternate rows to make a shallower slant. The increases and decreases are worked every fourth row.

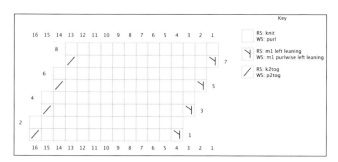

Diagram shows the direction of the stitches within the sloping shape.

A shallower 'lean', increasing at the RH edge and decreasing at the LH edge more gradually, on every fourth row.

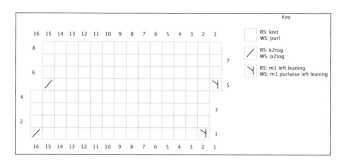

Chart for side slope, increasing at the RH edge, decreasing at the LH edge on alternate rows.

Chart for diagonals, with shaping every fourth row.

Bias within a rectangle

This sample keeps the *width of the fabric* the same, but alters the angle of the stitches. Supposing you wanted to make a rectangle, a 'normal' piece of straight knitting with the usual edges at right angles, keeping the *width of the fabric* the same, but altering the angle of the stitches? There are lots of variations within this structure, but it is possible to control the edges and make a bias fabric within a rectangle.

The sample begins with an even number of stitches (22 in this piece), and a few rows of garter stitch worked straight. To move from this straight edge to the angled rows (here worked in 2-row stripes), you must build up the shape with short rows.

Note: The chart shows the short-row section, not the borders, showing the total number of stitches. Begin on 22 stitches, as written below.

Row 1: col A, inc in first st (K into f&b), K1, turn (3 sts).
Row 2: S1, P2.
Row 3: col B, inc in first st, K4, turn (6 sts).
Row 4: S1, P5.
Row 5: col A, inc in first st, K7, turn (9 sts).
Row 6: S1, P8.
Row 7: col B, inc in first st, K10, turn (12 sts).

Row 8: S1, P11.
Continue in this way until you reach the end of the row:
Row 21: col A, inc in first st, K31 (33 sts).
Row 22: Sl, P30, turn (31 sts).
Now begin decreasing:
Row 23: col B, Sl, k28, K2tog.
Row 24: P (28 sts).
Row 25: col, A Sl, K25, K2tog.
Row 26: P (25 sts).
Row 27: col B l, k22, K2tog.
Row 28: P (22 sts).
Row 29: col A, Sl, k19, K2tog.
Row 30: P (19 sts).
Cont in this way in stripes, working in shorter rows and decreasing until you reach the end of the row.

During this process, you gain stitches at the widest part of the diagonal: on this sample, it increases from 22 to 32 stitches. These then decrease again naturally at the left-hand edge, and when all the stitches are incorporated, you will arrive back at the original number of stitches.

Straight bands of knitting alternating with bias knitting

Exploring this idea further, the multicoloured sample pictured shows bands of straight knitting alternating with

Keeping the edges straight, the stitches lean on the bias by beginning with short rows.

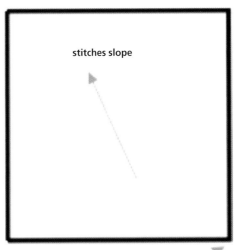

This diagram shows the straight sides with stitches on the bias.

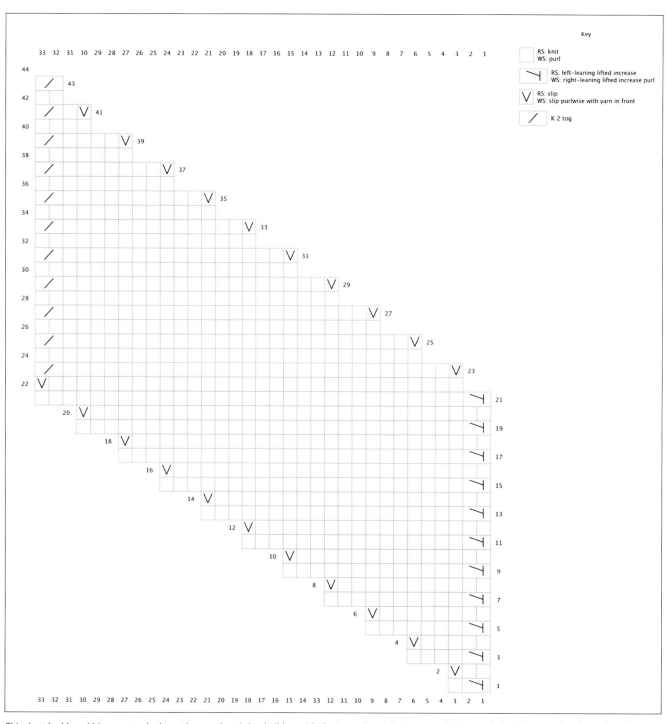

Key

RS: knit
WS: purl

RS: left-leaning lifted increase
WS: right-leaning lifted increase purl

RS: slip
WS: slip purlwise with yarn in front

K 2 tog

This chart for bias within a rectangle shows the way the stitches build up with short rows becoming longer until they reach the full width, then becoming shorter again to fit the rectangular shape.

Straight bands of knitting alternate with bias knitting: shaped gradually at the bottom and more steeply at the top.

bands of diagonal knitting. This is shown in a plain colour so the differences between the bias and the straight knitting are subtle, but with changes in colour or texture, you have a great design tool for playing with directions. The aim here is to create a bias fabric that fits with areas of straight knitting within a rectangular shape, so in order to keep the sides of the knitting travelling up in parallel, you need to increase at one edge and decrease at the other. During this process (as we saw in bias within a rectangle), the number of stitches increases to many more than you cast on, because the measurement of the diagonal is longer than the horizontal (normal) row, but as you continue to finish with a horizontal top edge, you will end up with the original number again. Of course, the top and bottom will also need to be shaped to fit the horizontal edges. This is done by working in short rows as before:

To make a sample, start with a number of stitches divisible by 4, knit a straight piece of stocking stitch, then begin the diagonal knitting as shown in the red strip in the image, showing straight bands of knitting alternating with bias knitting.

Note: There is no chart for this piece, as it is worked like the chart for the bias within a rectangle, but working in groups of 4 stitches instead of 2, and increasing every fourth row.

Row 1(RS): K4, turn.
Row 2: S1, P3 (always slip the first stitch to minimize a step or hitch here).
Row 3: K8, turn.
Row 4: S1, P7.
Row 5: increase into the 1st st, K11, turn.
Row 6: S1, P12.
Row 7: K17, turn.
Row 8: S1, P16.
Row 9: increase into the 1st st, K20, turn.
Row 10: S1, P21.
Continue like this, increasing at the beginning of every fourth row, and adding an extra 4 stitches each knit row until you reach the opposite edge, the end of the row.

Now you work in reverse with shorter and shorter rows and a decrease to match the increased edge:

Turn and P to the last 4 sts, turn and knit back (slipping the first st every time).

Turn and P to the last 8 sts, turn and knit to the last 2 sts and K2tog (this is the left-hand edge, at the end of the knit row).

Continue like this, purling 4 fewer sts every P row, and K2tog at the end of every 4th knit row, until you are back to working only 4 sts.

Your knitted piece should be more or less rectangular, with all the stitches still on the needle, so now you can continue in straight knitting as in the sample, or cast off.

You could work this diagonal piece from scratch without a 'straight' edge, by starting with casting on 4 stitches and casting on an extra 4 stitches on alternate rows, rather than knitting 4 more every knit row. The top edge would then be made by casting off 4 each row.

The top half (rust colour) shows a steeper diagonal made in the same way, but adding 2 sts every knit row, and increasing on alternate rows on the first stitch (*see* chart for bias within a rectangle). Again, always slip the first stitch after the turn.

With the stitches (divisible by 2) already on the needle:
Row 1: K2, turn.
Row 2: S1, P1.
Row 3: inc in first st, K3, turn.

Row 4: S1, P4.
Row 5: inc in first st, K6, turn.
Row 6: S1, P7.
Continue in this way until you reach the end of the row. Now, leave 2 behind every P row, and decrease on alternate rows at the end of every K row.

During this process, you gain stitches at the widest part of the diagonal: the 4-stitch gradual diagonal gained only 2 stitches over 32 stitches, but the steeper 2-stitch diagonal gains 12 stitches as the rows have to travel further to obtain the same width. These then decrease again naturally at the left-hand edge, and when all the stitches are incorporated, you will arrive back at the original number of stitches. You could alter the angle of slope by using longer groups of stitches between the turns for a more vertical angle, and by adjusting the increases and decreases at the edges accordingly.

Straight sides, with chevrons and zigzags

A simple chevron shape can be produced by increases and decreases. The whole fabric slants as we have seen,

1 increase at either edge and 2 decreases in the centre on alternate rows creates a chevron pattern, emphasized with 2-row stripes.

with the top and bottom edges sloping with the movement of the stitches. This idea can translate at any scale so, for example, you could design a sweater or jacket

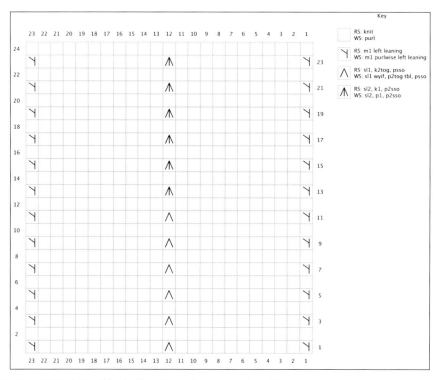

Chart for chevron pattern. To put in repeat, there will be double increases alternating with double decreases.

with zigzags all over, or one that simply dips in the centre at the front and back (decreases), and is raised at the sides (increases). The steepness of the angle of the sloping rows depends how frequently the shapings are made, so if you increase and decrease on alternate rows you will get a steep chevron (even steeper if you shape on every row), and a shallow dip can be made by shaping every 4 or 6 rows, or even slighter movement with more rows between the shapings.

These instructions show two different ways of decreasing in the centre.

Cast on 23 sts.
Row 1(RS): K into f&b, K10, S1, K2tog, psso, K10, K into f&b.
Row 2 (and all WS rows): Purl.
Row 3: rep row 1.
Row 5: rep row 1.
Row 7: rep row 1.
Row 9: rep row 1.
Row 11: rep row 1.
Row 13: K into f&b, K10, S2, K1, p2sso, K10, K into f&b.
Row 15: rep row 13.
Row 17: rep row 13.
Row 19: rep row 13.
Row 21: rep row 13.
Row 23: rep row 13.

You can also put a chevron into repeat with any number of stitches between the increases and decreases, fewer for smaller zigzags, and more stitches to extend to wider zigzags: the steepness depends on how many plain rows are between the shapings.

Similarly with decreases, a double decrease could be worked over 4 stitches as a 'K2tog, S1, K1, psso (SSK)', or the other way round, depending on which way you want the top stitch to slope. Or you could decrease 3 stitches into 1 by either 'S1, K2tog, psso', or 'S2 (as if you were knitting them together), K1, p2sso'. The first makes a mark sloping to the left, the second places the left-hand stitch on top and makes a strong vertical line if you purl this stitch on the reverse rows.

We've been looking at zigzag stitches made by regular *double* increases and *double* decreases throughout the row, which also push the stitches into a diagonal slant,

first one way, then the other, but these balance each other to make a piece of 'bias' knitting where the side edges stay vertical and the rows travel up and down – but what happens to the bottom edge? This will also be pushed into a zigzag, which can be used as a decorative edge. If you launch straight into a zigzag stitch from a piece of straight knitting, depending on how steep the zigzags are, there will be some distortion, but knitted fabric is very accommodating, so if the zigzags are shallow, it will find a way of adjusting. The most gradual zigzags would have the increases and decreases spaced with several rows between, whereas a steeper zigzag is achieved by shaping frequently, perhaps alternate rows, or even every row. This vigorous movement of the bias stitches affects the width of the knitting quite dramatically (*see* the graduated chevrons sample in the next section).

Ways to increase

There are several different ways of increasing and decreasing, which have very different visual effects, so choose the best one for you, depending on your stitch pattern and how prominent you want these to be.

Three ways of making 2 new stitches, written as 'M1' x 2:

1. *K into front and back of next st* x 2.
2. YO, K1, YO.
3. pick up and knit bar before next st, K1, pick up and knit bar before next st.

Each kind of increase makes a different mark, with the 'yarn over' producing a lacy hole, the picked-up stitch leaving a small hole, and the 'M1' being the most solid, but making a little 'blip' for the new stitch, which shows clearly in stocking stitch.

Ways to decrease 2 stitches

1. over 4 stitches: K2tog, S1, K1, psso (or SSK).
2. over 4 stitches: SSK, K2tog (*the stitches slope the other way*).
3. Over 3 stitches: S1, K2tog, psso (*slopes left*).
4. Over 3 stitches: S2 (as if knitting them tog), K1, p2sso (*this places the LH stitch on top and makes a strong vertical line if you purl this stitch on reverse rows*).

Graduated chevrons

Cast on a multiple of 10 sts.

This sample has a few rows of garter st to give a firm edge, then start the shaping in stocking stitch:

Row 1: *K into f&b of first st, K3, S1, K2tog, psso, K2, K into front and back of next st*, rep to end.

Row 2: P.

These 2 rows form the pattern, but the decreases are placed at different intervals.

Band 1 (turquoise): the shaping (row 1) is every 8th row, with plain st st worked between.

Band 2 (pink): is shaped every 4th row, with plain st st between.

Band 3 (mauve-blue): is shaped on alternate rows.

Band 4 (turquoise): is shaped every row, not just on the knit rows, so the purl row is worked like this:

Row 2: *purl into front and back of st, P3, P3tog, P2, P into front and back of st*, rep to end.

This shows clearly how the width is gradually pulled in by the more frequent zigzagging of the stitches.

Using this method of increasing causes a central knit stitch to travel upwards between the new (increased) stitches, and the decrease makes a regular pattern of textured spots. Another way of decreasing would create a central stitch running up the knitting, which works like this: put the needle through 2 stitches as if to slip them (so insert needle through the back), K1, pass 2 slip stitches over.

Graduating chevrons in small repeats of 10 stitches: the increases and decreases happen more frequently moving up each band, pulling the width of the fabric inwards.

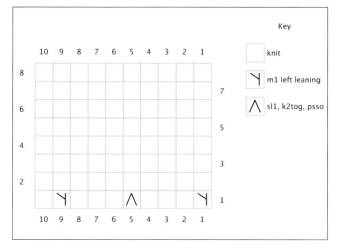

Graduated chevrons chart showing shaping for every eighth row.

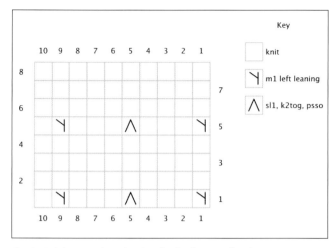

Graduated chevrons chart showing shaping for every fourth row.

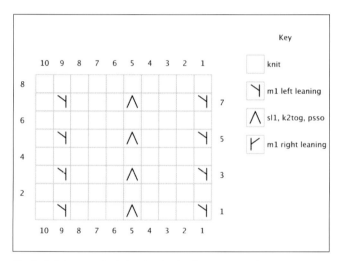

Graduated chevrons chart showing shaping for every second row.

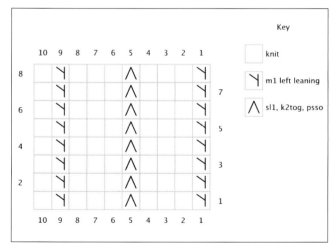

Graduated chevrons chart showing shaping for every row.

Chevron placed between strips of straight garter stitch

Here, the first sample has straight bands at the top and bottom and a bias chevron between, shaped to lie flat and fit the flat edges by using short rows, as in the bias within a rectangle sample shown earlier, whereas the second sample moves directly from straight to chevron knitting.

Short-row shaped sample

For a chart, *see* the chart for the bias within a rectangle sample for the first (RH) part, then reverse it for the LH part.

Shaping one half at a time:

Row 1: K 2, turn.
Row 2: S1, P1.
Row 3: inc in first st (knit into f&b), K3, turn.
Row 4: S1, P 4.
Row 5: inc in first st, K5, turn.
Row 6: S1, P6.

Continue in this way until you reach the middle of the row, so you have worked 16 sts, but because of the increases, you now have 23.

Now continue to knit across the remaining 16 sts.

Beginning this half on the P row:

Row 1: inc into first st, P1, turn.
Row 2(RS): S1, K2.
Row 3: inc into first st, P4, turn.
Row 4: S1, K5.
Row 5: inc into first st, P7, turn.
Row 6: S1, K8.

Continue like this, increasing at the beg of each P row until you P all the way back to the centre again: continue to P all the way across, turning before the last 2 sts.

Now you are beginning on the RS again.

K to 2 sts before the centre, and S1, K1, psso (or SSK), K2tog, knit to last 2 sts, turn.

Carry on leaving 2 more sts behind at the end of every row, and decreasing as above on RS rows, until you end up having filled in the middle section completely, by which time you should have 32 sts again.

Again, there is a V-shaped chevron, increasing at the outer edges and with a double decrease in the centre, so

Chevron fabric worked with short rows to lie flat between bands of straight knitting.

Chevron fabric worked from a straight band of garter stitch into a chevron zigzag. Compared to the short-rows sample, this technique distorts the straight bands and draws the fabric inwards.

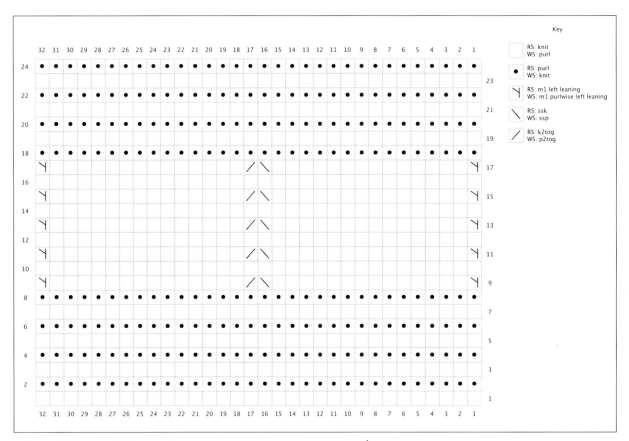

Chart for the straight bands with bias zigzag between.

the stitches angle from both sides towards the centre, as in the striped chevron piece earlier; but in this case, there are no short rows, the stitches are pushed away from the sides by the increases, and 'swallowed' up in the centre by the decreases. There is a strip of garter stitch at the top and bottom, which is used as it has more strength and rigidity across the rows than stocking stitch, to illustrate the energy and strength of the V-shape, which now cannot lie flat but is trying to push and pull these strips, and they have nowhere to go except to buckle the fabric three-dimensionally. This might be the kind of thing we would normally try and avoid, but it shows really clearly how something as slight as a change of direction sets up forces and movement within the fabric, and gives lots of scope for creating surface texture and interest. Understanding how this happens enables us to control and use these forces and tensions.

The other difference between the short-row sample and the sample that moves directly from straight to chevron knitting, is the width. The garter-stitch strips are wider than the chevron, pulling in by 2.5cm (1in) on this small piece of 32 stitches. This is because a given number of stitches knits wider when horizontal than when used diagonally.

The fabric wants to dip down in the middle, and if this piece was knitted with no straight knitting above or below, it would simply make a V-shape (*see* the 'straight sides with chevron' sample). But as it's gripped at the bottom and top edges by straight knitting, its only way out is to push upwards and outwards, making a 3D shape.

Sample without short rows

Cast on 32 sts.
Work a band of g st (this sample has 10 rows).
Mark the centre; 16 sts either side.
Chevron pattern:
Row 1: M1 in first st (by knitting into f&b of st), K13, K1, S1, psso (or SSK) (centre marker), K2tog, K13, M1 in next st.
Row 2: P.
Repeat these 2 rows for as long as you want.
Make another g st strip at the top and cast off.

More texture

We've seen the energy set up in bias stitches fighting against straight knitting. With nowhere to go, they are forced up and

Beginning by working increases at the edges and decreases in the centre, when these are reversed, the fabric pushes and pulls into 3D. Follow the chevron chart from earlier, swapping the increases and decreases every 16 rows.

down three-dimensionally. This can be taken further by not just changing from bias to straight knitting, but from one bias to its opposite, which intensifies the effect.

This piece shows a chevron, as before, simply reversing the increases and decreases every 14 rows, pushing and pulling the stitches into a bubbling, undulating surface. On a smaller scale, sample 60 shows the same effect with 4 plain stitches between the increases and decreases.

Chevrons in a repeating pattern for all-over texture

Small chevrons

Here are two pieces showing zigzags in a smaller repeating pattern with garter stitch bands between. Playing with the idea of putting strips of plain, unshaped garter stitch through the fabric as before, but in a smaller repeat, the knitting is forced to buckle and move into a 3D textured pattern.

This sample uses the same structure as the single chevron, with bands of garter stitch knitted straight across between smaller zigzags, which push and pull to buckle the surface.

The same effect as the previous sample, worked on a small scale to create a bubbled surface.

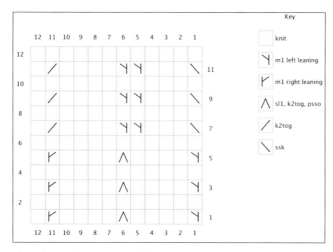

Chart showing the increases and decreases with 4 stitches between each shaping.

The alternate bands of garter stitch and zigzag create a textured surface, with the garter-stitch bands trying to remain horizontal. They are also naturally wider than the zigzag area.

Small zigzags with bands of 'straight' garter stitch
Cast on a multiple of 10 sts.
Work 10 rows g st (K).
Zigzag pattern:
Row 1: *M1 (by knitting into f&b of stitch), K4, S2 (slip these tog as if knitting them together), K1, p2sso, K3, M1*, repeat to last st, K1.
Row 2: P.
These 2 rows form the pattern.

A small zigzag pattern, shaped with increases and decreases over the stocking-stitch areas, but with garter-stitch bands knitted straight, pushed and distorted by the zigzag bands.

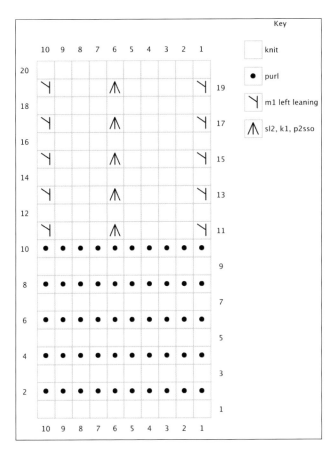

Key

□	knit
●	purl
⅄	m1 left leaning
⋀	sl2, k1, p2sso

Chart showing straight garter-stitch bands and shaped stocking stitch.

Small zigzags with bands of shaped garter stitch

The second, longer zigzag sample shown is worked in a repeating pattern of zigzags or chevrons, in stocking stitch alternating with garter stitch. The garter-stitch bands are shaped in the same way as the zigzag stocking-stitch bands, so they also zigzag and the whole piece settles into a bias zigzag fabric lying flat.

Cast on a multiple of 10 sts.
Work 10 rows of g st (K) with incs and decs.
Zigzag pattern:
Row 1: *M1 (by knitting into f&b of stitch), K4, S2 (slip these tog as if knitting them together), K1, p2sso, K3, M1*, rep to last st, K1.
Row 2: K.
Rep these 2 rows for 10 rows, then work 10 more, purling the even rows.

Note: different increases and decreases could be used. The ones described give a clear stitch travelling up through the centre of the increase and the decrease.

The same small zigzag pattern, but this time shaped over the stocking stitch and the garter-stitch bands, so it lies flatter (see chart overleaf).

Work the pattern for 8 more rows (10 altogether), then work another garter-stitch band.

A normal cast-off edge is very forceful and would push the edge to straighten rather than follow the zigzag movement: casting on is more flexible and easily influenced by the movement within the fabric. So in this piece, the cast-off used gives it the flexibility to move up and down by incorporating the increases and decreases *(the increase used is 'picked up' as this is easier to do while casting off):*

K 1, K the bar before the next st, and cast off first st; K and cast off the next 4 sts, then S2, K1, p2sso and cast off, K and cast off the next 4 sts, K the bar before the next st, and cast off, rep from * to * to the end.

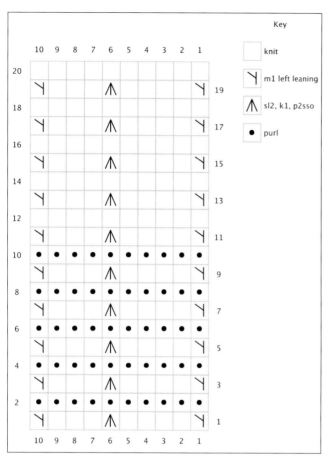

Chart for small zigzags with bands of shaped garter stitch, showing increases and decreases throughout.

Key
- knit
- m1 left leaning
- sl2, k1, p2sso
- purl

Added to the stretchiness of the bias chevron pattern, this piece is very stretchy vertically, as it's worked in a 'welting' stitch of 4 rows knit-side and 4 rows purl-side stocking stitch, making a reversible fabric.

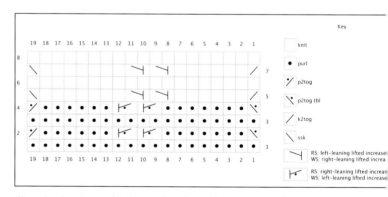

Key
- knit
- purl
- p2tog
- p2tog tbl
- k2tog
- ssk
- RS: left-leaning lifted increase / WS: right-leaning lifted increase
- RS: right-leaning lifted increase / WS: left-leaning lifted increase

Chart showing 4 rows of knit-face alternating with 4 rows of purl-face stocking stitch. Increases/decreases are paired to keep the edges straight.

What would happen if...?

In considering how to develop ideas in designing with zig-zags, you could try using different stitches. We've looked at how garter stitch next to stocking stitch is thicker and stronger horizontally, trying to push the fabric straight. You could alternate knit- and purl-faced stocking stitch for added surface texture.

Combining zigzags with welting stitch

Working on a multiple of 19 sts, in two colours:
Row 1: col A, P.
Row 2: *K2tog, K6, (K into f&b of next st) x 2, K7, SSK* rep to end.
Row 3: P.

Row 4: as row 2.
Row 5: change to col B, as row 2.
Row 6: P.
Row 7: as row 2.
Row 8: P.

These 8 rows form the pattern. Note that rows 8 and 1 are both purl. This stitch is reversible, with each colour showing on the side where it is in purl.

Sloping bias stitches with single incs and decs throughout

At the beginning of this chapter, we looked at what happened if you increased at one end of the row and decreased at the other end, as in the 'side slope' sample, so the whole piece slopes either to the left if you begin with an increase, or to the right if you begin with a decrease. The chevron pieces keep the sides travelling up vertically by using double increases and double decreases.

Separated single increases and decreases

Spaced single increases and decreases

Single increases and decreases repeated within the row have a similar effect of pushing the whole piece off at an angle, and creating more movement within the rows, as shown in this piece; but they also have the effect of slanting the fabric itself either one way or the other. There is lots of action going on here, as each increase and decrease will push and pull into bands of stitches so that, rather than tilting in mirror image one way then the other, some appear to travel upwards and the neighbouring group go at an angle.

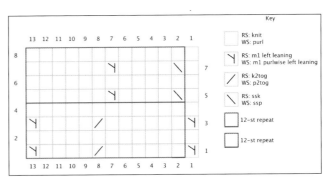

The bottom half of the chart will slope to the left, the top half to the right.

The spaces between the decreases and increases could be of any width. The stripes and changes in colour are there to show the movement of the stitches within the rows.

Cast on a number of stitches divisible by 12, plus 1 edge st.
Row 1: M1 (by knitting into f&b of 1st st), *K6, K2tog, K4, M1*, rep from * to * to last st, K1.
Row 2 (and all even rows)**:** P.
Rep these 2 rows, and the knitting slopes to the right, with the groups of stitches zigzagging to right and left (more gradually than on the chevron sample with double incs and decs).
To make it change direction and slope to the left, reverse the incs and decs:
Row 1: K1, *SSK, K4, M1, K6*, rep from * to * to last st, K1.
Row 2 (and all even rows)**:** P.

Narrow bands between repeated single increases and decreases

Here, we continue this theme but with fewer stitches between the increases and decreases making narrow diagonal bands of stitches, or a ripple or soft zigzag effect if stripes are placed across it. The increase is slightly different from the previous pieces: this is something to experiment with as each increase makes a different mark. The 'M1' increase leaves slightly more room for the stitches to adjust and move than a 'K into the f&b' increase. Using a 'YO' would be more flexible again, and would create a more marked hole than M1.

This piece has a multiple of 7 sts:
Row 1: *K2tog, K3, M1 (by picking up and knitting bar before next st), K2*, rep.
Row 2: P.
Rep these 2 rows.

Repeating single (not paired) increases and decreases across the row makes the whole fabric slope, reversing the shaping for the other direction.

Narrow bands between repeated single increases and decreases show alternate columns of stitches sloping and remaining upright.

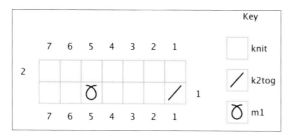

Chart showing spaced out single increases and decreases.

You can change direction by reversing the incs and decs like this: *K2, M1, K3, SSK*, rep.

Narrow bands worked in rib with alternate row shaping

What would happen if you worked this as a rib, with columns of knit- and purl-faced stitches?

With a multiple of 7 sts:
Row 1: *P2tog, P3, M1 (by knitting into f&b), K2*, rep.
Row 2: *P2, K5*, rep.

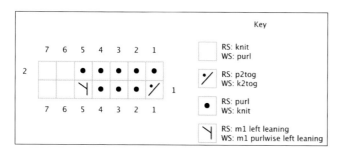

Chart for narrow bands worked in sloping rib.

Narrow bands between repeated single increases and decreases alternating knit-face and purl-face to create a sloping rib, lightly pressed to flatten the fabric.

The energy in this diagonal rib shows when it is on the needle, and wants to curl into a spiral. (Photo: Author)

This piece is shown in progress as well as lightly steamed flat, showing the knit and purl diagonal columns. On the needle, it has a strong inclination to spiral. The stitches push and curl, coming forward at the right edge (the increase edge) and wanting to coil into a spiral tube. It invites knitting in the round!

Narrow bands worked in rib, with shaping every row

Taken a stage further, this sample had the shaping carried out on every row instead of on alternate rows. The angle of the bias stitches becomes steeper, meeting the more vertical stitches almost at right angles, causing something different to happen. The knitted stitch is wider than it is long, so placing stitches against each other at this angle with top of stitch against side of stitch, means the widthways stitches will buckle. Another design discovery is that this stitch creates a kind of seersucker-ruched stripe in the fabric. Alternate bands of knit-side and purl-side stocking stitch are used.

Working on a multiple of 12 sts:
Row 1: *YO, P5, K2tog, K5*, rep to end.
Row 2: *P5, P2tog, K5, pick up bar before next st and K*, rep to end.

Adjusting stitch pattern to flatten fabric

If you like this idea but want the stitches to fit together more comfortably, this sample shows a way of overcoming the seersucker effect. It has been worked with columns of stocking stitch for the more vertical stitches, and the alternate columns are in K1, P1 rib which, because it pulls the width in, it takes in the excess and lies flat, creating a decorative stitch contrast.

Working on a multiple of 12 sts:
Row 1: *SSK, (K1, P1) x 3, M1 (by picking up and knitting bar before next st), K4*, rep to end.
Row 2: *P4, M1 purlwise, (P1, K1) x 3, K2togb*, rep to end.

This could be worked in the round (as illustrated).
Working on a multiple of 12 sts:
Round 1: *SSK, K6, M1 (pick up bar), K4*, rep all round.
Rep every round.

The puckered bands caused by increasing and decreasing every row have been replaced with K1, P1 ribbing, which pulls in enough to flatten the fabric. This stitch would also work well in the round.

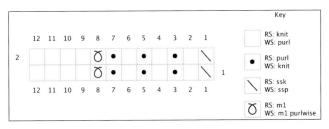

Chart showing alternate columns of ribbing and stocking stitch, and shaping every row, to flatten the fabric.

If the increases and decreases are made every row, the slope or bias is steeper and the pattern begins to pucker like a seersucker fabric.

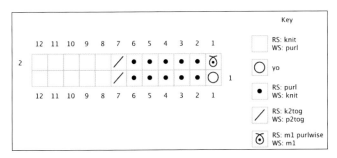

Chart showing the knit and purl columns, with increases and decreases every row.

Increases and decreases placed together

It is the separation of the increases and decreases that causes the stitches to slope in groups or columns, growing away from the increases and towards the decreases where they are 'swallowed' into the fabric. If you place an increase next to a decrease, you can still make the fabric slant, but

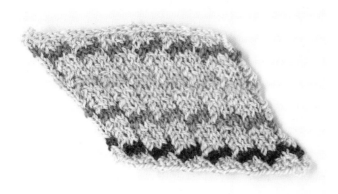

Increases and decreases placed next to each other, making a bias fabric with a 'hitch' or step when a coloured stripe is knitted. Wider stripes would create the illusion of blocks of colour.

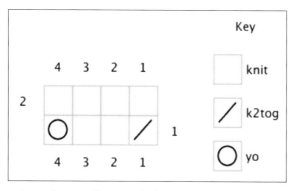

Chart shows a 'yarn over' increase, which gives the stitches more space to move and make a clear step.

the stitches travel vertically up the fabric. This piece places a single increase next to a single decrease, with just 2 stitches between. This eliminates the column of stitches travelling at one angle seen in the sample with narrow bands between repeated single increases and decreases above. It leaves clear columns all travelling parallel, with a 'hitch' or step where the increase and decrease takes place, shown very clearly and intriguingly by knitting stripes across. These appear to be disconnected, stepping clearly up and down, so that by knitting stripes (the easiest way of patterning knitting) this movement turns them into dots and dashes. The stitches have once again created a new pattern for you.

Worked on a repeat of 4 sts:
Row 1: *K2tog, K2, YO*, rep.
Row 2: P.

Note: a 'yarn over' increase is used here to allow the stitches maximum movement to create the step. Picking up the strand before the next stitch works well too, but if you were to use a solid or firm increase such as knitting into the front and back of the stitch, this holds the stitches more firmly and prevents room to manoeuvre, so you get a slightly stilted hitch rather than a definite step.

To reverse this pattern, begin *SSK, K2, YO*, rep.

How could these be sloping pieces be used?

A simple sloping fabric is perfect for a scarf, shawl or throw, and if knitted in the round, it will spiral. Another idea is to use the 'slope' in one direction, together with its mirror image sloping the other way, to make a chevron fabric but with added changes of direction within the fabric, shown here. This is similar to the zigzag knitted in two-colour 'welting' stitch shown earlier in the chapter, but placing the increases and decreases next to each other with 4 sts between the shapings.

Reversing the pattern of increases and decreases placed next to one another creates a chevron, but with added changes of direction within the fabric.

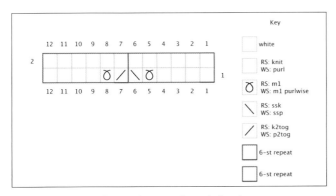

Chart for this pattern showing the repeat for each direction.

Cast on a multiple of 6 sts:

Row 1: *K4, M1 (pick up bar before next st and K), SSK*, rep.

Row 2: P.

To change direction (shown in sample 14 in the middle of the row):

Row 1: *K2tog, M1 (pick up bar before next st and K), K4*, rep

Row 2: purl

Overspun yarn

There is another way of achieving a bias fabric, not often seen or discussed unless you have access to hand-spun wool, as it involves knitting with an overspun or high-twist yarn: something that is not readily available for knitters in the retail market, except as a fine yarn from weaving suppliers. People who knit hand-spun yarn will be aware of it as it is – usually – something to avoid, but if you take the attitude that if something unexpected happens, even if it looks 'wrong' it's worth trying to understand what is going on, it can be hugely interesting to explore[1]. The kind of effect we are talking about here applies especially to wool, which has more spring and energy than most other fibres. Plant fibre yarns and silky animal fibres such as alpaca, or any very soft yarns are less affected: it needs wool with some bounce and life to make the most of this effect. A high-twist yarn has an extraordinary influence not just in knitting, but in other constructive textile techniques too. What it can do in weaving is described in depth in Ann Richards' books[2], where she explores how the high twist can affect woven fabric, releasing its extra energy to force the structure of the cloth to react and behave in unexpected ways; this can then be used to create special effects that change the surface texture and shape the fabric. The same approach can be used in knitting.

To understand what's going on, first we need to look at a normal, stable knitting yarn, which is formed from two or more spun threads, each known as 'singles'. These are spun in one of two directions, usually described as S-twist or Z-twist, with the diagonal of each letter illustrating the direction, so with either a clockwise or anticlockwise spin. The spin gives the yarn its strength: a bunch of fibres without spin will pull apart, but when spun into a thread they become strong. A yarn can have different amounts of spin according to its intended use, sometimes classified by the angle of the spin, or the number of turns per inch or centimetre.

To create a 'balanced' yarn, these single threads are plied or twisted together in the opposite direction to the original spin, giving greater strength to the finished yarn, but also balancing out the excess twist so it lies flat and inert and will stay where it's put and do what we expect. The number of threads gives the terms 2-ply, 4-ply and so on, but in general terms these plies don't necessarily tell you the thickness of the yarn: the single threads from which they are plied can be fine or chunky. However, it's not singles yarn that's always a problem: singles can behave properly if it doesn't have too much spin –

Detail of grey jacket in simple blocks of knit- and purl-faced stocking stitch using energized yarn. (Photo: Author)

at an angle of less than 20 degrees it will not distort the fabric. The catch, then, is that it won't be a very strong yarn as it's the spin or twist that gives any yarn its strength, with plying adding to the strength. If it is spun more tightly the extra spin can distort the fabric, which is not generally what you want, but experimenting with this tendency can have startling and exciting results if you have time to explore.

So what is this mystery? What happens if you knit with overspun singles yarn? If you take a piece of yarn and hold a length of it out straight, then let go, it will twist back on itself and coil up. It is full of spring and bounce and sometimes correctly described as 'energized', so as you can imagine it

is difficult to handle and knit, as it wants to spring into coils under your hands, and this energy then transfers to the knitted fabric. If you knit stocking stitch with an energized yarn, it pushes the knitting off at an angle or bias, which would certainly be a problem if you were following a specific knitting pattern: you may not want a jumper with a twist around the body.

There is one way to correct the leaning tendency in the knitting, which is to use 'balanced' stitches. So, for example, suppose the knit stitch pushes to the left (and conversely, the purl stitch pushes to the right); if you were to knit every row in knit (garter stitch), the inclination will be cancelled by pushing one way then another. Any pattern with an even distribution of one or two knit stitches and one or two purl stitches such as ribbing or moss stitch will not show a definite lean in the fabric, although the overall texture might be a bit chaotic, as the individual stitches are still trying to twist. The pattern that reflects the twisted angle the most, or best, is stocking stitch where the stitches are all facing the same way: knit on one side, purl on the other, and this is where the bias inclination will show up most clearly.

It can be unruly to work with this spiralling yarn and the result may look disturbed and distorted, but don't be put off as the results are fascinating. When it comes off the needles, if you then gently wash or soak the piece of knitting in warm water the energy will be transferred from fighting within the yarn to pushing the stitches into a settled diagonal, biased fabric (see next sample below).

This is a great design tool for creating texture and movement. Using stocking stitch, the stitches will slope in one direction on the knit side, but looked at from the purl side they go the opposite way. What happens if the two surfaces are combined? It needs a few stitches of each stitch to react: in K1, P1 rib or garter stitch there is not enough space for the stitches to create the bias. You need a larger group of each surface to really show the effect.

It may be difficult to get hold of an over-twisted energized yarn, unless you know someone who can spin some for you: some weaving suppliers keep fine, energized yarns (such as the Handweavers Studio in London[3]), which may be too fine to knit by hand, but can be combined with a balanced yarn to influence the lean of the knitting. Another approach is to try other ways to get a similar effect using balanced yarn and creating bias fabric which pushes in different directions, as shown at the beginning of this chapter. Two alternative methods are compared here; firstly, twisting each stitch as you knit it, creating a lean in one direction, and secondly using increases and decreases to make the fabric lean. The following samples will show all three methods in order to compare the effects, their similarities and their differences: firstly, energized yarn, secondly, twisting the stitches as you knit, and thirdly, using increases and decreases to make the knitting slope in different directions.

In all these samples, for simplicity and comparison, the fabric leans in one direction only (knit surface to the left) and to make the reverse slope, the purl side is used. This adds to the texture as well, as the knit and purl areas also want to move forward and back against each other.

In each case, you could make the stitches lean the other way, by:

1. using a singles overspun yarn spun in the opposite direction. Here, an S spin is used, so as indicated in the S, the diagonal bias is to the left. Z would lean to the right.
2. twisting the stitches in the opposite way. Here, they are knitted and purled into the back of the stitch. The opposite way is more laborious because of the way the stitches sit on the needle at an angle: they must be passed to the right needle, twisted and returned before knitting.
3. placing the increases and decreases at opposite edges to cause the knitting to slope in the other direction.

In the first two examples, the overspun yarn and the twisted-stitch shaping, the stitches themselves slope, taking the fabric with them. In the third method, the edges of the fabric are sloped by the increases and decreases, but the rows of stitches remain normal, pointing vertically and horizontally in their usual grid format.

Each set of three pieces has the same number of stitches and rows although the singles yarn is finer, so it's apparent that in the vertical bands of knit and purl, the singles yarn has shrunk in width in its efforts to transfer the twist into the fabric; on the other hand, the twisted-stitches piece is quite wide. In the horizontal bands, the difference is less, but the singles yarn and the twisted stitch piece are narrower than the third sample made with increases and decreases.

Comparing knit with purl in horizontal stripes

In these pieces, the top and bottom of the knitting lie normally, with the energized yarn and the twisted stitch examples showing the stitches themselves sloping, causing the whole piece to distort in that direction so that the sides slope. In the third method, the edges of the fabric are sloped by the increases and decreases, but the rows of stitches remain vertical.

As always happens when a knit-face and a purl-face stocking stitch are neighbours, one pushes forward, and the other back. In horizontal bands, the purl comes forward. So, this energy is combined with the fact that one group leans one way and the other leans the opposite way, and a lot of movement is occurring.

Horizontal bands of knit-face and purl-face stocking stitch in overspun, energized yarn, which pushes the stitches sideways.

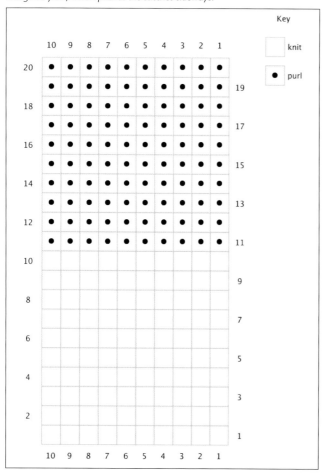

Chart showing bands of stocking stitch reversing.

1.) Energized yarn

Cast on any number of sts.

Row 1: K.

Row 2: P.

Continue these 2 rows for (in this sample) 10 rows.

Row 11: P.

Row 12: K.

Continue these 2 rows for the next band, making bands of knit- and purl-faced stocking stitch.

2.) Twisted stitches

Cast on any number of sts.

Row 1: K every stitch into the back of stitch.

Row 2: P every stitch into the back of stitch.

Continue these 2 rows for (in this sample) 10 rows.

Row 11: P every stitch into the back of stitch.

Row 12: K every stitch into the back of stitch.

Continue these 2 rows, making bands of knit- and purl-faced stocking stitch.

Note: this is slow work, and twists the stitches left side over right side, pushing to the left. If you want to slant the other way, lift the next stitch off the needle, return it with the left edge in front, and knit or purl into this, twisting the stitch to the right.

3.) Increases and decreases

Row 1: K2tog, K to last st, K into f&b of last st.

Row 2: P.

Continue these 2 rows for (in this sample) 10 rows.

Row 11: P.

Row 12: K2tog, K to last st, K into f&b of last st.

Continue these 2 rows, making bands of knit- and purl-faced stocking stitch.

Note: M1 by picking up the bar before the next stitch, returning it to LH needle twisted, and K into back of it. If this is difficult in

Horizontal bands of knit-face and purl-face stocking stitch in ordinary (balanced) yarn, the stitches pushed diagonally by knitting and purling into the backs of the stitches to twist them.

Horizontal bands of knit-face and purl-face stocking stitch, the edges of the fabric here pushed diagonally by using increases and decreases, with the stitches travelling straight up.

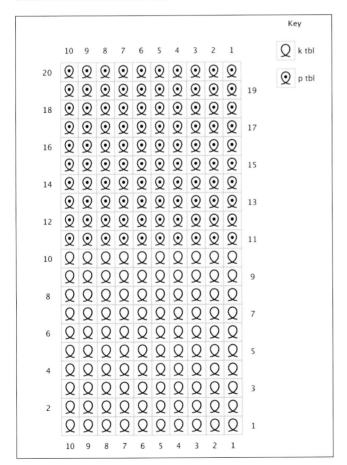

Chart showing bands of stocking stitch in twisted stitches.

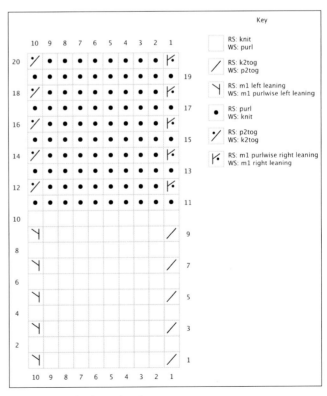

Chart showing shaping at the edges.

the first row after casting on, M1 in any way that seems possible!
After this, use the method described as any other way can leave
a gap.

Comparing knit with purl in vertical stripes

Here the opposite happens with the side edges sitting straight. In the energized yarn and the twisted stitch pieces, the slope is indicated by the top and bottom edges forming a zigzag, but the stitches run vertically up the knitting. In the third method, the increases and decreases cause the zigzag edges at the top and bottom, and the resulting vertical bands contain stitches sloping at an angle.

Once again, the knit-face and purl-faced fabrics are jostling and fighting for their place, but in this case the knit-face pushes forwards, as happens in ribbing.

Vertical bands of knit-face and purl-face stocking stitch in energized yarn, pushing the stitches onto the bias and forcing the fabric to shift up and down.

1.) Energized yarn
Cast on 40 sts.
Row 1: K10, P10, rep to end.
Row 2: K10, P10, rep to end.
These 2 rows form the pattern.

2.) Twisted stitches
Row 1: K10b, P10b, rep to end.
Row 2: K10b, P10b, rep to end.
These 2 rows form the pattern.

3.) Increases and decreases
Row 1: *K2tog, K8, M1, P10* rep to end.
Row 2: *K10, M1 purlwise, P8, P2tog*, rep to end.
These 2 rows form the pattern.

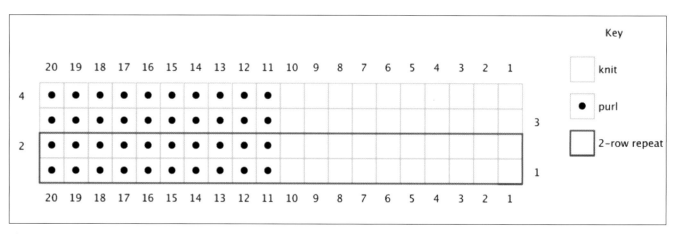

Chart for reversing stocking-stitch bands.

Vertical bands of knit-face and purl-face stocking stitch: the stitches pushed diagonally by knitting and purling into the back of the stitches, forcing the fabric to shift up and down.

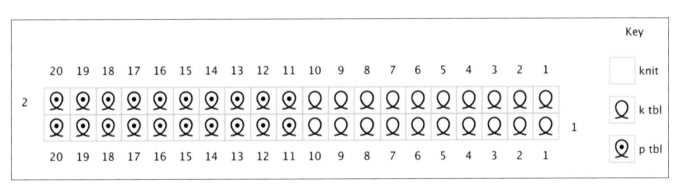

Chart for reversing stocking-stitch bands in twisted stitches.

Vertical bands of knit-face and purl-face stocking stitch: here, increases and decreases force the stitches to travel diagonally (unlike the previous two methods), therefore pushing the fabric to zigzag up and down.

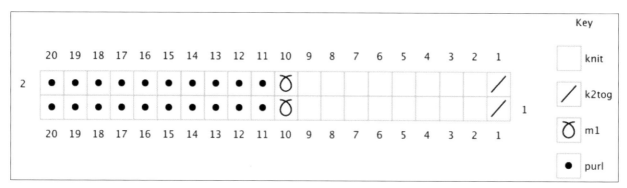

Chart for vertical bands with shaping.

Comparing knit with purl in blocks or squares

Here, the two previous ideas are combined in blocks of knit- and purl-faced stocking stitch, 10 stitches x 12 rows. We have seen how the borders of these blocks move, almost fighting with each other in their efforts to find their place when one set of stitches is pushing and the next is pulling. In these pieces the increases and decreases methods are effective. Although it's constructed quite differently from the two where the stitches do the twisting, the end result is similar. So this time, there is the push and pull of knit against purl on the horizontal edge, with the same thing happening in the opposite way at the vertical join, and then the diagonal push and pull also changing direction at every junction. What happens? There is nowhere for the fabric to go except forwards and back, and a three-dimensional texture is formed.

1.) Energized yarn

Row 1: K10, P10, rep to end.
Row 2: K10, P10, rep to end.
Rep these 2 rows for 12 rows.
Row 13: P10, K10, rep to end.
Row 14: P10, K10, rep to end.
Rep these 2 rows for 12 rows.
Make as many blocks as you want.

Blocks of knit-face and purl-face stocking stitch in energized yarn, where the stitches are pushed by the force of the spin to gather in alternating peaks and troughs.

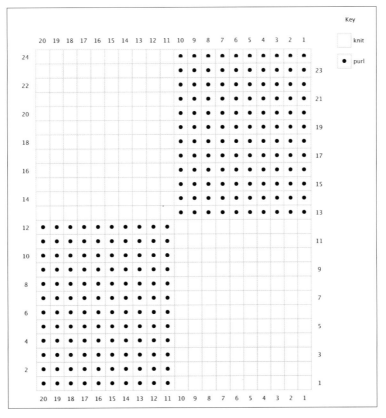

Chart showing knit and purl blocks.

2.) Twisted stitches

Row 1: K10B, P10B, rep to end.

Row 2: K10B, P10B, rep to end.

Rep these 2 rows for 12 rows.

Row 1: P10B, K10B, rep to end.

Row 2: P10B, K10B, rep to end.

Rep for 12 rows.

Rep these 2 rows for 12 rows.

Make as many blocks as you want.

Blocks of knit-face and purl-face stocking stitch, pushed diagonally by knitting and purling into the back of the stitches, forcing the squares to rise and fall in an alternating pattern.

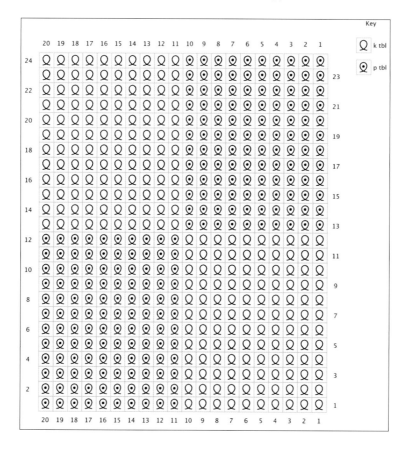

Chart for twisted-stitch blocks.

3.) Increases and decreases

Row 1: *K2tog, K8, M1, P10*, rep to end.

Row 2: *K2tog, K8, M1, P10*, rep to end.

Rep these 2 rows for 12 rows.

Row 13: *P10, K2tog, K8, M1*, rep to end.

Row 14: *P10, K2tog, K8, M1*, rep to end.

Rep these 2 rows for 12 rows.

Make as many blocks as you want.

Blocks of knit-face and purl-face stocking stitch, with increases and decreases pushing each square onto the bias, causing alternate peaks and troughs where the squares meet.

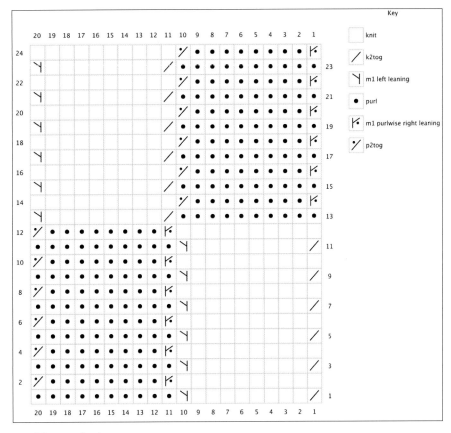

Chart for blocks with increase and decrease shaping.

CHAPTER 4

TWISTS, TURNS, CABLES AND CROSSOVERS

The word 'knitting' derives from the old Saxon *cnyttan* and is in itself derived from *cnotta* – the intertwining parts of one or more ropes forming a knot.

Heinz Edgar Kiewe, The Sacred History of Knitting, 1971

Cables can be thick, rope-like columns of several stitches, or fine single-stitched lines crossing each other. We looked at moving stitches gradually across the surface of the knitting with increases and decreases in Chapter 3, where they are pushed into curves and diagonals but still lie beside each other. In cabling this happens in a different way: they cross over each other physically, swapping positions, and are then worked in their new position. Cabled patterns can be disciplined, regular twists travelling vertically; they can create intricate plaited or knotted effects or can meander in a random fashion here and there (but always upwards, not directly sideways) across the fabric.

This method of patterning is richly decorative and very familiar, famously used in Aran knitting, with cables forming complex twists, plaits and knots highlighted by a purl ground or edging, or they can be smoother and more subtle against a knit ground. The textures and patterns they produce are tactile and inviting, rising up from the fabric in low relief, casting shadows and creating wonderfully rich, intricate patterns reminiscent of carved stone, but at the same time soft and warm. Used traditionally in working men's sweaters around the coasts of Britain and Ireland to provide extra thickness and warmth, and constantly occurring in fashion knitting, often in soft, luxurious yarns, we know how attractive and decorative they can be. Here we're going to look at the way they change

the shape and structure of the knitted fabric as well as their pattern-making.

The vertical smooth 'V' of knit stitches shows the direction of the cable more clearly than purl, where the rough, slightly horizontal texture of the stitch interferes with the direction of the columns of curving stitches, but purl stitches (or purl-sided stocking stitch) are a great tool used *beside* a cable to push it forward and show it off. Although you can still see the twists and crossovers in a cable pattern worked entirely in knit-faced stocking stitch, they merge more generally with the background, whereas a small column of purl stitches outlines or emphasizes the cable. There is so much to explore: soft, blending patterns, or strong, clear dramatic twists, and rather than using them all over, they can be used in columns, bands or patches to shape the knitting.

When we think of cables, vertical columns come to mind, but there are many other possibilities: trellis patterns work very well, from a dainty single knit stitch trellis on a purl background, to bolder, heavier trellis patterns, creating a somehow satisfying and decorative effect reminiscent of Elizabethan embroidery or Celtic patterns. In a regular trellis pattern, you can follow a stitch with your eye as it leaves its original position and travels across the fabric, weaving up and down across the other strands. However, it doesn't have to be entirely geometric; it could be more adventurous and travel some way across, change its mind and travel back. There is lots of scope for more organic, fluid random patterns, although these are often more difficult to plan and achieve than something regular.

What happens to the fabric during all this busy crossing of stitches? It's easy to see and to feel how this action pulls it in widthways. The more crossovers there are in a row, the more it will pull in. It will also affect the length, as it has an overall firming effect on the fabric, restricting the stretchiness in all directions. This is evident in the actual working of a cabled stitch as well: it is often quite hard physically to move or even force one group of stitches across another, necessitating a few plain rows to ease the tension back to a comfortable knitting action. Obviously, the size of the groups of stitches that cross over, and the frequency this happens in rows will affect the firmness. An average cable pattern (if there is such a thing) might have two or three stitches crossing each other perhaps every eight or ten rows, with plain rows between the cabling rows, making for a relaxed feel, but the option to improvise is there. Think it through to create some interesting effects ranging from really strong, tough, heavily cabled stitches to something much softer and lighter, with less frequent cabling.

And so to shaping the fabric: if cabling pulls in, can this be used in a design to shape a garment? What stitches would emphasize this tendency and show well against a cabled area?

Fine trellis

The repeat in this fine trellis pattern is 8 stitches, but it has been knitted with a plain border to see how it alters the width and length of the fabric, so there are 7 edge stitches at each end of the row. The chart shows the repeat.

Cast on 38 sts and knit 10 rows in garter stitch, then about 6 rows in stocking stitch. The purl side is the right side.

Row 1: P7, *K1, P6, K1*, rep to last 7 sts, P7.
Row 2: K7, *P1, K6, P1*, rep to last 7 sts, K7.
Row 3: P7, *C1F, P1, K1C, P4, cable L over R by knitting 2nd st, bring wool forward, P 1st st, slip both off*, rep to last 7 sts, P7.
Row 4: K7, *K1, P1, K4, P1, K1*, rep to last 7 sts, K7.
Row 5: P7, *P1, cable R over L, P2, cable L over R, P1*, rep to last 7 sts, P7.
Row 6: K7, *K2, P1, K2, P1, K2*, rep to last 7 sts, K7.
Row 7: P7, *P2, cable R over L, cable L over R, P2*, rep to last 7 sts, P7.
Row 8: K7, *K3, P2, K3*, rep to last 7 sts, K7.
Row 9: P7, *P3, cable L over R in K, P3*, rep to last 7 sts, P7.
Row 10: as row 8.
Row 11: P7, *P2, cable L over R, cable R over L, P2*, rep to last 7 sts, P7.
Row 12: K7, * as row 6.
Row 13: P7, *P1, cable L over R, P2, cable R over L, P1*, rep to last 7 sts, P7.
Row 14: as row 4.
Row 15: P7, *cable L over R, P4, cable R over L*, rep to last 7 sts, P7.
Row 16: as row 2.
Row 17: P7, * K1, P6, cable R over L in K*, rep to last 8 sts, K1, P7.
Row 18: K7, *P1, K6, P1*.

Repeat from row 3. This is a trellis with a light touch, hardly altering the width of the fabric, but it is firmer than it looks and will not be as stretchy as a 'flat' pattern.

A single-stitch crossover trellis creates a fine trellis with a little firmness but without much effect on the width of the fabric.

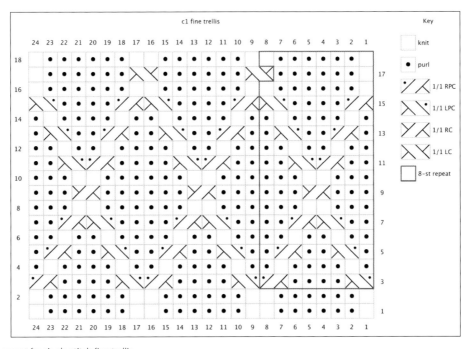

Chart showing pattern repeat for single-stitch fine trellis.

2-stitch trellis

This is worked on 34 stitches, with 7 stitches at each edge. Again, a plain border shows how the stitch pulls in the fabric. A few rows of garter stitch help it to lie flat, then a few rows of stocking stitch (with purl used as right side), which is more flexible but lets the knitting spread to its full width.

Row 1: P7, *K2, P6, K2*, rep ending P7.

Row 2: K7, *P2, K6, P2*, rep ending K7.

Row 3: P7, *C2f, P1, K2C, P4, C1b, K2, P1C*, rep ending P7.

Row 4: K7, *K1, P2, K4, P2, K1*, rep ending K7.

Row 5: P7, *P1, C2f, P1, K2C, P2, C1b, K2, P1C, P1*, rep ending P7.

Row 6: K7, *K2, P2, K2, P2, K2*, rep ending K7.

Row 7: P7, *P2, C2f, P1, K2C, C1b, K2, P1C, P2*, rep ending P7.

Row 8: K7, *K3, P4, K3*, rep ending K7.

Row 9: P7, *P3, C2f, K2, K2C, P3*, rep ending P7.

Row 10: as row 8.

Row 11: P7, *P2, C1b, K2, P1C, C2f, P1, K2C, P2*, rep ending P7.

Row 12: as row 6.

Row 13: P7, *P1, C1b, K2, P1C, P2, C2f, P1, K2C, P1*, rep ending P7.

Row 14: as row 4.

Row 15: P7, *C1b, K2, P1C, P4, C2f, P1, K2C * rep ending P7.

Row 16: as row 2.

Row 17: P7, *K2, P6, C2b, K2, K2C* rep, ending K2, P7.

Row 18: as row 2.

Repeat from row 3. The sample illustrated finishes with a few rows of stocking stitch then garter stitch.

A trellis pattern with 2 stitches crossing over 1 pulls in slightly.

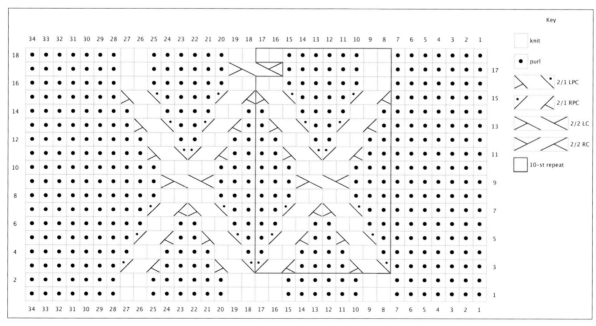

Chart showing 2-stitch trellis pattern.

3-stitch trellis

This has a repeat of 10 stitches with 4 edge stitches each side. The cables are wider, crossing over either 3 over 2 purl stitches, or 3 over 3 where the knit stitches cross, making a much firmer fabric, pulling in more than the single stitch and 2-stitch trellis samples.

The garter and stocking-stitch border illustrates the amount the cables pull in.

Row 1: P4, *K3, P4, K3*, rep, ending P4.
Row 2: K4, *P3, K4, P3*, rep, ending K4.
Row 3: P4, *C3f, P2, K3C, C2b, K3, P2C*, rep ending P4.
Row 4: K4, *K2, P6, K2*, rep ending K4.
Row 5: P4, *P2, K6, P2*, rep ending P4.
Row 6: as row 4.
Row 7: P4, *P2, C3b, K3, K3C, P2*, rep ending P4.
Row 8: as row 4.
Row 9: as row 5.
Row 10: as row 4.
Row 11: P4, *C2b, K3, P2C, C3f, P2, K3C*, rep ending P4.
Row 12: as row 2.
Row 13: P4, K3, P2 *P2, K4, P2*, rep ending P2, K3, P4.
Row 14: as row 2.
Row 15: P4, K3, P2 *P2, C3f, K3, K3C, P2*, rep ending P2, K3, P4.
Row 16: K4, P3, K2 *K2, P6, K2*, rep ending K2, P3, K4.

Row 17: P4, K3, P2 *P2, K6, P2*, rep ending P2, K3, P4.
Row 18: as row 16.

Making the cables and crossovers every 4 rows pulls this fabric in, but this could be adjusted to a more relaxed fabric crossing every 6 or 8 rows, or tightened up with alternate row cabling.

A trellis pattern with 3 stitches crossing over 2, creates a much firmer, narrower fabric.

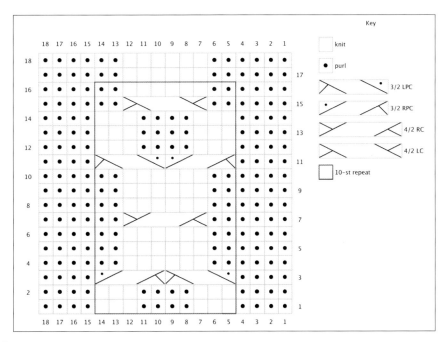

Chart for 3-stitch trellis pattern.

Criss-cross cables

Cabling doesn't get much tighter than this; 2 stitches are crossed over 2 neighbouring stitches on alternate rows. This pulls in widthways a lot, as shown in the frilling of the plain band of garter and stocking stitch. The garter-stitch strip up the sides of this piece is designed to lie flat, but remembering that garter stitch also pulls up lengthwise, it illustrates that the crossover pattern pulls up the same amount as garter stitch.

Criss-cross cable makes a very firm, thick fabric: on alternate rows, 2 stitches cross the neighbouring 2 stitches all along the row, pulling in tightly.

The pattern is a simple repeat of 4 rows over 4 stitches. This piece is knitted on 38 stitches so it can be compared in width with the previous pieces, but the actual pattern is worked on 26 stitches, with 6 stitches for each side border. If you follow these instructions on a number of stitches divisible by 4, you will end up with vertical ropes of 2 over 2-stitch cables. To achieve this alternating pattern, either work on a number divisible by 4 with 2 extra (like this on 26 sts), or stagger the cables.

Cast on 38 sts and work a band of garter stitch then stocking stitch.
Row 1: K4, P2, *C2f, K2, K2C*, rep to last 8 sts, K2, P2, K4.
Row 2: K6, P to last 6 sts, K6.
Row 3: K4, P2, K2 *C2b, K2, K2C*, rep to last 6 sts, P2, K4.
Row 4: as row 2.
These 4 rows form the pattern.

The 2-row stripes have been introduced at the top of this piece to show how the cabling breaks up the stripes into tiny diamonds of alternating colours.

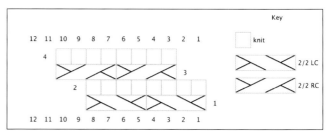

Chart showing the criss-cross pattern: the crossover shifts to pair a different group of 2 over 2 each time.

4-stitch criss-cross

On a slightly larger scale, this is worked with 4 stitches crossing 4, with 3 rows between the cable rows. This produces an extremely tough, solid fabric with very little stretch. It would work well for a firm edging, blooming out into the full width in a blouson effect, or as a way of pulling part of a garment

Four stitches cross over 4 every fourth row, pulling in very tightly to make a thicker criss-cross pattern. Stripes of colour are transformed into a pattern of diagonal blocks, flaring out into a frill when the cables finish.

or item into a tight band. If you work this stitch right to (or from) the top or bottom edge, it creates a decorative zigzag edging.

This piece is worked on more stitches than the previous samples, as the width is pulled in so much.

Cast on 48 sts, and P one row.
Row 1: *C4f, K4, K4C*, rep to end.
Row 2: P.
Row 3: K.
Row 4: P.
Row 5: K4, *C4b, K4, K4C*, rep to last 4 sts, K4.
Row 6: P.
Row 7: K.
Row 8: P.

These 8 rows form the pattern. On this piece, a band of stocking stitch above the cables shows how much the width has been pulled in, finishing with the even wider moss stitch to highlight this effect. If you want to experiment further, what would happen if you always cabled in the same direction?

Playing with colour can give different emphases, and simple stripes are distorted by the cabling to give the illusion of small diamonds of colour. It would be simple to produce a basket weave effect by using just two colours, changing colour on each cable row. Here, a sequence of colours has been used in 4-row stripes.

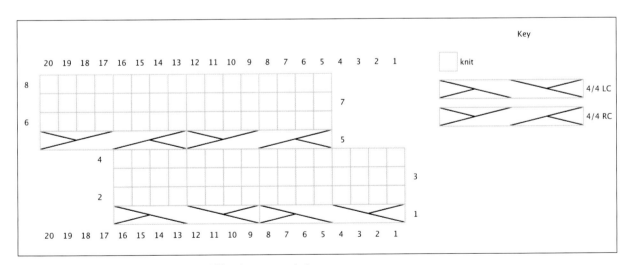

Chart showing how 4 stitches cross over a different neighbouring group each time.

Trellis with moss stitch

Another way of introducing a cabled trellis pattern is to introduce it gradually rather than all at once, bringing in the fullness of the width of the knitting more slowly, making a decorative V-shaped panel with gathers below it and enabling a body-shaped garment.

This piece is worked on 42 sts, with a moss stitch ground to provide the fullness to contrast with the trellis pattern.

Cast on 42 sts and do a few rows in moss stitch (MS), then introduce the bottom of the V-pattern:

Row 1: MS20, K2, MS20.
Row 2: MS20, P2, MS20.
Row 3: MS19, K4, MS19.
Row 4: MS19, P4, MS19.
Row 5: MS17, C2b, K2, P2C, C2f, P2, K2C, MS17.

Beginning with moss stitch, the cabled trellis-pattern is introduced gradually, pulling the fabric in gently and causing a slight dip down in the centre against a moss stitch edging.

Row 6: MS17, P2, K4, P2, MS17.
Row 7: MS15, C2b, K2, P2C, P4, C2f, P2, K2C, MS15.
Row 8: MS15, P2, K8, P2, MS15.
Row 9: MS13, C2b, K2, K2C, P8, C2f, K2, K2C, MS13.
Row 10: MS13, P4, K8, P4, MS13.
Row 11: MS11, C2b, K2, K2C, C2f, P2, K2C, P4, C2f, P2, K2C, C2b, K2, K2C, MS11.
Row 12: MS11, (P2, K4) x 3, P2, MS11.
Row 13: MS9, (C2b, K2, P2C, P4, C2f, P2, K2C) x 2, MS9.
Row 14: MS9, (P2, K8, P2) x 2, MS9.
Row 15: MS7, C2b, K2, K2C, P8, C2F, K2, K2C, P8, C2f, K2, K2C, MS7.
Row 16: MS7, (P4, K8) x 2, P4, MS7.
Row 17: MS5, (C2b, K2, P2C, C2f, P2, K2C, P4) x 2, C2b, K2, P2C, C2f, P2, K2C, MS5.
Row 18: MS5, (P2, K4) x 5, P2, MS5.
Row 19: MS3, (C2b, K2, P2C, P4, C2f, P2, K2C) x 3, MS3
Row 20: MS3, (P2, K8, P2) x 3, MS3
Row 21: K1, C2b, K2, K2C (P8, C2f, K2, K2C) x 2, P8, C2f, K2, K2C, K1
Row 22: K1, (P4, K8) x 3, P4, K1

The trellis pattern has now reached the edges.
To continue the trellis pattern:
Row 23: K1, P1, K1, (C2f, P2, K2C, P4, C2b, K2, P2C) x 3, K1, P1, K1.
Row 24: K1, P1, K1, K2 (P2, K4) x 5, P2, K2, K1, P1, K1.
Row 25: K1, P1, K1, P2 (C2f, P2, K2C, C2b, K2, P2C, P4) x 2, C2f, P2, K2C, C2b, K2, P2C, P2, K1, P1, K1.
Row 26: K1, P1, K1, (K4, P4, K4) x 3, K1, P1, K1.
Row 27: K1, P1, K1, (P4, C2b, K2, K2C, P4) x 3, K1, P1, K1.
Row 28: as row 26.
Row 29: K1, P1, K1, P2 (C2b, K2, P2C, C2f, P2, K2C, P4) x 2, C2b, K2, P2C, C2f, P2, K2C, P2, K1, P1, K1.
Row 30: as row 24.
Row 31: K1, P1, K1, (C2b, K2, P2C, P4, C2f, P2, K2C) x 2, K1, P1, K1.
Row 32: K1, P1, K1, (P2, K8, P2) x 3, K1, P1, K1.
To continue the trellis pattern, repeat from row 21.

Chart showing the trellis with moss stitch pattern, which could continue on a wider piece, letting the trellis spread across the width to draw in the fabric.

Moss stitch and gradual cables

This piece uses columns of twisted stitches repeated in a simple vertical, but rather than all beginning at the bottom, these are introduced gradually as the knitting travels upwards, with the effect that the width is slowly drawn in, and the sides also drawn up by the tight twists. These 'ropes' contrast well with moss stitch, which knits up wider than stocking stitch, is lighter and less rigid than garter stitch, but lies flat without any tendency to curl or bounce up, and with an attractive, pebbly texture that sets off the smoothness of the cables.

The cabled unit is 6 stitches wide, 3 crossing over 3, with a 2-stitch column of purl-faced stocking stitch edging each 'rope'. There are 8 rows between the twists, and new ropes are introduced every second twist, so are 16 rows apart. The instructions are given for this sample worked on 50 stitches, but it could be made in a much wider panel or across a garment. The moss stitch border is used to illustrate how the cables pull in.

Ropes of cabling introduced from the centre out towards the sides in steps also pull in gradually, causing a dip in the centre.

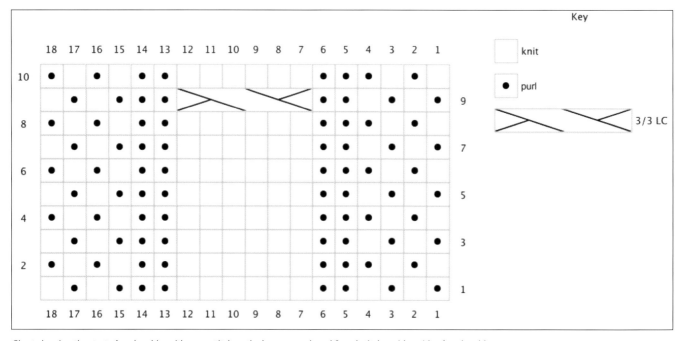

Chart showing the start of each cable, with moss stitch as the base ground, and 2 purl stitches either side of each cable rope.

The chart shows the first cable 'rope' with its edging of purl and moss stitches.

Cast on 50 sts, and work in moss stitch:
Row 1: *K1, P1*, rep to end.
Row 2: *P1, K1*, rep to end.
Repeat these 2 rows for a border.

Step 1: first cable sts

The first cable stitches are introduced on the centre 6 sts:
Row 1: MS20, P2, K6, P2, MS20.
Row 2: MS20, K2, P6, K2, MS20.
Repeat these 2 rows until you have done 8 rows.

Note: When starting row 2, be careful to keep the moss stitch in pattern, not turning into rib: check whether to start each row with a knit or a purl stitch.

<u>**First cable row:**</u> MS20, P2, C3f, K3, K3C, P2, MS20.
Row 2: MS20, K2, P6, K2, MS20.
Row 3: MS20, P2, K6, P2, MS20.
Row 4: as row 2 of this section.
Rep rows 3 and 4 until you have done 8 rows of this section, then rep the cable and 7 more rows.

Step 2: second cables sts

The second cable stitches are introduced, and more cabling:
Row 1: MS12, P2, K6, P2, C3f, K3, K3C, P2, K6, P2, MS12.
Row 2: MS12, (K2, P6) x 3, K2, MS12.
Row 3: MS12, (P2, K6) x 3, P2, MS12.
Row 4: as row 2.
Rep rows 3 and 4 until you have done 8 rows of this section, then rep the cable and 7 more rows.

Step 3: third cables sts

The third cable stitches are introduced, and more cabling:
Row 1: MS4, P2, K6, P2, (C3f, K3, K3C, P2) x 3, K6, P2, MS4.
Row 2: MS4, (K2, P6) x 5, K2, MS4.
Row 3: MS4, (P2, K6) x 5, P2, MS4.
Row 4: as row 2.
Rep rows 3 and 4 until you have done 8 rows of this section, then rep the cable and 7 more rows.

Continue in this way as long as you like; they could expand to cover the width of a sweater.

Cables for texture

Random-effect texture

Randomness is quite difficult to achieve as the surface can become unevenly buckled and look chaotic. This may be what you want, but it must look as if it was intentional to avoid looking wrong! In this piece, worked on a knit-faced stocking stitch background, simple twists form pinch points, pulling the fabric in. They are made by crossing 4 stitches over 4 twice, with one row between, each pair of twists in a different direction. There are 12 plain stitches between the crosses, and 8 rows before a twist is placed in the space between the previous twists. The different directions of the twists influence the fabric around them so that, although the twists are at regular intervals, the effect is random, pushed this way and that.

As before, there is a border to show how much the fabric is pulled in, this time in moss stitch.

Cast on 44 sts and work a border in moss stitch (K1, P1), then keeping 5 sts at either edge in moss st, work 8 rows in st st.

Row 1: K1, P1, K1, P1, K1, K3, C4f, K4, K4C, K12, C4b, K4, K4C, K3, P1, K1, P1, K1, P1.
Row 2: P1, K1, P1, K1, P1, P to last 5 sts, K1, P1, K1, P1, K1.
Row 3: as row 1.
Row 4: as row 2.

Work 8 rows in st st with MS edges, then make a cross in the centre in the same way.

Here 4 stitches cross over 4 to create pinch points all in stocking stitch, repeating again after a plain row, pulling the fabric in, making a random-effect textured surface rather than a distinct pattern.

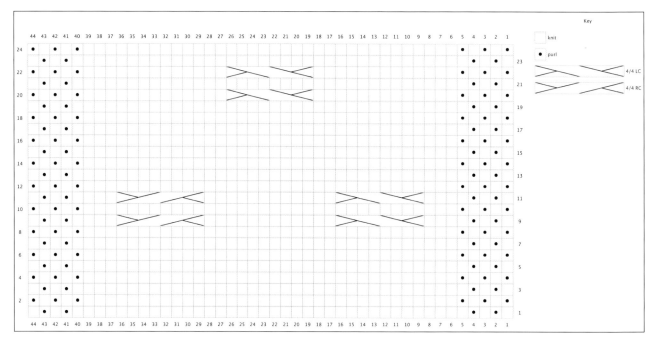

Chart showing pinch points repeated each time on the second row.

Pinch points

This has the same 'pinch points' as the random-effect texture sample above, but is worked on a moss stitch ground with only one twist, rather than repeated 2 rows later.

Cast on 44 stitches, and work in moss stitch:
Row 1: *K1, P1*, rep to end.
Row 2: *P1, K1*, rep to end.
Work for about 10 rows, finishing on a WS row.

Pattern
Row 1: MS8, K8, MS12, K8, MS8.
Row 2: MS8, P8, MS12, P8, MS8.
Row 3: MS8, C4f, K4, K4C, MS12, C4b, K4, K4C, MS8.
Row 4: as row 2.

Work 8 rows in moss st, then introduce new cable/pinch point:
Row 1: MS18, K8, MS18.
Row 2: MS18, P8, MS18.
Row 3: MS18, C4f, K4, K4C, MS18.
Row 4: as row 2.

Work 8 rows in moss st, then make 2 cables like the first 2, but cabling the first to the back, and the second to the front.

Pinch points in stocking stitch on a moss stitch ground, with a single twist of 4 over 4 stitches in an alternating dot pattern.

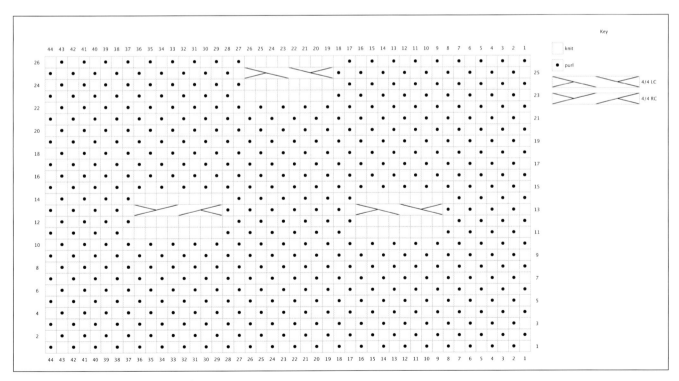

Chart showing pinch points which change direction.

Gathered surface pattern

Here, pinch points are placed regularly, 4 stitches crossing over 4 again. They are repeated over these 8 stitches with 8 plain stitches between, travelling to the right in one row, and to the left in the next crossover row. Originally, the crossing stitches or cables were planned in knit-face stocking stitch on a purl background, but as it progressed, the reverse side became more interesting and makes a clearer design, with the plain stitches pulled by the cables into a regularly patterned buckled surface texture. It's always worth checking what is happening on the back in case it is more interesting! This patterning would be satisfying as an all-over effect, or could be used in an area of gathering such as embroidered smocking, contrasting with a fuller fabric.

Illustrated on 48 stitches, the chart shows a repeat of 16 stitches, and shows the *reverse side to the photo*.

Cast on 48 sts and work 4 rows in g st as a foundation, then P 1 row on WS:

Row 1: K.
Row 2: *P8, K8*, rep to end.
Row 3: *P8, K8* rep to end.
Row 4: *P8, K8* rep to end.
Row 5: *P8, C4f, K4, K4C*, rep to end.
Row 6: *P8, K8*, rep to end.
Row 7: K.
Row 8: P.

Row 9: K.
Row 10: *K8, P8*, rep to end.
Row 11: *K8, P8*, rep to end.
Row 12: *K8, P8*, rep to end.
Row 13: *C4b, K4, K4C, P8*, rep to end.
Row 14: *K8, P8*, rep to end.
Row 15: K.
Row 16: P.

These 16 rows form the pattern.

Pinch points of 4 stitches crossing 4 in purl on a knit ground, crossing first one way then the other, gather the fabric in strongly, like the effect of smocking.

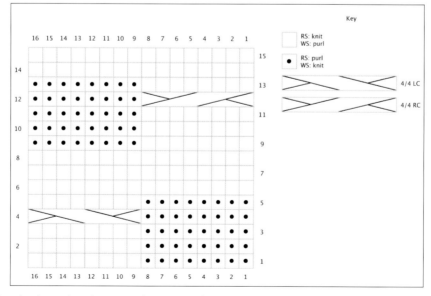

The chart shows reverse side to the photo, where the crossover happens in purl.

Summary of trellises and cables

A review of this chapter so far shows that all-over patterns of trellises and cables used in a formal, repeated pattern are both attractive and functional. They make a thicker fabric, but as we have seen, this thickness comes at the cost of pulling in the width in order to build that extra layer and density. Once again, here is an opportunity to shape the fabric or to give form to a garment by using the cables to pull in.

Braided and twice-knit stitches

Braiding in knitting

Another form of knitting where crossing stitches alters the fabric both visually and structurally involves something different again. In cabling, stitches swap places, crossing over each other at an angle. The steepness of the angle is controlled by how often this happens, with frequent crossings making for an angle nearer horizontal, but with several rows between the cabling, the angle moves closer to vertical. There's another very obvious stitch we use frequently, a method of laying stitches over each other, which we take for granted without really examining it: casting (or binding) off. Here, the stitches are laid down completely flat, horizontally one over another. We think of this process as final, as the finish to a piece of knitting, but there are ways of using it within the knitting to produce extraordinary effects, changing the stretch, feel and drape of the knitted fabric and giving it both a horizontal emphasis visually and a built-in stiffness as well. A row of cast-off in knitting is described as a 'braid'. These are not formed like woven or plaited braids, but they give the appearance of a raised braid crossing the knitting, almost contradicting the familiar look of a knitted fabric by travelling sideways. If two colours are used, they can look like a plaited braid. There are traditions of using braids in knitting decoratively and functionally. As each stitch is cast off, another is created, so that a chain is laid horizontally across the knitting with new stitches remaining on the needle to continue upwards. These braids or chains are often used as an edging to mittens in Estonia[1] and other countries in the area, usually one stitch wide, but the idea can be developed with more stitches, until with enough stitches, it turns into an i-cord or thicker rope across the knitting. We know from experience that there is not much stretch in a cast-off edge, so what happens to the knitted fabric? The effect of making this line across the stretchiest (widthways) direction of the knitting is of a stiffening or strengthening, altering the movement of the fabric and the way it hangs, rather such as the action of a stiff edge of piping used in sewn fabric. There are times when this is useful and it is a great design tool, either used occasionally in a band to build up an area travelling at right angles to the rest of the knitting as a kind of horizontal punctuation, or repeated to form a regular (or irregular) pattern.

First method: Yarn-over braid

The braid travels in the direction of the knitting, so the right-hand stitch is laid over the left-hand stitch, as in casting off (binding off). This can also be done by making a decrease with the right stitch on top, made by K1, S1, psso (or SSK) which, if done continuously, has a similar effect. A new stitch is created before each decrease or bind off, so the number of stitches remains the same.

One-stitch braid

Knitted in blue yarn in the sample pictured, this is the first braid from the book, after the band of garter stitch.

On any number of stitches, knit to the place you want to make your braid. The 'YO's create the new stitches that remain on the needle.

Knitted braids of different thicknesses: the blue section shows a 1-stitch yarn-over braid; green shows 2-stitch braids, and the grey section is 3-stitch braiding, or a travelling i-cord.

Row 1 (RS facing): YO, S1, K1, psso (or SSK)*, put st back on LH needle, YO, SSK*, rep to end.

If you continue in stocking stitch, purl the next row.

You can also make this braid on the purl row, forming a chain facing the opposite way on the knit side:
Row 2 (purl side facing): *YO, bring yarn forward, P2tog, put st back on LH needle*, rep ending P2tog.

This braiding can be made as often as you want, on a ground of stocking stitch, or spaced with plain rows between. Working braids on the knit and purl rows produces a solid area of braiding in alternating directions, making a horizontal pattern of chains.

The characteristic of this 1-stitch braid is that it stands forward from the ground with the cast-off chain tilting forwards, making a very pronounced ridge. If you stretch it out, it will (surprisingly) easily stretch to the full fabric width (*see* the Vikkel braid, below).

Two-stitch braid

This is worked in a similar way, with 2 stitches travelling across. It is shown in green in the knitted sample.

Row 1 (RS facing): cast on 2 sts, K2, return 2 sts to LH needle, YO, K1, S1, K1, psso (or SSK)*, put 2 sts back on LH needle, YO, K1, SSK*, rep to end of row.

At the end of the row, check you have the same number of sts, and if an extra one appears, K2tog at the end.

To make this braid on a purl row, work in a similar way:
Row 2: cast on 2 sts, P2, return 2 sts to LH needle, YO, P2tog*, put 2 sts back on LH needle, YO, P2tog*, rep to end of row.

This braid is firmer than the 1-stitch braid, with less stretch and more horizontal strength.

3-stitch braid (or i-cord)

This 3-stitch braid is the top braid on the sample, knitted in grey yarn. An even stronger braid, this is the horizontal version of the i-cord, first named by Elizabeth Zimmerman in her books of the 1970s[2]. An i-cord produces a knitted cord like the 'French knitting' kits usually used by children, where as few as 4 stitches are worked on pegs or loops in the round on a bobbin. To make this work on knitting needles, the stitches are knitted, then passed back to the left-hand needle and knitted again, always in the same direction. The yarn pulls around the back to close the gap and a narrow tube is knitted. The great thing about knitting an i-cord is that as well as making an independent cord, it can be combined with and incorporated within a flat knitted fabric. It can form a cord along the side edge of the knitting, vertically, or across as shown in the knitted sample, or as a cast-on or a cast-off edge. It is stronger and firmer than the 2-stitch braid, acting as a definite stabilizing influence on the fabric, restricting its stretch. It also makes a great cast-off edge (without the YOs, which make new stitches), giving a firm, professional finish when a strong, inflexible edge is appropriate.

Row 1 (RS facing): cast on 4, K3, place 3 sts back on LH needle, YO, K2, SSK*, put 3 sts back on LH needle, YO, K2, SSK*, rep to end of row, slip last 3 sts back on LH needle, K1, SSK, slip 2 sts back, K2tog.
You need to pull the yarn quite firmly on the first stitch to make a neat cord.

This cord can also be made on a purl row:
Row 2: cast on 4 sts, P3, place 3 back on LH needle, YO, P2, P2tog*, put 3 sts back on LH needle, YO, P2, P2tog*, rep to end of row, slip last 3 sts back on LH needle, P1, P2tog, slip 2 sts back, P2tog.

Note: It is hard to make the purl cord as neat as the knit one, as shown in the sample where it is wider than the knit, but this may vary with individual knitters.

The braids in this piece are finished with an i-cord cast-off:
Cast on 3 sts. Knit 2, SSK, put 3 sts back on LH needle, K2, SSK, rep to end, slip 3 sts back, K1, K2tog, slip 2 sts back, K2tog and finish off.

All these braids or cords become firmer with greater numbers of stitches, although there is a limit to how many stitches can be handled. The 1-stitch yarn-over braid is not particularly tight or firm, so this method would be useful if you want to retain some stretch. The knitted sample shows how much more the 3-stitch i-cord is pulling in and stiffening the fabric.

However, there is another way of making a 1-stitch braid: a very different action in the knitting, but again resulting in the 1-stitch chain lying along the front of the fabric, but this time much flatter and firmer. This is described by Nancy Bush in *Folk Knitting in Estonia* under 'Vikkel braid'.[1]

Second method: Vikkel braid

Row 1: K1, then replace this st onto the LH needle, *bring the right needle behind this st, K the next st through back of loop, then knit into the 1st st through the front as usual, and slip both sts off. Place the st just made back onto the LH needle, and repeat from *.

Again, you can use this braid occasionally or set closely together in rows, with the purl-row braid formed like this:

Row 2: with P side facing, P1, then replace this st onto the LH needle, *bring the yarn and right needle forward and P the second st, then P into the 1st st through the front as usual, and slip both sts off. Place the st just made back onto the LH needle, and repeat from *, ending by purling and slipping last sts off.

Third method: 2-yarn braid

Another way of making a raised horizontal pattern across the knitting is to carry yarn across in front of the stitches when working in two colours. In some Scandinavian knitting traditions this is used in one colour to created extra warmth and texture, but can also be used to make colour patterns, often called twined knitting. In this piece, the bottom two braids are made in this way, with the pattern of vertical stripes made by simply knitting alternate stitches in each of two colours (purling on the reverse). This is the 2-row pattern:

Row 1: on RS bring the yarns to the front, P1 col A, lift yarn A up, P1B, lift yarn B up. Repeat, but always twist the yarns in the same direction. By the end of the row, the yarns will be twisted around each other, but working back, they will untwist.

This shows Vikkel braid worked on both knit and purl rows, travelling in both directions, firstly spaced with bands of stocking stitch and moss stitch, then worked as a repeated band of solid braiding.

A 2-yarn braid: working from the bottom, the first rows of striped braiding are made by knitting the stitches in alternate colours, carrying the spare yarn in front for 2 rows. The plain grey area is done in the same way using 2 strands of grey yarn. The next braid up is a two-colour braid using the yarn-over method, and the top shows a (flatter) Vikkel braid.

Row 2: with yarns at the back, *K1A, K1B*, twisting the yarns in the opposite direction (they will unwind), and always in the same direction.

To achieve this twisting, you need to hold the yarns so you can easily twist them and pick up alternate strands. This is not so easy if you are used to knitting with a yarn in each hand for two-colour knitting – in fact it is counter-intuitive to the usual way of weaving in a second colour where you do *not* want to twist the yarns. But whether you usually hold the yarn in your left or right hand, they need to twist round one way for one row, and the reverse on the next to produce the neat chevron-patterned braid. There are many videos easily found on the internet showing this technique, but as with most YouTube videos, it's worth watching a few before deciding which is the most efficient, and which suits your own way of knitting.

The plain grey raised ridge in the two-yarn braid sample is done in the same way with two strands of grey, so the herringbone pattern doesn't show so clearly. Above this is a two-colour yarn-over braid, worked like this:

Row 1: *using col A, YO, K2togb, return stitch to LH needle, change to col B, YO, K2togb, return stitch to LH needle*. Rep, alternating stitches and being careful to keep the tension even. This is made in one row.

The final braid in this piece is a Vikkel braid using two colours, lying flatter against the background, as we saw in the Vikkel braid sample.

Row 1: K1A, put st back on LH needle, K 2nd st through the back in A, K 1st st B, put st back on LH needle, K 2nd st through the back in B, K 1st st A, put st back on LH needle, rep to end.

This is also a 1-row braid.

More on the i-cord

The i-cord deserves a little more examination and a section in its own right. It's an extraordinary tool, both decorative and useful, and surprising if you haven't come across it before, linking with both cables and crossovers and braids. This little tube of knitting can be made independently, or travel upwards or across the knitting, within the fabric or at the edge. It makes a great finish (or start) if you want a fairly rigid edging, or as already mentioned, provides a stiffening or 'piping' within the knitted fabric. It makes a satisfying and strong edge to a knitted hat or bag, where it helps to hold a firm shape. Forming a natural knitted piping, an i-cord used to edge a knitted cushion gives a professional finish. The back and front can be placed together, and the 'cast-off' i-cord

formed through both sets of stitches, simultaneously joining them and making a neat edge. There is something very pleasing about incorporating this technique into the body of the knitting, or using it as an edge or join that is integral and doesn't need attaching separately. It can, of course, be made to detach itself and become independent at any time to form loops or cords from the knitted surface (*see* below).

These instructions for i-cords travelling in different ways are given individually for each separate movement. These are for a 4-stitch i-cord, but other sizes could be used.

Self-coloured i-cord
This piece shows i-cord cast-on, travelling up one side edge, across the rows, vertically up the centre, up the other edge and finishing with an i-cord cast-off.

i-cord cast-on
Cast on 4 sts. *YO, K4, return 4 to LH needle*, rep until you have enough sts, ending with K4.
Note: always pull the yarn firmly behind the i-cord.

Beginning with an i-cord cast-on, the cord becomes independent and creates a free loop at the side. A new blue cord is picked up from the right corner, looped at the side and knitted across, looped again, then travels across the fabric from left to right. It is looped again, then creates an i-cord cast-off. The cords show up well on a stocking stitch or moss stitch ground.

This i-cord cast-on, which travels up the side edge of the knitting, begins to travel from left to right on the purl row, then makes a vertical i-cord travelling upwards, continues across, up the other edge, and finishes with an i-cord cast-off.

All these are written for an i-cord on a knit (stocking stitch) ground. The horizontal i-cords stand out clearly, but the vertical i-cords are less prominent. You could make them more visible on a purl-faced ground.

i-cord at left edge
The 4 sts are extra to the number of sts in your main fabric.
Knit row: K to last 4 sts, return 4 to LH needle, K4.
Purl row: S4, and P to end.
Rep these 2 rows for as long as you want.

i-cord at right edge
The 4 sts are extra to the number of sts in your main fabric.
Knit row: K4, return 4 to LH needle, K4, K to end.
Purl row: P to last 4 sts, slip these and turn.
Rep these 2 rows for as you long as you want.

Horizontal i-cord travelling from right to left
At beginning of **knit** row, *YO, K3, K2tog B, return 4 to LH needle * rep to end, return 4 to LH needle and K4 again.

Horizontal i-cord travelling from left to right
At beg of **P** row, *YO, P3, P2tog, return 4 to LH needle, rep from * to end, then return 4 to LH needle, P them again.

Note: I find it particularly difficult to make a neat cord travelling on the purl row. The YO makes a long journey because of the angle of the needles, although this may vary with different knitting styles. I find it works to omit the YO, just purl 4. When you begin the next P4, pick up the strand that was pulled across before the P4: this makes the new stitch with less wasted yarn, and is neater. Repeat across the row.

Vertical i-cord mid-row
This is shown in the sample as a continuation of the cord crossing the rows, but you could begin one from scratch: to create an i-cord within the knitting, you need to create 4 stitches. Work to where you want it to begin, and make 4 stitches. This is tricky to do neatly, so the neatest and firmest way might be to grow it gradually:

Make a st by picking up the bar before the next st and knitting it.

Slide 2 sts back to the LH needle and (K1, make a st with a thumb twist) twice.

Slide these 4 sts back and K4. Work to end of row.
Purl row: P to the i-cord, S4, P to end.
Knit row: K to the i-cord, K4, return 4 to LH needle, K4 and K to end.
Rep these 2 rows for as long as you want.

Diagonal i-cord
Moving from RH edge diagonally to the left:
Knit row: YO, K3, K2togb, return sts, K4, cont with pattern.
Purl row: purl, slip the 4 sts of the i-cord, pulling the yarn across firmly.
Note: the 'YO' may seem loose, so work through the back of st to twist it more firmly.
Next Knit row: K1, YO, K3, K2togb, return 4 sts, K4, cont with pattern.
In each following knit row, there will be an extra K st before the 'YO' as the i-cord travels across.

Moving from LH edge diagonally to the right
Knit row: work to the last 5 sts, K2tog, K3, return 4 sts, K3, K into f&b of 4th st.
Purl row: slip the 4 sts of the i-cord, pulling the yarn across firmly.
Next **Knit row**: work to last 6 sts, K2tog, K3, return 4 sts, K3, K into f&b of 4th st, K1.
In each following knit row, there will be an extra K st after the last increase as the i-cord travels across.

Note: the sample shows that it is more difficult to make this diagonal i-cord neat and cord-like. Remember to pull the yarn behind it as firmly as possible.

Random and detached i-cords
The i-cord can be made independently, or it can leave the surface of the knitting and move freely, making a cord for tying, or landing back into the surface at any time to create a loop.

A simple i-cord knitted independently is easier to work on two short double-ended needles. This removes the need to slip the stitches back onto the LH needle: you can simply swap the needle to the other hand, slide the stitches to the other end and knit in the same direction again. Repeat this for as long as you want it.

Using an i-cord cast-on, the cord then travels randomly back and forth, with a second cord picked up and travelling up the other side diagonally. The blue area is not attached, and crosses the brown cord before joining in with the background again, then both cords continue independently.

If you have an integral i-cord and want it to take flight from your knitting, simply put the i-cord sts onto a short double-ended needle and work the cord as described above for as long as you want.

i-cord cast-off
Knit row: K4, return these to LH needle, *K3, K2togb, return 4 to LH needle, rep from * until you reach the end, return 4 to LH needle, K2, K2tog, return 3 to LH needle.
K1, K2tog, return 2 to LH needle.
K2tog and fasten off.

Twice-knit stitches

Although this stitch looks very different from the braiding, the similarity is that the stitches are locked together, but this time by knitting two together (rather than dropping one over another), which places the left stitch on top of the right. This action of K2tog is done all the way across the row, but,

of course, this would also reduce the number of stitches by half. In order to keep the original number, as you knit the 2 together, you drop only one stitch from the needle and knit into the remaining stitch again together with the following stitch, thus knitting into each stitch twice. So from knitting into 2 stitches, you are left with 2 stitches with a firm 'lock' below, which pulls in, but in fact surprisingly it still retains some stretch. As illustrated in the following pieces, this action can be done in knit or purl, on every row or alternate rows, or occasionally. One point to bear in mind is that it's quite tricky to keep a definite edge to vertical patches or blocks of this stitch (so this only applies to the pieces with blocks, dots or vertical stripes). Each block loses a stitch at the beginning with the first K2tog, so has to create one at the end of the block by knitting the last stitch again, as written in the instructions.

Stripes of twice-knit stitch
These bands of twice-knit stitches alternated with stocking stitch create a slightly gathered or seersucker effect.
Cast on 40 sts (any number can be used).
This piece shows a band of garter stitch and stocking stitch, then 4 rows of twice-knit stitch, which go like this:
Row 1: *K2tog, but only drop one st off the needle*, rep to end of row, K last st again, (so the second K2tog knits the one remaining on the needle with the next st, and so on). *Don't forget to knit the last stitch again at the end of the row or the number of sts will decrease!*
Row 2: *P2tog, but only drop one off the needle*, rep to end of row, purl last st again.

The 3 bands of twice-knit stitch show how much this stitch pulls in: the bottom band is knit-side, the second band is worked in purl-side (or twice-purl), and the top band in twice-knit garter stitch.

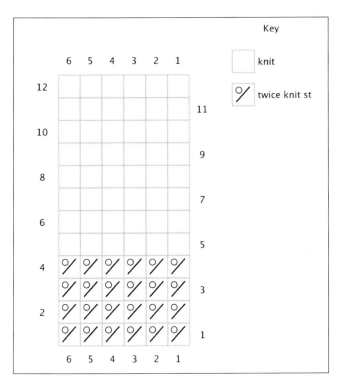

Key
☐ knit
◿ twice knit st

Chart showing the knit-side band of twice-knit.

The chart shows one repeat, but there are 8 rows of stocking stitch on the piece illustrated, then the next band of twice-knit stitch is worked on the purl side: work row 2, then row 1, row 2, and row 1.

Work 8 more rows of stocking stitch, then the top band is in garter stitch, so do 4 rows of row 1.

If you stretch this out widthways, the twice-knit areas are happy to stretch to the full width, but will then pull back in again.

Columns of twice-knit stitches

This piece is not as visually striking as the stripes, showing that the columns of twice-knit stitches don't shorten the length; all the tightness is in the width. A band of stocking stitch and

moss stitch has been added at the top to show how much the columns have pulled in. From left to right, the columns are twice-knit purl side, knit side in the centre, and garter stitch on the right.

Cast on 42 sts.

Row 1: K4, *K2tog, slipping only the first st off the needle*, rep for 5 sts: K the remaining st again, K8, *K2tog, slipping only the first st off the needle*, rep for 5 sts: K the remaining st again, K8, *P2tog, slipping only the first st off the needle*, rep for 5 sts, P the remaining st again, K4.

Row 2: P4 *K2tog, slipping only the first st off the needle*, rep for 5 sts, K the remaining st again, P8*, P2tog, but only drop one off the needle*, rep for 5 sts, P last st again, P8, *K2tog, slipping only the first st off the needle*, rep for 5 sts, K the remaining st again, P4.

These 2 rows form the pattern. The knit column sinks into the knit background and is hardly visible, but both the other columns show well on both sides of the fabric.

The moss stitch edging shows that these columns of twice-knit stitch don't pull in as much as horizontal bands. The 5-stitch columns are purl on the left, knit in the centre, and garter stitch on the right.

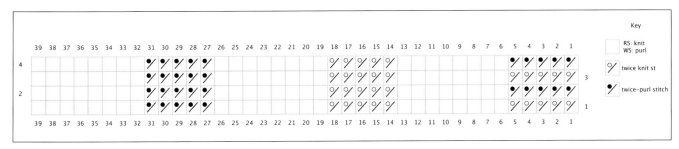

Chart showing knit-side, purl-side, and garter stitch twice-knit.

Blocks of twice-knit stitches

Placing this stitch in blocks creates a texture on the surface, but also draws the stitches in to distort the fabric into a bubbled effect. Here, the twice-knit blocks are in garter stitch, making a definite ridged pattern.

This piece has a band of K1, P1 rib, which pulls in to highlight the fullness of the band of stocking stitch before the pattern begins.

The chart shows a repeat of 24 sts.

Blocks of twice-knit garter stitch in an alternating pattern, pulling in the width to create a bubbled texture with columns of stocking stitch being pulled to left and right between the blocks.

Pattern:

Row 1: K15, *K2tog, slipping only the first st off the needle (so the second K2tog knits the one remaining on the needle with the next st)*, rep for 9 sts: K the remaining st again, K15.
Row 2: P15, *K2tog, slipping only the first st off the needle*, rep for 9 sts, K the remaining st again, P15.
Rep these 2 rows until you have 6 rows of pattern.

New blocks:

Row 7: K3, *K2tog, slipping only the first st off the needle*, rep for 9 sts, K the remaining st again, K14, *K2tog, slipping only the first st off the needle*, rep for 9 sts, K the remaining st again, K3.
Row 8: P3, *K2tog, slipping only the first st off the needle*, rep for 9 sts, K the remaining st again, P14, * K2tog, slipping only the first st off the needle*, rep for 9 sts, K the remaining st again, P3.

Rep for 6 rows, then go back to the first blocks and repeat as often as you like.

'Spot' twice-knit stitch

Spots of 4 stitches are placed regularly with 8 stitches between, and after 4 plain rows, another row is staggered between the first row. In order to make the spots stand out and contrast, they are knitted in purl on the knit background. In both this piece and in the previous blocks, the stitches either side of each block of twice-knit form a strong part of the pattern, being pushed and pulled by the tighter stitches to snake prominently up the fabric.

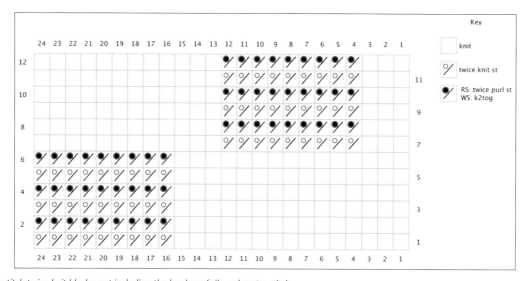

Chart for garter stitch twice-knit blocks, not including the borders of rib and garter stitch.

Cast on a repeat of 24 sts.

Row 1: K6, *(P2tog, but only drop one off the needle) x 4, P the last stitch, K8*, rep to last 6 sts, (P2tog, but only drop one off the needle) x 4, P the last stitch, K2.

Row 2: P2, *(K2tog, but only drop one st off the needle) x 4, K last st again, P8*, rep to last 10 sts, *(K2tog, but only drop one st off the needle) x 4, K last st again, P6.

Row 3: K.

Row 4: P.

Row 5: K.

Row 6: P.

Row 7: *(P2tog, but only drop one off the needle) x 4, P the last stitch again, K8*, rep.

Row 8: P8, *(K2tog, but only drop one st off the needle) x 4, K last st again, P8*, rep to last 4 sts, K2tog, but only drop one st off the needle) x 4, K last st again.

Smaller blocks or 'spots' of twice-knit create a textured, all-over pattern, creating snaking columns of stocking stitch between the spots.

Row 9: K.

Row 10: P.

Row 11: K.

Row 12: P.

These 12 rows form the pattern.

Summary and comparison of braids and twice-knit stitches

In the braid patterns, each stitch is worked into twice by knitting or purling it once, returning the new stitch to the LH needle and working it again, so the first stitch has dropped down a row, while another stitch passes across it in a cast-off chain. In 'twice-knit' knitting, each stitch is worked twice *within* the same row together with its neighbouring stitch (first the previous stitch, then with the following stitch) before being dropped off, making a much tighter fabric: very evident in the knitted samples.

There is some similarity in both these methods with Tunisian crochet, where a knit row forms stitches and alternates with a row of crochet, meaning the stitches are cast off on alternate rows. The look is very different although the structure within the stitches is similar. The surface pattern produced depends a lot on how the stitches are picked up (as there are several strands available), and where the discarded loops are placed, whether they are made in a purl or a knit fashion. All these techniques lose a little, or a lot, of the elasticity we expect of knitting, but sometimes this is useful: if you want a firm fabric for jackets, bags, cushions or anything else, it's good to know knitting can make a firmer, stronger fabric as well as the more predictable soft and stretchy material.

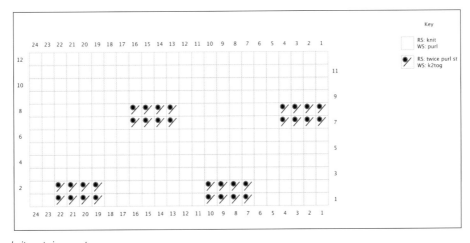

Chart showing the twice-knit spots in repeat.

CHAPTER 5

SHAPING WITH COLOUR

There are several ways of making colour patterns in knitting, all very familiar to us: we know the way they look and the kind of patterns they can create, from simple stripes of colour to intricate geometric patterns. However, this book is about how different stitches shape the fabric, and these different colour methods also have clear effects on the stretch, drape and thickness. Separating these techniques might seem a bit restrictive, as though they can only be used one at a time, but once the differences are understood, there's nothing to stop you using them in all sorts of combinations and ways; in fact, changing from one method to another is not only interesting visually, but would be another way of shaping the knitting.

So we have simple one-colour-at-a-time striped patterns, which can be developed into slip stitches. These are also knitted with one colour per row, but by slipping some of the stitches, patterns are formed. Then Fair Isle knitting or Jacquard knitting uses two or more colours travelling across the row to make different coloured patterns, with yarns stranded or woven at the back (while not making stitches). Finally, there is intarsia knitting, which uses as many colours as needed, each keeping to its own area of pattern, not crossing other colours. This last gives freedom to make designs of any kind, but is best suited to larger areas of colour. In smaller

repeating patterns it would become impractical to manage individual yarns to each patch of colour, but in abstract, figurative or any larger design, it is ideal. The weight and thickness of the knitted fabric is not changed but remains the same as any single-yarn knitting, therefore as intarsia does not alter the fabric in any way, we are not going to look in detail at this method here. However, slip stitch and Fair Isle knitting can produce repeating patterns in different ways, and it's interesting to compare the differences between these two techniques and how they alter the width, length, texture and thickness.

Slip stitches

Slip stitches are a great method of pattern-making with several different uses, both decorative and functional. The name says it all: in this way of knitting, not all the stitches are worked in a row – some are slipped (directly from one needle to the other without making a new stitch), making an interestingly textured, firm fabric. The action of slipping the stitches tends to pull the knitting upwards, and also inwards, as the yarn is then stranded or passed behind (or in front of) the slipped stitch, limiting the usual stretchiness. Lengthwise, the slipped stitch is pulled up across the row or rows, again limiting stretch, and creating a thicker fabric. Preventing stretch can be a great asset if you are working with a yarn without much body or bounce, any yarn that might 'drop' letting the fabric stretch too much: these stitches will act as a brake or strengthener to hold the fabric together. Worked in a single colour, slip stitches will make textural patterns – anything from small dots and ridges to larger, more definite patterns, giving it the name 'mosaic knitting'. If two or more colours are used in different rows, this enables coloured patterns to form, as the stripe of colour is punctuated by the slipped stitches crossing it.

Stitches can be slipped occasionally or frequently, and can be slipped over one, two or several rows. They can be slipped individually or several together, so the pattern-making opportunities are almost limitless, ranging from small, textural patterns or mosaics to bolder effects where the slipped stitches progress gradually across the fabric to form bold lines, curves or blocks. The great advantage of creating colour patterns in slip stitches is that you only need to handle one colour at a time: the stitches mix the colours and create the patterns for you, so if you work in two-row stripes in two colours, the stripes are transformed into patterns.

There is a disadvantage to this way of working, though: it is slow. The fabric grows more slowly than single-colour knitting or Fair Isle knitting, where you knit all the stitches using two or more colours along each row. If you slip alternate stitches, you are only working half the stitches in each row, so this inevitably slows up production. The length grows more slowly as the slipped stitches hold it back, and the width tends to be pulled in by stranding the yarn across the slipped stitches, so you need more stitches to achieve the width you want. The fewer the 'slips', the less the knitting is affected in speed of growth, width and length. Sometimes this can be frustrating, especially if the pattern is something as simple as stripes of 'knit 3, slip 3' in one colour for two rows, then in the second colour working the alternate groups, 'slip 3, knit 3'. This is a slow process! If you are comfortable with knitting two colours in a row, why not 'knit 3 colour A, knit 3 colour B' and do it all in one row, as in a Fair Isle pattern? However, the result is different (*see* overleaf). Slip stitches produce more texture and pull in more than Fair Isle knitting (unless you knit Fair Isle with a very tight tension). Looked at closely, the rows are actually staggered as well, so rather than your 'K3' in one colour lying next to the 'K3' in the contrast colour,

Charts for coloured slip-stitch patterns

Note: the charts for the coloured patterns show the working method, the rows of different colours as they are knitted: the slipped stitches don't show in their true colour in the charts, only as a symbol. So, for example, the vertical stripes look like horizontal stripes in the chart, as this is how they are worked, with the vertical effect created in practice by the action of the slipped stitches being stretched across the rows. The charts show the working method, and the knitted stitches show the effect.

they slot in between each other like building bricks in the separate rows.

In this section we are going to look at some different slip stitches: at how much they shape the length and breadth of the knitting, and at the kind of patterns they can create. Without changing colour there will still be a textured pattern, but with different colours, the fun begins. In some samples, stitches have been worked both in a single colour, then with two colours to compare the effect, but if you experiment, this can be taken much further; the balance of the pattern changes radically according to the colours used, and the number of colours.

Comparing width of knitting with slip stitches – texture only

The three stitches chosen for this sample are related, all having a moss-stitch-like texture. Firstly, plain moss stitch

Note

In all the slip stitches here, slip the stitches purlwise, holding the yarn at the back of the work *unless the instructions say 'yf' and 'yb'. Note:* yf (yarn forward) does not necessarily mean to the right side of the work, but the side facing you in that row, towards you. Slipping purlwise means the stitches are in the correct position when you come to knit them again.

Three stitches to compare the width:
a) moss stitch in green
b) slip tweed stitch in pale blue
c) slip moss stitch in sky blue.

(no slip stitches) is used as a contrast in width and texture (a), then slip tweed stitch (b), with slip moss st at the top (c).

Cast on 31 sts or any odd number.

a) Moss stitch

This makes a lightweight textured reversible stitch which lies flat without curling.

Row 1: *K1, P1 * rep to last st, K1.
Row 2: *K1, P1 * rep to last st, K1.

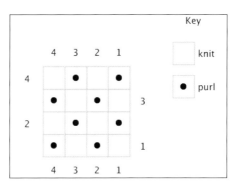

Chart for moss stitch (a).

b) Slip tweed stitch

This stitch slips alternate stitches on alternate rows, with the odd numbered rows working every stitch. It is thicker than plain moss stitch, with a smooth back and textured front. Each little 'knot' appearing on the front represents two rows.

Row 1: P1, *K1, P1*, rep to end.
Row 2: K1, *S1, K1*, rep to end.
Row 3: K1, *P1, K1*, rep to end.
Row 4: K2, S1, *K1, S1*, rep to last 2 sts, K2.

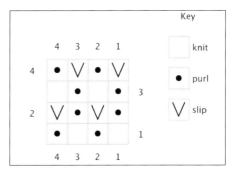

Chart for slip-tweed stitch (b).

c) Slip moss stitch

Here, alternate stitches are slipped on every row, with the same stitch being slipped for 2 rows, and the alternate stitch slipped on the following 2 rows. It is much closer-textured, very dense and warm, again with a rough-textured front and a smooth back. The little dots represent 2 rows.

Row 1: K1, * S1, K1*, rep to end.
Row 2: K1, *yf, S1, yb, K1*, rep to end.
Row 3: K2, *S1, K1*, rep to last st, K1.
Row 4: K2, *yf, S1, yb, K1*, rep to last st, K1.

As this stitch pulls in a lot, it is best cast off with a very firm cast-off:
K3, *pass 1st knitted st over 3rd, K1*, rep to last 2 sts, pass st over as usual, fasten off.

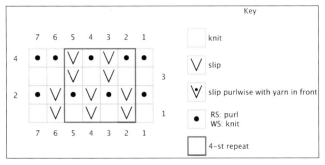

Chart for slip moss stitch (c).

The difference in width is obvious, and these three could be used in conjunction to create a garment with an overall moss stitch texture shaped by the stitches.

Comparing width of knitting with slip stitches – texture and colour

Here we have the same stitches using two colours, in 2-row stripes of each colour.

The moss stitch section is included as a contrast in width, but also to show how this simple stitch can break up the stripes of colour, simply by the stitches being pushed to the front and back in knit and purl, creating a much softer and more blurred effect than stocking-stitch stripes.

a) Moss stitch

Row 1: col A *K1, P1*, rep to last st, K1.
Row 2: col A *K1, P1*, rep to last st, K1.
Row 1: col B *K1, P1*, rep to last st, K1.
Row 2: col B *K1, P1*, rep to last st, K1.
These 4 rows form the pattern (the chart shows the repeat on an even number of sts).

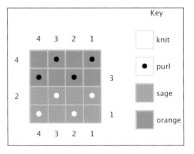

a) chart showing stripes of plain moss stitch.

b) Slip tweed stitch

Row 1: col A K1, *S1, K1*, rep to end.
Row 2: col A K1, *P1, K1*, rep to end.
Row 3: col B K2, S1 *K1, S1*, rep to last 2 sts, K2.
Row 4: col B P1, *K1, P1*, rep to end.

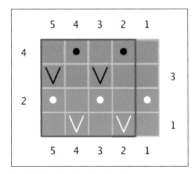

b) chart for slip tweed stitch, still showing the stripes, which become almost vertical in the knitting.

These stitches compare the width, worked in 2-row coloured stripes, which become disguised by the stitches:
a) bottom is moss stitch
b) middle is slip tweed stitch
c) top is slip moss stitch.

c) Slip moss stitch

Row 1: col A K1, *S1, K1*, rep to end.
Row 2: col A K1, *yf, S1, yb, K1*, rep to end.
Row 3: col B K2, *S1, K1*, to last st, K1.
Row 4: col B K2, *yf, S1, yb, K1*, rep to end.

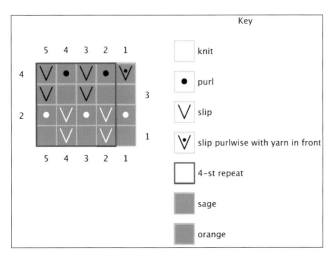

c) chart for slip moss stitch, where the stripes again are hidden in the knitting.

Comparing the length of knitting with slip stitches

In this piece, three different slip stitches are compared side by side to show the difference in length, so the number of rows is the same in each one. In each case, stitches are slipped in different groupings, some more and some less frequently. From left to right, they are 'tweed stitch' (a), 'colour slip stitch' (b) and 'ribbon stitch' (c). Although tweed stitch has alternate stitches slipped, it does not pull up nearly as much as colour slip stitch, where groups of 3 stitches are alternately knitted and slipped. Ribbon stitch has the least effect on the length. They are all knitted in a sequence of three colours, with two rows of each single colour, and the main characteristic that these three stitch combinations share is that each does a good job of disguising what would normally be a striped pattern, mixing the colours into small geometrics and textures.

3 stitches to compare the length of slip stitches, each worked in 2-row stripes in a three-colour repeat. From left to right:
a) tweed stitch
b) colour slip stitch
c) ribbon stitch.

Tweed stitch reduces the colours to dots of single stitches of each colour, in the same way as a woven tweed. There is a suggestion of a soft horizontal stripe: this would be less obvious if only two colours were used. Colour slip stitch manages to get rid of the stripe altogether, and if you played with the balance of colours, the pattern could be changed dramatically. In ribbon stitch, the stripes are broken gently by the one slipped stitch being pulled across on every fourth stitch.

In tweed stitch, the yarn is always carried to the front of the slipped stitches, making a flat fabric with a smooth front and tightly textured reverse, rather than such as a tight moss stitch. Colour slip stitch and ribbon stitch both carry the yarn across the back only.

a) Tweed stitch

For tweed stitch (TS) use an odd no of stitches (the chart shows the repeat). This has a 2-row pattern repeat. Always carry the yarn at the back, unless you see 'yf' and 'yb'.

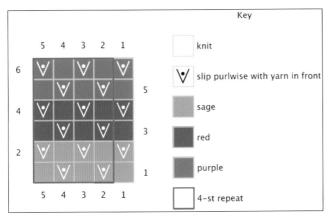

a) tweed stitch chart, the colours become blended in the knitting.

b) Colour slip stitch

For colour slip stitch (CSS) use a multiple of 6 stitches plus 5 extra. The chart shows the 4-row pattern repeat.

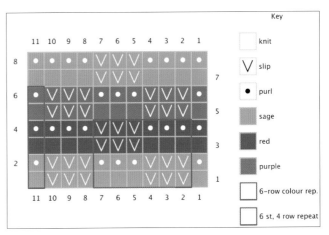

b) colour slip-stitch chart, which mixes the colours into little blocks rather than stripes. The colour repeat and stitch repeat are shown separately.

c) Ribbon stitch

For ribbon stitch (RS), use a multiple of 8 stitches and 2 extra. This has an 8-row pattern repeat.

However, using three colours in rotation means the complete pattern takes 24 rows to repeat.

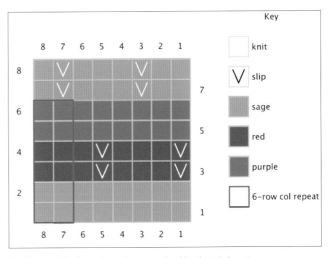

c) ribbon stitch chart: the stripes are mixed by the stitch pattern.

Put a marker between each group of sts, and follow the direction for that stitch to the marker, written as a /.

Row 1: col A: **RS**, K/**CSS** K1, *S3, K3* to last 4 sts, S3, K1/**TS** K1, *wf, S1, wb, K1*, rep to end.

Row 2: col A: **TS** P1, *P1, wb, S1, wf*, rep to end, P1/**CSS** K1 *yf S3, yb K3*, rep to last 4 sts, S3, K1/**RS** P to end.

Row 3: col B: **RS** K1, *S1, K3*, rep to last 2 sts, S1, K1/**CSS** K4, *S3, K3*, rep to end, K1/**TS** K1 *wf, S1, wb, K1*, rep to end.

Row 4: col B: **TS** P1, *P1, wb, S1, wf*, rep to end, P1/**CSS** K1, *K3, yf S3, yb* to last 4 sts, ending K4/**RS** P1, *S1, P3*, rep to last 2 sts, S1, P1.

Row 5: col C: **RS**, K/**CSS** K1, *S3, K3* to last 4 sts, S3, K1/**TS** K1 *wf, S1, wb, K1*, rep to end.

Row 6: col C: **TS** P1, *P1, wb, S1, wf*, rep to end, P1/**CSS** K1, *yf S3, yb K3*, rep to last 4 sts, S3, K1/**RS** P to end.

Row 7: col A: **RS** K3, *S1, K3*/**CSS** K4, *S3, K3*, rep to end, K1/**TS** K1 *wf, S1, wb, K1*, rep to end.

Row 8: col A: **TS** P1, *P1, wb, S1, wf*, rep to end, P1/**CSS** K1, *K3, yf S3, yb* rep to last 4 sts, ending K4/**RS** P3, *S1, P3*, rep to end.

Row 9: col B: **RS**, K/**CSS** K1, *S3, K3* to last 4 sts, S3, K1/**TS** K1 *wf, S1, wb, K1*, rep to end.

Row 10: col B: **TS** P1, *P1, wb, S1, wf*, rep to end, P1/**CSS** K1 *yf S3, yb K3*, rep to last 4 sts, S3, K1/**RS** P to end.

Row 11: col C: **RS** K1, *S1, K3*, rep to last 2 sts, S1, K1/**CSS** K4, *S3, K3*, rep to end, K1/**TS** K1 *wf, S1, wb, K1*, rep to end.

Row 12: **TS** P1, *P1, wb, S1, wf*, rep to end, P1/**CSS** K1, *K3, yf S3, yb* to last 4 sts, ending K4/**RS** P1,*S1, P3*, rep to last 2 sts, S1, P1.

Row 13: col A: **RS**, K/**CSS** K1, *S3, K3* to last 4 sts, S3, K1/**TS** K1, *wf, S1, wb, K1*, rep to end.

Row 14: col A: **TS** P1, *P1, wb, S1, wf*, rep to end, P1/**CSS** K1 *yf S3, yb K3*, rep to last 4 sts, S3, K1/**RS** P to end.

Row 15: col B: **RS** K3, *S1, K3*/ **CSS** K4, *S3, K3*, rep to end, K1/**TS** K1, *wf, S1, wb, K1*, rep to end.

Row 16: col B: **TS** P1, *P1, wb, S1, wf*, rep to end, P1/**CSS** K1 *K3, yf S3, yb* to last 4 sts, ending K4/**RS** P3, *S1, P3*, rep to end.

Row 17: col C: **RS**, K/**CSS** K1, *S3, K3* to last 4 sts, S3, K1/**TS** K1, *wf, S1, wb, K1*, rep to end.

Row 18: col C: **TS** P1, *P1, wb, S1, wf*, rep to end, P1/**CSS** K1 *yf S3, yb K3*, rep to last 4 sts, S3, K1/**RS** P to end.

Row 19: col A: **RS** K1, *S1, K3*, rep to last 2 sts, S1, K1/**CSS** K4, *S3, K3*, rep to end, K1/**TS** K1, *wf, S1, wb, K1*, rep to end.

Row 20: col A: T**S** P1, *P1, wb, S1, wf *, rep to end, P1/**CSS** K1, *K3, yf S3, yb* to last 4 sts, ending K4/**RS** P3, *S1, P3*, rep to end.

Row 21: col B: **RS** K/**CSS** K1, *S3, K3* to last 4 sts, S3, K1/**TS** K1, *wf, S1, wb, K1* rep to end.

Row 22: col B: **TS** P1, *P1, wb, S1, wf*, rep to end, P1/**CSS** K1 *yf S3, yb K3*, rep to last 4 sts, S3, K1/**RS** P to end.

Row 23: col C: **RS** K3, *S1, K3 */ **CSS** K1, *S3, K3*, to last 4 sts, S3, K1/**TS** K1 *wf, S1, wb, K1*, rep to end.

Row 24: **TS** P1, *P1, wb, S1, wf*, rep to end, P1/**CSS** K1 *K3, yf S3, yb* to last 4 sts, ending K4/**RS** P3, *S1, P3*, rep to end.

Comparing different textured slip-stitch patterns – texture only

In this sample, three stitches are compared for width and to look at the kind of textured patterns that can be made in a single-coloured slip stitch.

Slip stitches don't have to be small textures – this way of patterning has the potential to be developed into larger designs. The first stitch [a] in this example using three patterns shows how a diagonal texture can be achieved; here two diagonals cross each other to make diamonds, but space

Comparing the width of different textured slip-stitch patterns, from bottom to top:
a) bottom is diagonal texture
b) middle is bubble stitch
c) top is a ribbed slip stitch, with the rib only showing on one side: finished with a band of moss stitch to compare width.

these differently and the diagonals can travel as far as you like and make large-scale designs.

a) Diagonals and ridges

Cast on a multiple of 10 sts + 2 edge sts. Here, 32 sts are used.
Row 1: K.
Row 2: P.
Row 3: K1, *S2, K6, S2*, rep to last st, K1.
Row 4: K1, *yf S2, yb K6, yf S2*, rep to last st, yb K1.
Rows 5 & 6: as rows 1 & 2.
Row 7: K1, *K1, S2, K4, S2, K1*, rep to last st, K1.
Row 8: K1 *K1, yf S2, yb K4, yf S2, yb K1*, rep to last st, K1.
Rows 9 & 10: as rows 1 & 2.
Row 11: K1, *K2, S2, K2, S2, K2*, rep to last st, K1.
Row 12: K1, *K2, yf S2, yb K2, yf S2, yb K2*, rep to last st, K1.
Rows 13 & 14 as rows 1 & 2.
Row 15: K1, *K3, S4, K3*, rep to last st, K1.
Row 16: K1, *K3, yf S4, yb K3*, rep to last st, K1.
Rows 17 & 18: as rows 1 & 2.
Row 19: as row 11.
Row 20: as row 12.
Rows 21 & 22: as rows 1 & 2.
Row 23: as row 7.
Row 24: as row 8.
Rep from the beginning.

b) Bubble stitch

This is a softer, more subtle pattern, using some stocking stitch to contrast with garter stitch and create 'bubbles'. Cast on a multiple of 8 stitches + 4 extra (the chart shows just the repeat). In this sample, continuing from 'diagonals and ridges', decrease 4 stitches at the edges to make 28. The yarn is always carried on the wrong side when slipping the stitches, but there's no need to write this into the pattern, as the yarn is already in the correct place while purling on the wrong-side rows.

Row 1: K.
Row 2: K.
Row 3: K1, S2, *K6, S2*, rep to last st, K1.
Row 4: P1, S2, *P6, S2*, rep to last st, P1.
Rows 5 & 6: as rows 3 & 4.
Rows 7 & 8: as rows 3 & 4.
Row 9: K.
Row 10: K.
Row 11: K5, S2, *K6, S2*, rep to last 5 sts, K5.
Row 12: P5, S2, *P6, S2*, rep to last 5 sts, P5.
Rows 13 & 14: as rows 11 & 12.
Rows 15 & 16: as rows 11 & 12.
Rep from the beginning.

c) Rib slip stitch

Looking at the back of this stitch, you wouldn't imagine it was ribbed; it looks like plain garter stitch, but has a chunky rib travelling up the front face of the knitting. As garter stitch pulls up slightly, it balances the slight shortening of the slipped stitch, making a stable, flat, thick fabric.

Cast on a multiple of 5 stitches, or if following bubble stitch as illustrated, increase one at either edge to make 30 stitches.

Beginning on the right side, knit a foundation row, as the pattern begins on the wrong side (the chart shows just the repeat):
Row 1(WS): K2, *P1, K4*, rep to last 3 sts, P1, K2.
Row 2: K2, *S1, K4*, rep to last 3 sts, S1, K2.
Rep these 2 rows.

In the sample, there is a band of moss stitch to finish off, to show how much (or how little) this slip stitch pulls in.

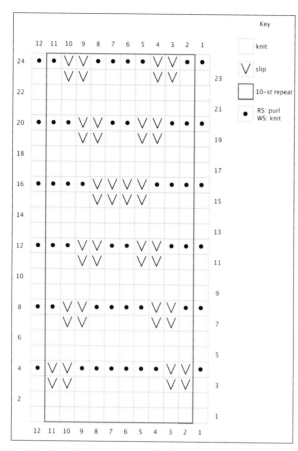

a) chart for diagonal texture pattern, which can be scaled up to make bold designs.

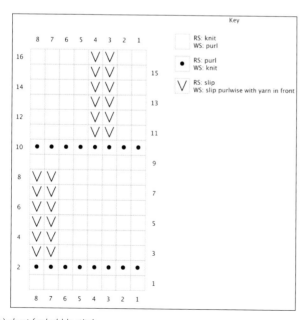

b) chart for bubble stitch.

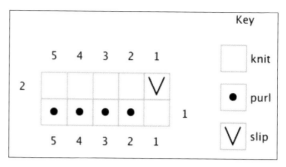

c) chart for ribbed stitch, which is actually garter stitch with one stitch slipped to look like ribbing.

Comparing different slip-stitch patterns – texture and colour

As well as looking at the width and thickness of these stitches, they have been chosen to illustrate the versatility of slip stitches in disguising the fact that each is knitted in stripes of each colour, with two colours to each pattern.

a) Houndstooth pattern

Worked in stocking stitch in 4 rows of each colour, this little interlocking shape does not lie flat but bubbles up slightly with the pull of the slipped stitches.

Cast on a multiple of 6 stitches + 2 extra.

Note: the yarn is always carried on the wrong side, but this happens automatically as it is held in the right place by the purl stitches.

Row 1 (WS): col A P.
Row 2: col B: K3, S2, *K4, S2*, rep to last 3 sts, K3.
Row 3: col B: P3, S2 *P4, S2 * rep to last 3 sts, P3.
Row 4: col B: as row 2.
Row 5: col B: P.
Row 6: col A: K5, S2, *K4, S2*, rep to last st, K1.
Row 7: col A: P1, S2, *P4, S2*, rep to last 5 sts, P5.
Row 8: col A: as row 6.
Rep these 8 rows.

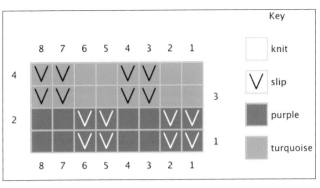

b) chart for slip stitch-stripe shows clearly how the bands of colour are changed to vertical stripes. Half the stitches are slipped every row, pulling in the width and the length.

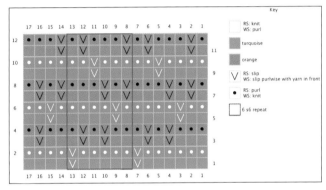

c) Moroccan slip stitch is a garter-slip-stitch, making thick fabric and also disguising the stripes in the knitting.

3 slip-stitch patterns worked in two colours each. Although each is knitted in 2 rows of each colour, different numbers of stitches are slipped in each one, and so they pull in different amounts. From bottom to top:
a) bottom is houndstooth pattern
b) middle is vertical stripes
c) top is 'Moroccan' slip stitch.

b) Slip-stitch stripe

Being able to produce verticals out of two-row horizontal stripes is intriguing; it is counter-intuitive and rather rewarding to experience the stripes emerging in verticals from simply knitting in rows in one colour at a time. This is illustrated clearly on the chart, which tells you it's knitted in horizontal stripes. It makes a much firmer stripe than knitting with the two colours in each row as in Fair Isle knitting, as it's more difficult to control the way the fabric pulls in.

Row 1: using col A: K1, *S2, K2*, rep to last st, K1.
Row 2: col A: P1, *P2, S2*, rep to last st, P1.
Row 3: change to col B: K1, *K2, S2*, rep to last st, K1.
Row 4: col B: P1, *S2, P2*, rep to last st, P1.

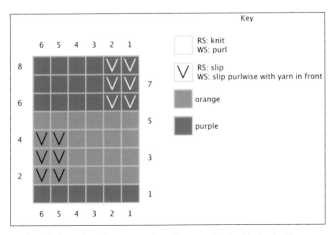

a) chart for houndstooth pattern: the stripes are disguised in the knitting.

c) 'Moroccan' slip-stitch pattern

This pattern is worked using a multiple of 6 sts + 5 edge sts. Work one row of purl in colour A.

Row 1: col B: K6, S1, *K5, S1, rep from * to last 4 sts, K4.

Row 2: col B: K4, *yf, S1, yb K5, rep from * to last 7 sts, yf, S1, yb, K6.

Row 3: col A: K3, (S1, K1) x 2 *K2, S1, K1, S1, K1, rep to last 4 sts, K2, S1, K1.

Row 4: col A: K1, yf, S1, yb, K2 *K1, yf, S1, yb, K1, yf , S1, K2, rep from * to last 7 sts, K1, S1, K1, S1, K3.

Row 5: col B: K2, S1, K4, *K1, S1, K4, rep from * to last 4 sts, K1, S1, K2.

Row 6: col B: K2, yf, S1, yb, K1, *K4, yf, S1, yb, K1, rep from * to last 7 sts, K4, S1, K2.

Row 7: col A: [K1, S1] twice, K3, *S1, K1, S1, K3, rep from * to last 4 sts, S1, K1, S1, K1.

Row 8: col A [K1, yf, S1, yb] twice, *K3, yf, S1, yb, K1, yf, S1, yb, rep from * to last 7 sts, K3, S1, K1, S1, K1.

Row 9: col B: K4, S1, K2, *K3, S1, K2, rep from * to last 4 sts, K4.

Row 10: col B: K4, *K2, yf, S1, yb K3, rep from * to last 7 sts, K2, yf, S1, yb, K4.

Row 11: col A: K1, S1, K3, S1, K1, *S1, K3, S1, K1, rep from * to last 4 sts, S1, K3.

Row 12: col A: K3, yf, S1, yb, *K1, yf, S1, yb, K3, yf, S1, yb, rep from * to last 7 sts, K1, S1, K3, S1, K1.

Rep these 12 rows.

Comparing slip-st stripes with Fair Isle knitting

The following pieces illustrate vertical stripes in a number of ways, but while they look similar, each produces a different thickness and texture of fabric. If you are used to two-colour knitting, you might find the one-colour slip stitches frustratingly slow, but they do in fact produce a different result and can be compared to create different effects.

A simple 2-stitch stripe

The bottom part of this sample is knitted in two colours per row in a 'Fair Isle' way. When not being used to knit, the second colour is woven behind the second stitch of each pair, by catching the strand in with the 'active' or knitting yarn. This is not essential when the gap between the colours

is only 2 stitches, and many knitters strand their colours over 2 or more stitches, but if you knit Fair Isle fluently, either with a yarn in each hand or over different fingers of one hand, weaving in becomes second nature and produces an even-textured, slightly stretchy fabric without any strain or strands.

Bottom sample (a) is 2-stitch stripes knitted in Fair Isle with two colours per row. Top sample (b) is in slip stitch, one colour at a time, in 2-row stripes, pulling in more tightly.

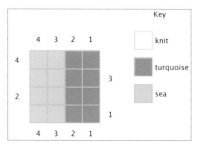

a) chart for Fair Isle stripes, 2 stitches to each colour.

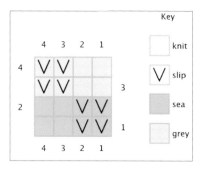

b) chart for slip-stitch stripes, showing the stripes as they are knitted, not how they appear.

a) Fair Isle, two colours per row
The bottom half is in Fair Isle knitting.

Cast on 30 sts.
Row 1: K1B, *K2A, K2B*, rep to last st, K1A.
Row 2: P1A, *P2B, P2A*, rep to last st, P1B.
Rep these 2 rows.

The top half of the sample is made in slip stitch.

b) Slip stitch, one colour per row
Row 1: using col A: K1, *S2, K2*, rep to last st, K1.
Row 2: col A: P1, *P2, S2*, rep to last st, P1.
Row 3: change to col B: K1, *K2, S2*, rep to last st, K1.
Row 4: col B: P1, *S2, P2*, rep to last st, P1.
Rep these 4 rows.
The slip-stitch pattern pulls in slightly and has much less stretch than the lower half knitted with both colours per row, but this will vary with different knitters' methods of knitting with two colours per row.

4-stitch stripe

Here, the sample is knitted in two halves again, with the bottom half using two colours per row in a Fair Isle technique, and the top half in slip stitch, one colour at a time. Each half reverses to show both the front and the back of the knitting, so you can see clearly what is going on in the method and resulting fabric.

a) Fair Isle, two colours per row
Cast on a multiple of 8 sts + 4 edge sts (a).
Row 1: K2A, *K4B, K4A*, rep to last 2 sts, K2B.
Row 2: P2B, *P4A, P4B*, rep to last 2 sts, P2A.
Rep these 2 rows, weaving in the unknitted yarn by crossing the yarns first one way and then the other between the stitches.[1]

4-stitch stripes knitted (a) bottom in Fair Isle, with two colours per row, and (b) top in slip stitch, one colour at a time, in 2-row stripes. Each pattern reverses halfway up to show the difference between the 'woven' back of the Fair Isle, and the stranded yarns in the slip stitch, which pulls in much more.

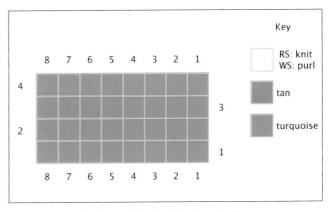

a) chart for Fair Isle stripes working 4 stitches in each colour.

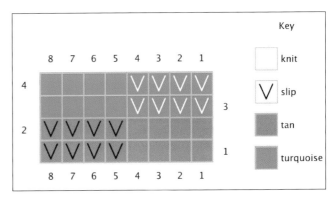

b) chart for slip stitch-stripes, again showing how they are knitted, not how they appear as vertical stripes.

Where the knitting reverses, you can see the pattern produced by the yarns gently 'weaving' up and down. This not only ties the yarn into the fabric so there are no loose strands, but the undulating movement of the second yarn gives a certain amount of stretch, unlike plain stranded yarn carried straight across.

b) Slip stitch, 1 colour per row
Row 1: using col A: K2, *K4, S4*, rep to last 2 sts, K2.
Row 2: col A: P2, *S4, P4*, rep to last 2 sts, P2.
Row 3: col B: K2, *S4, K4*, rep to last 2 sts, K2.
Row 4: col B: P2, *P4, S4*, rep to last 2 sts, P2.
Rep these 2 rows.

This stitch pulls in strongly compared to the bottom part of the sample, and where the pattern reverses, the strands can be seen in pairs of 2 rows of each colour.
What would happen if you stranded the yarns in the two-colour method rather than weaving them in? This is shown in the next sample, below.

6-stitch stripes

This stitch was popular for knitted tea cosies of the 1940s and 1950s when tea was brewed in teapots, using wide stripes of garter stitch perhaps 6 stitches per colour, where the slipping method pulled in across the back of each stripe so much that a tubular effect was created, with great heat-trapping properties.

Inspired by this idea, this piece uses the traditional garter-slip-stitch shown at the top (b) with 6 stitches of each colour. Garter stitch naturally makes a thicker fabric, and its rigidity helps to form the tubular structure.

The bottom part is worked in garter stitch in two colours per row, stranding the yarn behind the 6 stitches: it isn't possible to weave in on the wrong-side rows without the 'wrong' colour showing on the front, so the yarn is simply stranded across the back.

a) two colours per row
Cast on 28 sts. *Note: carry the unknitted yarns on the wrong side.*
Row 1: K2A, *K4B, K4A*, rep to last 2 sts, K2B,
Row 2(WS row): keeping the unknitted yarn forward, towards you, K2B, *K4A, K4B*, rep to last 2 sts, K2A.

6-stitch stripes in garter stitch. The bottom half (a) is in two colours per row, the top half (b) in slip stitch in 2-row stripes of each colour. This stitch pulls in to create columns of stitches with the yarn stranded across the back, making a very warm, heat-trapping fabric, traditionally used to make tea cosies.

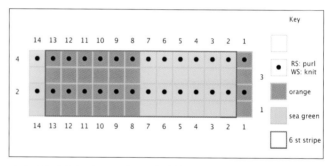

a) chart for knitting in two colours, 6 stitches to each stripe.

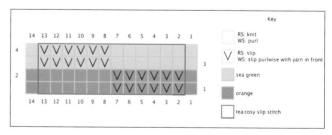

b) chart for the slip-stitch stripe, working 2-row stripes of each colour, but slipping half the stitches every row to make vertical stripes.

b) slip stitch (tea cosy pattern), 1 colour per row
Row 1: col A: K2, *S6, K6*, rep to last 2 sts, K2.
Row 2: col A: K2, *yf, S6, yb, K6*, rep to last 2 sts, yb, K2.
Row 3: col B: K2, *K6, S6*, rep to last 2 sts, K2.
Row 4: col B: K2, *yf, S6, yb, K6*, rep to last 2 sts, K2.
Rep these 4 rows.

Although the yarns in the bottom part (a) are stranded, not woven in, they don't pull the fabric so tightly, and there is still a noticeable difference between the two methods, with the slip stitch pulling in much more strongly. The stripes lie side by side in the two-colour piece, whereas the rows slot in between each other in the slip-stitch pattern.

Geometric slip-stitch pattern

This is one of many possible geometric patterns, which could be explored and designed on paper (or digitally) to create anything from squares, stripes and dots to Greek key patterns. It is composed of stripes, but this time combining the 'natural' knitted stripes with a vertical slip stitch: the horizontals are made with ridges of garter stitch, and the verticals by slipping a stitch and pulling it up across the horizontal. The same stitches are slipped for 2 consecutive rows, with the yarn always carried on the back. The band of stocking stitch and garter stitch below the pattern shows how much it pulls in.

Cast on a multiple of 6 sts + 5 extra: keep yarn at back of work when slipping sts.
Row 1 (RS): col B: K.
Row 2 (WS): col B: P1, *(K5, P1) × 2*, rep ending K5, P1.
Row 3: col A: K2, (S1, K1) × 2, *S1, K5, (S1, K1) × 3* rep, ending K1.
Row 4: col A: P1, *(P1, S1) × 3, K5, S1*, rep ending (P1, S1) × 2, P2.
Row 5: col B: (K1, S1) × 3, *K7, (S1, K1) × 2, S1*, rep ending K1.
Row 6: col B: P1, *(S1, P1) × 3, K5, P1*, rep ending (S1, P1) × 3.
Row 7: rep row 3.
Rows 8-11: rep rows 4–7.
Row 12: col A: rep row 4.
Row 13: col B: K.
Row 14: col B: rep row 2.
Row 15: col A: K6, *(S1, K1) × 3, S1, K5*, rep ending K1.
Row 16: col A: P1, *K5, (S1, P1) × 3, S1*, rep ending K5, P1.
Row 17: col B: K6, *(K1, S1) × 3, K6*, rep ending K1.
Row 18: col B: P1, *K5, (P1, S1) × 3, P1*, rep ending K5, P1.
Row 19: col A: rep row 15.
Rows 20-23: rep rows 16–19.
Row 24: rep row 16.

A geometric slip-stitch pattern, worked in 2 rows of each colour to make both vertical and horizontal stripes in a basket-weave effect, which shows as narrower and firmer than garter stitch.

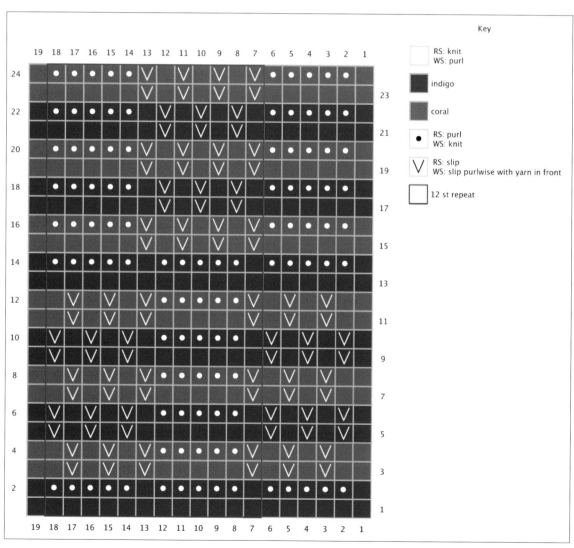

Chart showing the stripes of colour as they are knitted, which are then transformed by the slip stitches.

Comparing slip-stitch patterns with Fair Isle knitting

Many geometric patterns could be knitted in either slip stitches or Fair Isle, but the resulting fabric is quite different. Fair Isle knitting is thicker than one-colour knitting, and so is slip stitch, but the tendency for Fair Isle knitting is to pull in widthways (depending on your tension and how tightly the yarn is stranded or woven), not upwards, whereas slip stitches pull up *and* in.

Greek key pattern

In the first example, a Greek key pattern is shown in three variations, separated by garter-stitch ridges: the first one (a) is in

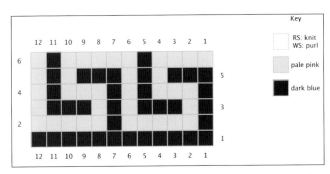

a) chart for Greek key Fair Isle pattern, worked in the bottom of the knitted piece 156 as in the chart, but at the top with 2 rows to each line of chart.

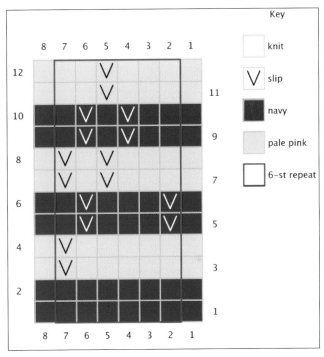

b) chart for Greek key slip-stitch section, again looking very different from the knitted example.

Greek key pattern. From bottom to top:
a) bottom is a Greek key pattern worked in Fair Isle with two colours per row.
b) middle is in slip stitch with 2 rows for each colour.
c) top is in Fair Isle again, but with 2 rows to each line of the chart, as in the slip-stitch pattern.

Fair Isle knitting, with two colours to each row, and a single row for each pattern line. The second one (b), in slip stitch, shows the same pattern, worked in 2 rows for each colour as shown on the chart (this means the colours always rest at the same end of the row, so are easy to pick up for the next row). Here, the pattern looks quite different: the chart shows the horizontal colours with the slip stitches shown as symbols, and the knitted piece shows the sharp edges of the rectangular pattern pulled into more rounded shapes, and a slightly more textured surface to the knitting. It also pulls in slightly. The third section (c) is the same pattern worked again in Fair Isle knitting, with two rows to each line of pattern (as in the slip stitch): but without slipping stitches, the motif grows longer and looks more angular, and surprisingly elongated compared to the slip-stitch area, showing that 36 rows of slip stitch is about the same length as 24 rows of Fair Isle knitting. The knitting appears wider in the Fair Isle areas, but in fact if you stretch it out by hand, the slip-stitch area is surprisingly more elastic.

Square and dot pattern. From bottom to top:
a) bottom is in slip stitch, which pulls inwards and upwards quite strongly.
b) top is with two colours per row in Fair Isle.

Fair Isle pattern
Casting on a multiple of 6 sts + 2 extra, follow the chart in stocking stitch.

Slip-stitch pattern
Work on a multiple of 6 sts + 2 extra.

Row 1: col A: K.
Row 2: col A: P.
Row 3: col B: K1, *K5, S1*, rep to last st, K1.
Row 4: col B: P1, *S1, P5*, rep to last st, P1.
Row 5: col A: K1, *S1, K3, S1, K1*, rep to last st, K1.
Row 6: col A: P1, *P1, S1, P3, S1*, rep to last st, P1.
Row 7: col B: K1, *K3, S1, K1, S1*, rep to last st, K1.
Row 8: col B: P1, *S1, P1, S1, P3*, rep to last st, P1.
Row 9: col A: K1, *K2, S1, K1, S1, K1*, rep to last st, K1.
Row 10: col A: P1, *P1, S1, P1, S1, P2*, rep to last st, P1.
Row 11: col B: K1, *K3, S1, K2*, rep to last st, K1.
Row 12: col B: P1, *P2, S1, P3*, rep to last st, P1.
Rep these 12 rows.

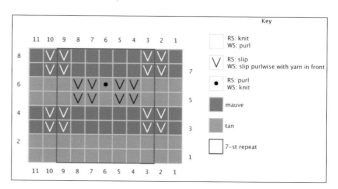

a) chart for slip-stitch square and dot pattern, showing the stripes as they are knitted, not as they appear in the example.

Top Fair Isle pattern
Follow the same chart (a) as for the first Fair Isle, working each row twice, comparing the length with the slip-stitch pattern.

Square and dot pattern

Beginning with the slip-stitch pattern and ending with Fair Isle, again there is a noticeable pull inwards and upwards in slip stitch, and a more textured surface. The squares are pulled slightly out of shape, so the slip stitch has a more varied, organic surface than the cleaner, sharper, flatter Fair Isle knitting.

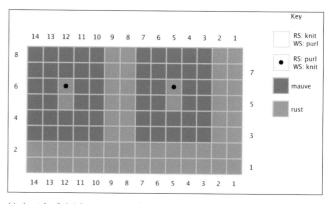

b) chart for Fair Isle square and dot pattern, knitted with two colours per row.

a) Slip stitch

Cast on a multiple of 7 sts + 4 extra.

Row 1: col A: K.

Row 2: col A: P.

Row 3: col B: K1, S1, *S1, K5, S1*, rep to last 2 sts, S1, K1.

Row 4: col B: P1, S1, *S1, P5, S1*, rep to last 2 sts, S1, P1.

Row 5: col A: K2, *K1, S2, K1, S2, K1*, rep to last 2 sts, K2.

Row 6: col A: P2, *P1, S2, K1, S2, P1*, rep to last 2 sts, P2.

Row 7: as row 3.

Row 8: as row 4.

These 8 rows form the pattern.

b) Fair Isle pattern

Follow the chart: the pattern changes every 2 rows, but the Fair Isle knitting looks elongated compared to the slip stitch. In this example, 40 rows are worked in slip stitch, and only 24 in Fair Isle to reach the same length. Is one thicker than the other? There are more horizontal floats travelling along the rows in Fair Isle knitting, but in the slip-stitch pattern there are also vertical 'hitches' where the rows are pulled across, so for warmth and thickness they are a similar weight.

Fair Isle stitches – not only for decoration

It's tempting to think of Fair Isle knitting as only used in stocking stitch, making a plain, smooth surface. It's the perfect way to knit repeating colour patterns, usually geometric, to produce any design you can annotate as a chart in a grid, and we are very familiar with the look of this method through the popularity of richly patterned and colourful Scandinavian and Baltic traditional sweaters, as well as those from Scotland and its islands. From a practical point of view, it works best with short runs of each colour rather than very large or separated areas, and you might choose a different method, such as intarsia, for a colour that only appears occasionally in the design. From two colours in a row you could increase the numbers to three or even four, but it then becomes very dense and a bit ungainly to work.

While one yarn is making the stitch, what happens to the unknitted yarn? There are strong opinions about the different ways of dealing with this among knitters, with each option having noticeably different results. Simply stranding the spare yarn at the back of the work is the easiest and most straightforward way to work. The advantages are clear colours on the front, with no extra movement needed in the knitting to weave or cross the yarns at the back. The downside is that the fabric will then pull in more tightly, limited in stretch by the straight strands, causing it to pull in more than you might want. If left too loose, the back can become loopy and the stitches uneven, with the edge stitch of each colour patch tending to loosen. These strands are not always practical for wearing: they can catch when putting on a garment and in the worst case, pull and distort the fabric.

The next option goes to the other extreme and weaves the spare yarn behind alternate stitches so that if, for instance, you have a run of 6 stitches in colour A, colour B would be held above colour A for one stitch, and below for the next (on the purl side), repeating along the 6 stitches, travelling lightly up and down and held in this position by crossing over and under colour A. The most efficient way to knit the Fair Isle technique is to carry the different colours either over separate fingers in one hand, or with a yarn in each hand, knitting right- and left-handed. If you can learn this method and become comfortable with it, it's possible then to weave the yarns neatly at the back while working at speed, never needing to drop one yarn and pick up another. You should never have to let go of the yarn in knitting, or the needles, whatever stitch you are knitting, except perhaps with cabling. With a good weaving technique, the yarns don't become twisted, but cross one way then back the opposite way so it can be just about as speedy as knitting with one colour. There are illustrations showing this method in many books including my previous books[1], inspired by *Mary Thomas's Knitting Book*, first published in 1938. It's worth searching for copies of her books: she was a knitter who understood knitting structure and technique absolutely, and was able to communicate so clearly. Other knitting books also discuss Fair Isle technique, and there are many YouTube tutorials showing different personal approaches: you have to decide which method looks the most efficient for you (*see* Further Resources section).

Another advantage of weaving-in is that this gentle up-and-down movement creates room to stretch; there are no loose strands, and if done well, the fabric does not pull in but has a good, regular evenness. The stitches are held more firmly, so at the edge of an area of colour they will not tend to loosen or spread. The disadvantage is that, depending on the yarn used, the second colour may show through slightly at the front of the pattern and this may not be what you want: a clear cotton would be more likely to show this effect than a softer woollier yarn. When done with a good tension, this method creates an even fabric, as attractive on the reverse as on the front.

Many people choose a middle road, catching the second yarn in every few stitches so the strands are not too long, and are less likely to show on the front. The examples knitted for this book don't use more than two colours per row, and they are woven on alternate stitches (by the author, out of habit!). It might sound restricting to limit a design to two colours each row, but it can be an interesting challenge to create designs within this limitation while keeping ease and speed of knitting to a maximum, and to produce a beautifully even fabric.

One reason for knitting Fair Isle in stocking stitch is because it's impossible to weave in the second colour if one yarn is at the back making knit stitches and the other at the front creating purl. So if we look at a piece of Fair Isle knitting, it will have all the usual characteristics of stocking stitch: the fabric wants to curl up at the bottom, and away towards the purl side at each side edge. If we want a flat fabric, this is a problem to be dealt with – we may not want the edges of a jacket or jumper to be curling back, but once again, it's worth thinking about taking these 'problems' on board as design opportunities, and exploring different ways of using Fair Isle knitting to create different textures, shaping, undulations, and anything else that single-colour knitting can do.

Beginning with the more usual stocking stitch Fair Isle fabric with its added weight of extra colours, it needs some determined flat or ribbed stitches to hold the edges of the garment in place, and these need to be of a similar weight. If you are making a colourful geometrically patterned jumper or jacket, it seems right to have a welt that is equally colourful and of a similar weight: a single-coloured rib might be a bit lightweight as an edging to a Fair Isle pattern. Traditionally, a two-coloured 'knit 2, purl 2' rib is often used, with colours stranded at the back of the knitting behind the knit stitches and behind the purls. What happens to this rib? Knits and purls appear forming a strong vertical striped pattern, but all the elasticity has vanished. We know that in a single-colour rib, knit stitches push forward and purls fall back, drawing the fabric in, but somehow if you change colour between these stitches, the energy of the 'push' of the stitch is lost and they lie flat, with the purl stitches appearing slightly raised: you have your strong, decorative edging, but it is as flat as the stocking-stitch areas. Supposing you want to keep the stretchiness of the rib and still use two colours to obtain a

stripe? This is possible if you carry the yarns at the back for the knit stitches, but bring both forward for purl. In effect, you are then making a right-side and wrong-side fabric, or a knit-face and purl-face, so it then buckles and closes in like a single-colour rib. One warning point here is that the second yarn *must* be woven over the second of each pair of stitches, or you will end up with a double-sided fabric with a different colour on each side, but no rib (as shown below, reversible stretchy rib and double-sided knitting.) This next piece shows firstly the flat two-colour rib, and at the top, the stretchy version.

More vertical stripes – Flat rib and reversible stretchy rib

Note: there is no chart for these stitches.

Comparing ribs. From bottom to top:
a) bottom: ribbing in two colours makes a striped but non-stretchy fabric, but weaving in the second yarn on knit and purl (taking it back for knit and forward for purl) restores the stretch of ribbing, making a reversible fabric.
b) middle: where the knit stitches come forward, showing the pale blue.
c) top: where the colours are swapped to show the reverse side, dark blue.

Flat rib

For the flat rib (bottom of sample), cast on a multiple of 4 sts.
Row 1: with both yarns at the back, *K2A, bring col B forward and P2, take B back*, rep to end.
Row 2: with col A forward, *take B back and K2, bring B forward and P2A*, rep to end.
Rep these 2 rows.

Stretchy rib

(Top of sample)
Row 1: *both yarns back: K1A, K1A weaving B, yarns both forward, P1B, P1B weaving A*, rep to end.
Row 2: *both yarns back: K1B, K1B weaving A, yarns both forward, P1A, P1A weaving B*, rep to end.
Rep these 2 rows.

In the sample shown, the colours are swapped halfway up the stretchy ribbing to show what happens on the reverse. What you get is the knit stitches in a solid colour, one colour showing one side, the second colour on the other, and the purl stitches show both colours as the strands weave across the purl. This creates a reversible fabric, showing a different colour each side, with a third colour produced by the mix on the purl stitches.

Reversible stretchy rib compared with double-faced knitting

This example shows the same reversible stretchy rib, changing halfway up into a double-faced stocking stitch. Just one small sleight-of-hand where you stop weaving in the second yarn, and the stitch is transformed into something completely different.

Instructions for the ribbed section are above; the only thing that changes to make the double-faced piece is not weaving in the yarn on the second stitch, instructions below. The K2 col A, P2 col B remains the same, but without that linking of yarns, the two colours are free to separate into two layers, both knit on the outside. This very same double-faced knitting can be made equally well using one colour at a time in slip stitch, or in K1, P1 rib in the same way as the K2, P2.

Double-faced knitting in two colours K2, P2

Row 1: *both yarns back: K2A, bring both yarns forward, P2B*, rep to end. *Be careful to keep the yarns free, not crossing each other, as you bring them to the front and back.* At the end of the row, twist the yarns once round each other before you begin the next row.
Row 2: *both yarns back: K2B, yarns both forward, P2A*, rep to end. Twist the yarns once round each other again before you begin the next row.

Because the knits and purls separate completely in this stitch, the fabric pulls in to be narrower than the ribbing, as only half the stitches are used for each side. Now you have the

Reversible stretchy rib (bottom section) depends on the way the colours are woven between stitches: a slightly different movement creates double-cloth fabric with two separate layers (top section).

option of casting off in K2, P2, therefore spreading the stitches out to their full width again, or separating the knits and purls onto two needles and casting each layer off individually to leave an open end, as illustrated.

Double-faced knitting in two colour K1, P1

Here is another way of achieving a double-faced fabric.
Row 1: *both yarns back: K1A, bring both yarns forward, P1B*, rep to end. *Be careful to keep the yarns free, not crossing each other, as you bring them to the front and back.* Twist the yarns once round each other before you begin the next row.
Row 2: *both yarns back: K1B, yarns both forward, P1A*, rep to end. Twist the yarns once round each other before you begin the next row.
The only slight difference between the K2, P2 version and this one is a faint pairing of the stitches in the K2, P2, depending on the yarns used.

Double-faced knitting in two colours in slip stitch

The same result as above can be achieved (a little more slowly) by working with two colours but only one colour per row, on an even number of stitches.
Row 1: col A: P1, *P1, yb, S1, yf*, rep to last st, P1.
Row 2: col A: K1, *K1, yf, S1, yb*, rep to last st, K1.
Row 3: col B: *K1, *yf, S1, yb*, rep to last st, K2.
Row 4: col B: P1, *P1, yb, S1, yf*, rep to last st, P1.

Double-faced fabrics can be explored endlessly:

• change the stitch so you have purl on the outside
• change the colours so they swap sides
• design two-sided colour patterns
• design two-sided colour and different textured patterns.

Colour patterns in double knitting will be clear and sharp with no interference from other colours stranded or woven behind, and each side will show the same pattern in positive and negative. Pattern making in this double fabric is a subject in itself, and much more can be found in Lucy Neatby's books and YouTube videos.[2]

Fair Isle using increases and decreases to create geometric patterns

This pair of mittens from Tromso, Norway[3] shows a simple geometric pattern in grey and white, but uses increases and decreases to create clean, sharp diagonal lines. If the triangular pattern had been knitted straight, the edges of the diagonals would have to be stepped, as shown in the sample overleaf, but the increases and decreases in the mittens tilt the rows to create a clean edge, giving a more satisfying pattern: the tilt of the stitches creates the clear diagonal. This idea could be applied to any colour pattern with diagonals, and progressed to using increases and decreases to create natural smooth curves and ripples in Fair Isle designs (*see* Chapter 6).

These mittens from Norway use increases and decreases to give this Fair Isle pattern clean, clear diagonal lines (photo: Angharad Thomas).

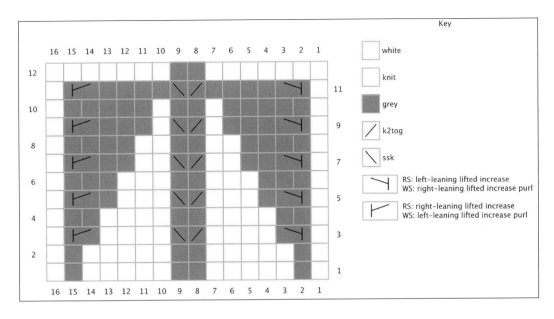

Chart showing the geometric
pattern of the Norwegian
mittens shaped by increases
and decreases.

Mitten pattern

Triangles and stripes

Worked on a multiple of 16 sts in two colours, A and B.

Row 1: *col A K1, col B K1, col A K5, col B K2, col A K5, col B K1, col A K1*, rep to end.

Row 2: *col A P1, col B P1, col A P5, col B P2, col A P5, Col B P1, col A P*, rep to end.

Row 3: *col A K1, col B K into f&b, col A K4, col B K2tog, SSK, col A K4, col B K into f&b, col A K1*, rep to end.

Row 4: *col A P1, col B P2, (col A P4, col B P2) x 2, col A P1*, rep to end.

Row 5: *col A K1, col B K into f&b, K1, col A K3, col B K2tog, SSK, col A K3, col B K1, K into f&b, col A K1*, rep to end.

Row 6: *col A P1, col B P3, col A P3, col B P2, col A P3, Col B P3, col A P1*, rep to end.

Row 7: *col A K1, col B K into f&b, K2, col A K2, col B K2tog, SSK, col A K2, col B K2, K into f&b, col A K1*, rep to end.

Row 8: *col A P1, col B P4, col A P2, col B P2, col A P2, Col B P4, col A P1*, rep to end.

Row 9: *col A K1, col B K into f&b, K3, col A K1, col B K2tog, SSK, col A K1, col B K3, K into f&b, col A K1*, rep to end.

Row 10: *col A P1, col B P5, col A P1, col B P2, col A P1, Col B P5, col A P1*, rep to end.

Row 11: *col A K1, col B K into f&b, K4, K2tog, SSK, K4, K into f&b, col A K1*, rep to end.

Row 12: *col A P1, col B P1, col A P5, col B P2, col A P5, Col B P1, col A P1*, rep to end.

Rep from row 3.

Working the same pattern as the mittens without the increases and decreases
means the diagonal lines are stilted or stepped rather than smooth
(photo author).

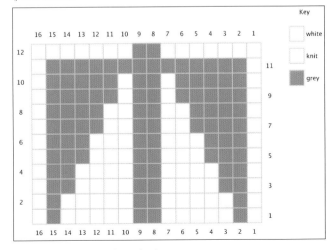

Chart for this pattern without shaping.

Diagonal striped pattern
This is worked on 16 sts.
Row 1: col A K1, into next st: col B K into f, col A into b (making 2 sts, cols B and A), (col B K1, col A K1) x 2, col B K2tog, SSK, (col A K1, col B K1) x 2, into next st: col A K into f, col B into b, col A K1, rep to end.
Row 2: (col A P1, col B P1) x 4, (col B P1, col A P1) x 4, rep to end.
Row 3: col A K1, col B K into f&b, (col A K1, col B K1) x 2, col B K2tog, SSK, (col B K1, col A K1) x 2, col B K into f&b, col A K1, rep to end.
Row 4: col A P1, col B P2, col A P1, col B P1, col A P1, col B P4, col A P1, col B P1, col A P1, col B P2, col A P1, rep to end.
These 4 rows form the pattern.
The tops of the mittens are shaped by omitting the increases, so the design decreases the whole shape naturally to the top.

'Straight' Fair Isle pattern
This piece shows the pattern charted without the increases and decreases, creating a more rigid effect, with the diagonal sloping line stepped as on the graph diagram, rather than the stitches leaning into a natural, smooth slant.

Fair Isle used right and wrong sides for pattern and movement

Another idea emerges from looking at the reversible two-colour ribbing, leading to the possibility of using larger areas of Fair Isle patterning alternating right and wrong sides to create movement in the fabric, such as larger ribs, pleats or flares. The movement is the same as any single-colour knitting: in a vertical rib the knit areas come forward, purl falls back: in bands of horizontal pattern, purl areas push forward and knit falls back. As well as this movement, here is an opportunity for patterning and colour mixing, as the woven back of Fair Isle knitting is very different on the purl side. On the knit (or right) side, you have a clear, sharply defined pattern, but on the reverse the colours become mixed and blurred as the yarns are woven over each other. If you are using a regular geometric pattern, this will still be visible as diagonals, diamonds, squares or whatever it is, but looking softer and out of focus on the purl side. Bringing the purl side to the front is another design tool, visually as well as practically. Using only two colours, you can create a third by mixing the two in the purl

areas. You may have two yarns, one turquoise-blue and one yellow yarn, and where the two weave and mix over the purl areas they will suggest a third, greenish shade. The actual Fair Isle pattern could be different in each area, so you could have turquoise dominating one knit area, yellow another, with the mixture on the purl side between creating green, a third colour. Again, questioning the 'right' and 'wrong' in knitting, whether right and wrong side, or the tendency of knitting to curl up, can lead to something new, and again the knitting technique has done some of the design work for you.

Reversible Fair Isle

Pattern 1 – diamonds and diagonals
Allowing 8 sts for the diagonals and 9 sts for the diamonds, cast on 42 sts.

Follow the chart for the colours, and weave in the yarns over the purl stitches in both patterns.
The knits and purls stay in columns, producing a rib effect.

Row 1: P8, following chart and using each colour for 2 sts each, *both yf, K9 following chart for diamonds, both yb, purl 8 in diagonals*, rep to end.

A two-colour pattern of diamonds and diagonals using knit-face and purl-face stocking stitch with colours woven on the purl sides, giving a strong, ribbed effect, and mixing the colours on the purl side.

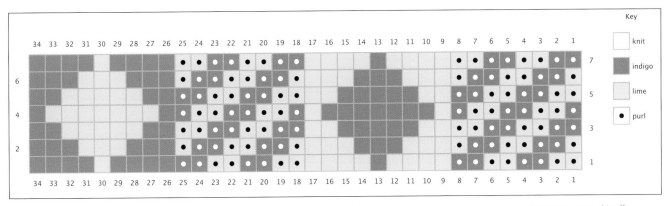

The chart for diamonds and diagonals showing knit and purl sides, but the yarns need to be neatly woven up and down on the purl areas to create this effect.

Row 2: K8 in diagonals pattern, * both yb, K9 in diamonds pattern, both yf, K8 diagonals*, rep to end.
These 2 rows form the pattern, using the chart for the colours.

Pattern 2 – triangles and pleats
In the previous pattern, the knits and purls were in columns, whereas here they follow the shape of the triangle motif,

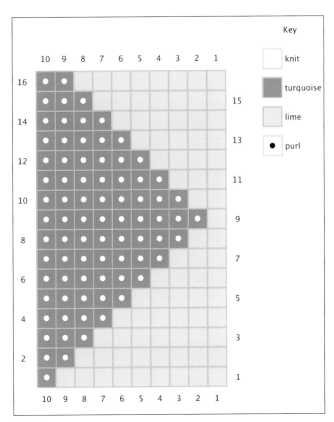

The chart shows the triangle pattern and the knit and purl, but the yarns also need to be neatly woven up and down on the purl areas to create this effect.

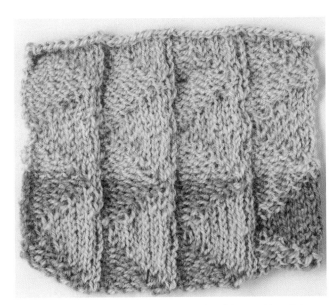

In this pattern with triangles using knit-face and purl-face stocking stitch (with colours woven on the purl areas), a pleat is created by the vertical line between the knit and purl sides.

creating a sharp knit/purl boundary at one edge, causing the fabric to pleat. The colours are varied throughout to show different plain colours against the mixed effect in the purl.

Cast on a multiple of 10 sts.

Follow the chart for the colour, either keeping one colour for knit and one for purl, or swapping them as you like, and weave in the yarns over the purl stitches on both sides.

Row 1: *K1A, P9B*, rep to end.
Row 2: *K8B, P2A*, rep to end.
Row 3: *K3A, P7B*, rep to end.
Row 4: *K6B, P4A*, rep to end.
Row 5: *K5A, P5B*, rep to end.
Row 6: *K4B, P6A*, rep to end.
Row 7: *K7A, P3B*, rep to end.
Row 8: *K2B, P8A*, rep to end.
Row 9: *K9A, P1B*, rep to end.
Row 10: *K2B, P8A*, rep to end.
Row 11: *K7A, P3B*, rep to end.
Row 12: *K4B, P6A*, rep to end.
Row 13: *K5A, P5B*, rep to end.
Row 14: *K6B, P4A*, rep to end.
Row 15: *K3A, P7B*, rep to end.
Row 16: *K8B, P2A*, rep to end.
Rep these 16 rows, changing the colours as you like.

Moss stitch Fair Isle

Another stitch that works well with a two-colour Fair Isle is moss stitch, using one colour for knit and the other for purl, so that the colours alternate each stitch and row, as do the knits and purls. This gives the added pebbly texture of the moss stitch as another design element, which if you use it with plain areas, will contrast with the smoothness of the knit. Either of the two colours can predominate, so you have two plain colours to play with and an added bonus of a mixed colour in the texture of moss stitch. Looking more closely, the texture of the mixed moss stitch also changes depending on which colour is used for knit and which for purl, as is shown in this example.

This sample begins with an ordinary K1, P1 moss stitch in single-colour stripes (a) (two rows each colour) to compare the width, then progresses to the following.

b) two-colour moss st, first band
Cast on an uneven number of sts. A = orange, B = pale green
Row 1: carrying the yarns at the back, *K1A, yBf, P1B, yBb*, rep ending K1A.
Row 2: carrying the yarns at the front, *yBb, K1B, yBf, P1A*, rep to last st, K1B.
Rep these 2 rows.

c) Two-colour moss st, second band
The colours are swapped for this section, with colour B showing more strongly.
Row 1: carrying the yarns at the back, *K1B, yAf, P1A, yAb*, rep ending K1B.
Row 2: carrying the yarns at the front, *yAb, K1A, yAf, P1B*, rep to last st, K1A.
Rep these 2 rows.
These three variations are shown in the chart for the first band, with a) at the bottom and working up through b) to c) at the top.

The top section is knitted with both colours per row, in blocks 6 stitches wide and 6 rows long, with some areas in plain stocking stitch in A or B (weaving the other colour behind), and some in mixed moss stitch in both variations. Looking at the right side, the colour of the knit stitches will be dominant, as the top of the stitch is pushed forward on the following row, so the first mixed moss stitch section shows more colour A, and the second colour B.

These moss stitches don't alter the width or length of the knitted fabric very much when knitted in two colours – the moss stitch stripes at the bottom are just a little wider – but the texture is different with two-colour knitting: carrying the yarns at the back gives a smoother feel than the textured front of the stitch. The blocks knit up almost square. Different knitting tensions may indicate more rows or stitches to produce a square block.

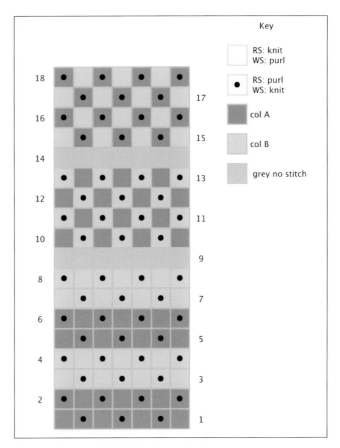

By knitting with two colours and playing with different stitches, colours can appear mixed, producing more shades. From bottom to top:
a) 2-row stripes in moss stitch.
b) to two-colour moss st, using one colour for knits, one for purls, which pulls in the width a little.
c) the colours are swapped, giving a different shade. The 6-stitch blocks at the top play with plain coloured squares alternating with mixed-colour moss stitch squares.

The chart for moss stitch Fair Isle. From bottom to top:
a) stripes in moss stitch
b) alternate colour moss stitch
c) the same with the colours swapped over.

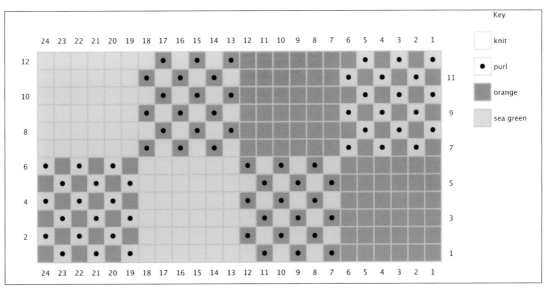

The chart for the moss stitch and plain colour blocks.

CHAPTER 6

CREATING CURVES

Looking at the structure of knitting, even though the yarn moves in fluid loops to make a flexible fabric, it is still built on a grid, as the stitches are placed in columns beside each other and in rows above each other. The usual or traditional way of designing a pattern in knitting is to use symbols in a chart as shown in this book, with a square representing each stitch. With colour patterns, this gives an instant visual impression of how the stitch will look, in the same way as charts for weaving, cross-stitch embroidery, and other textile techniques using repeating patterns or single motifs. This grid structure can suggest curves by moving the pattern gradually stitch by stitch, or square by square, so curves can be implied, but with slightly angular edges.

Any design with curves is possible to knit and notate in this way, whether coloured or using different stitches represented by symbols on the chart, but it will have the slightly stilted look of any pixelated shape where curves are built from dots or units. There are wonderful examples of knitting in museums, ranging from fifteenth century through to the twentieth century (and later). The V&A Museum in London has a Dutch petticoat knitted finely in wool, with sophisticated patterning of foliage, flowers, birds and animals all described simply in knit and purl stitches. There are areas of knit-side and purl-side stocking

OPPOSITE PAGE: Six methods of knitting circles

stitch, moss stitch, garter stitch and other combinations of knit and purl, all in undyed wool so that the textures show. The design incorporates curves to depict the motifs in a free and decorative way, but the stitches don't move – they stay in position. It works because of the fine scale, but looking closely, if you copy the design onto a squared chart, the curves are not smooth, but pixelated by the grid.[1]

However, the stitches don't have to stay in their correct position or groove in knitting: if they themselves move they form natural curves and so can be used to create curves for you. A stitch such as cabling illustrates how simple it is to bend or move the columns of stitches so they curve in a more fluid way, travelling back and forth, helped by the elasticity of knitting in the accommodating way stitches bending round angular corners can transform to a smooth curve. Increases and decreases have the same effect, so, for example, moving a stitch by knitting 2 together on alternate rows makes it travel diagonally, but if you alter the angle or change direction by using more or fewer rows between, the stitches can appear to curve. The stretchiness of knitting makes this change smooth and rounded, rather than stilted.

With cables, increases and decreases, we can make vertical curves formed by stitches travelling up the rows, gradually crossing other columns of stitches as they go. What about the horizontals? In the same way, we can make the rows of stitches travel up and down by repeated increases and decreases within a row, moving the rows up at the point of increase and dipping down at the point of decrease. We have seen it's possible to get quite sharp changes of direction according to the kind of increase or decrease used, for example in the zigzag samples in Chapter 3, but there is a way of softening angles by spacing out several decreases and increases to curve the row gently up and down in a more rounded way.

Short rows also move the horizontal rows of stitches, building some areas up higher and holding other areas back so the knitting tilts. If planned carefully, again the rows will bend in a fluid way.

This chapter looks at ways of using stitches to create curves in knitting, beginning with some simple ideas examining how to make a complete knitted circle. There are several ways to achieve this, some knitted along the radius in segments, and some working from the centre outwards or the edge inwards in a spiral or circular motion.

Circles – six ways

Six ways of making a circle: the first piece is taken from a design by Britt-Marie Christoffersson[2] and is in garter stitch on two needles, so is very simple to make. It is knitted back and forth, with a small seam sewn at the end.

A circle worked back and forth in garter stitch in 2 rows to each colour, decreasing towards the centre; this has a seam sewn to join.

Back-and-forth circle

The chart shows the repeat of 6 sts.
Cast on 84 sts in col A.
Foundation row (WS): col A K.
Row 1 (RS): col B *K4, K2tog*, rep to end.
Row 2: col B K.

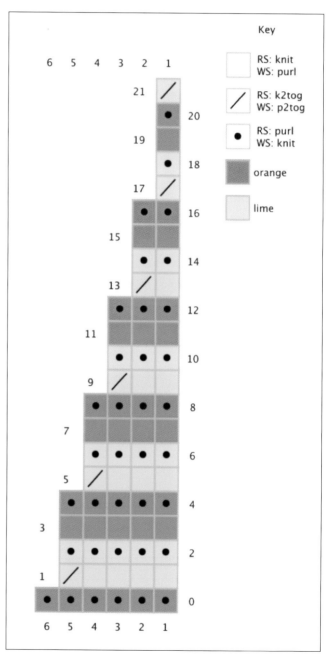

Chart for back-and-forth garter-stitch circle, beginning at the circumference and working towards the centre.

Rows 3 & 4: col A K.

Row 5: col B *K3, K2tog*, rep to end.

Row 6: col B K.

Rows 7 & 8: col A K.

Row 9: col B *K2, K2tog*, rep to end.

Row 10: col B K.

Rows 11 & 12: col A K.

Row 13: col B *K1, K2tog*, rep to end.

Row 14: col B K.

Rows 15 & 16: col A K.

Row 17: col B *K2tog*, rep to end.

Row 18: col B K.

Rows 19 & 20: col A K.

Row 21: col B *K2tog*, rep to end.

7 sts remain, cut yarn and thread onto a tapestry needle. Thread through the 7 sts, pull tight and sew the piece into a circle.

14 decreases are placed evenly along the row every 4 rows. It would be equally possible to knit in the round.

A circle worked in the round decreasing at eight points towards the centre .

8-decrease circle (octagon)

Here is another circle, this time knitted in the round with no seam, on a set of five double-ended needles, with the stitches evenly distributed on four needles and knitting with the fifth, again working from the outer edge in towards the centre. It is worked in 2 rows of stocking stitch, 2 rows of garter stitch. The chart shows the repeat of 11 stitches.

Cast on 88 sts in col A, casting 22 sts onto each of 4 needles.

Round 1: col B: *K9, K2tog*, rep to end of round.

Round 2: col B: P.

Round 3: col A: *K8, K2tog*, rep to end of round.

Round 4: col A: K.

Round 5: col B: *K7, K2tog*, rep to end of round.

Round 6: col B: P.

Round 7: col A: *K6, K2tog*, rep to end of round.

Round 8: col A: K.

Round 9: col B: *K5, K2tog*, rep to end of round.

Round 10: col B: P.

Round 11: col A: *K4, K2tog*, rep to end of round.

Round 12: col A: K.

Round 13: col B: *K3, K2tog*, rep to end of round.

Round 14: col B: P.

Round 15: col A: *K2, K2tog*, rep to end of round.

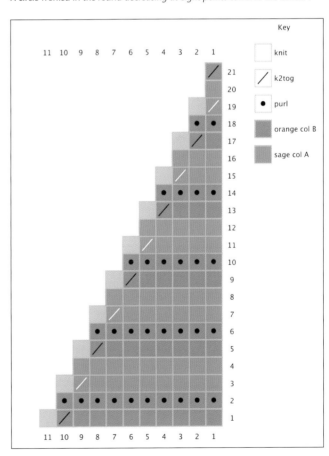

Chart showing the decreasing circle, with stocking stitch and garter-stitch stripes.

Round 16: col A: K.
Round 17: col B: *K1, K2tog*, rep to end of round.
Round 18: col B: P.
Round 19: col A: *K2tog*, rep to end of round.
Round 20: col A: K.
Round 21: col B: *K2tog*, all round to make 4 sts.
Cut yarn and thread onto a tapestry needle: pass thread through these sts, pull tight and fasten off.

The stocking-stitch stripes are more open than if knitted in garter stitch, but with eight decreases on alternate rows, the circle is about the same size as the back-and-forth circle.

Circle with 6 increases (hexagon)

This piece is also worked in the round but this time from the centre outwards, and with six increases on alternate rounds, with the chart showing a repeat of 14 stitches.
Cast on 6 sts in col A, casting 2 onto each of three needles.

A circle worked in the round from the centre outwards, increasing at six points, casting off the outer edge, becoming rather hexagonal.

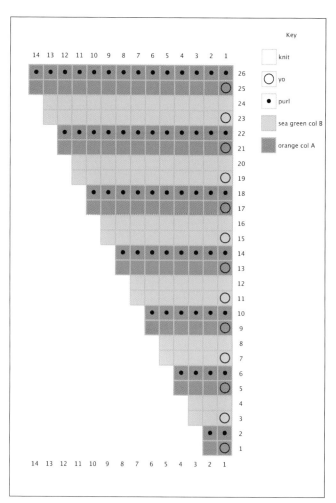

Chart showing the hexagonal shape worked from the centre in stocking stitch and garter-stitch stripes.

Round 1: col A: *YO, K1, YO, K1*, rep on each needle.
Round 2: col A: P.
Round 3: col B: *YO, K2*, rep all round.
Round 4: col B: K.
Round 5: col A: *YO, K3*, rep all round.
Round 6: col A: P.
Round 7: col B: *YO, K4*, rep all round.
Round 8: col B: K.
Round 9: col A: *YO, K5*, rep all round.
Round 10: col A: P.
Round 11: col B: *YO, K6*, rep all round.
Round 12: col B: K.
Round 13: col A: *YO, K7, *rep all round.

Round 14: col A: P.
Round 15: col B: *YO, K8*, rep all round.
Round 16: col B: K.
Round 17: col A: *YO, K9*, rep all round.
Round 18: col A: P.
Round 19: col B: *YO, K10*, rep all round.
Round 20: col B: K.
Round 21: col A: *YO, K11*, rep all round.
Round 22: col A: P.
Round 23: col B: *YO, K12*, rep all round.
Round 24: col B: K.
Round 25: col A: *YO, K13*, rep all round.
Round 26: col A: P.
Cast off in A.

Comparing this piece using six increases with the previous sample worked with eight decreases, it appears that for this size of sample, both create a circle: or more precisely, an octagon or hexagon, which could be used as a circle. To make a bigger circle, depending what stitch is used, six shapings

(whether worked inwards or outwards) can produce a more domed, less flat circle than eighty shapings. But using this particular increase of 'YO' seems to allow freedom of movement for the stitches so they can expand more easily, and the garter-stitch stripe draws the shape up a little more than plain stocking stitch would have. If you use this method for the top of a hat, a slight dome is fine, and six shapings is usually enough. In order to make a much bigger circle, working from the centre, you would need to introduce more increases to keep it flat. Similarly, eighty increases would need to be added to a larger circle.

Random-increase circle

In this next sample, working from the centre again, the six increases are staggered and moved around rather than always occurring over the same stitches, which removes the angular hexagonal shape and allows a more rounded circle.

A circle worked from the centre outwards in the round, increasing six times but in different places creating a smoother circle.

Short-row circle

A completely different approach is to knit the circle sideways across the radius, using short rows to build up segments until you have enough for a flat circle. It's a very adaptable way of working; you can keep adding and testing to see if it is as flat as you want, or you can stop short of a circle to make a cone shape. Small segments will make a smoother circle, while larger segments create a more angular edge.

Using garter stitch in stripes of 2 rows in alternating colours shows the structure clearly. The short rows leave one more stitch behind on alternate rows, and in this case take nine segments to make a circle. Stocking stitch would stretch out further and require fewer segments.

The right-hand edge of the chart represents the outer edge of the circle.

Using col A, cast on 11 sts.
Row 1: col A: K11, turn.
Row 2: col A: K.
Row 3: col B: K10, w&t.
Row 4: col B: K.
Row 5: col A: K9, w&t.
Row 6: col A: K.
Row 7: col B: K8, w&t.

Row 8: col B: K.
Row 9: col A: K7, w&t.
Row 10: col A: K.
Row 11: col B: K6, w&t.
Row 12: col B: K.
Row 13: col A: K5, w&t.
Row 14: col A: K.
Row 15: col B: K4, w&t.
Row 16: col B: K.
Row 17: col A: K3, w&t.
Row 18: col A: K.
Row 19: col B: K2, w&t.
Row 20: col B: K.
Row 21: col A: K1, w&t.
Row 22: col A: K.

This makes one segment. Repeat these 22 rows until you have a circle and sew invisibly to join.

A circle worked sideways in short-row segments in garter stitch in 2-row stripes to show the direction, continuing until the circle is complete and joining by grafting.

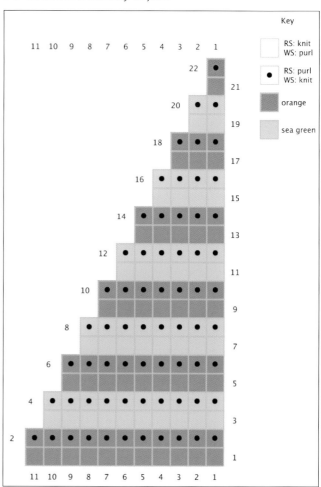

Chart showing one segment of the circle, which pulls up much shorter than the chart shows when knitted in garter stitch.

Smooth short-row circle

This sample is made in a similar way, but in much narrower segments and in stocking stitch.
Cast on 12 sts.

Row 1: K12, turn.
Row 2: P.
Row 3: K9, w&t.
Row 4: P.
Row 5: K6, w&t.
Row 6: P.
Row 7: K3 w&t.
Row 8: P.

Repeat these 8 rows to build up segments to create a circle. Because stocking stitch is so smooth and revealing, a provisional cast on was used in this sample so that it could be joined by Kitchener stitch to make an invisible join.

A circle worked sideways in narrow short-row segments in stocking stitch, grafting an invisible join.

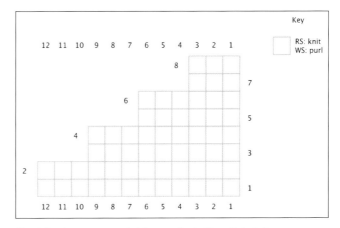

Chart showing one segment of the smooth stocking-stitch circle.

A circle or circular motif within the fabric

A circular motif can be drawn on graph paper and copied in knitting, here shown in two colours. Bearing in mind that the knitted stitch is wider than it is tall, the chart shows a taller circle than the knitted piece. Knitting tensions vary, and the Fair Isle technique can pull the tension in to make stitches that are almost square, so it's worth checking your tension before a project, measuring how many rows and stitches you have to a given measurement over the pattern. For example, stocking stitch in a plain colour usually works out at roughly 3 stitches to 4 rows to make a square.

The sample illustrated shows the bottom circle (a) knitted with two colours travelling across and woven at the back, resulting in this circle becoming wider than the top circle (b). This will vary with individual knitting tension in Fair Isle knitting.

The second circle (b) is knitted in intarsia, with a separate ball of yarn for each area, so is only a single yarn's thickness. Both these circles have noticeably rough edges: a smooth circle is very difficult to achieve when composed of individual stitches in stocking stitch. The same thing happens on the chart; a smooth curve is pixelated, but in knitting the top of the stitch is not a square, but a spiky V-shape with sharp corners, and the circle becomes more untidy at the top than round the bottom edge.

These circles are both 15 stitches wide with a few stitches in the darker colour at each edge.

Circular motifs within the fabric. From bottom to top:
a) circular shape knitted in Fair Isle with two colours across the row, woven at the back.
b) follows the same chart in intarsia, each colour in its own area.

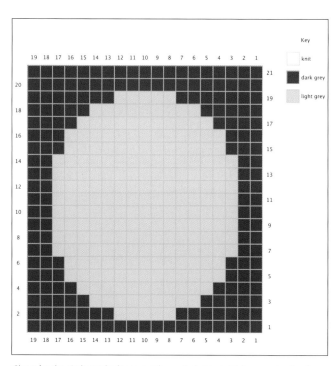

Chart for the circle worked in two colours. As knitted stitches are shorter than a square, the chart looks taller than the finished knitting.

Smooth-edged circles

This piece has been knitted in intarsia again, but the stitches at the side edges of the circle have physically travelled to create a smoother line, moving away from the vertical by increasing and decreasing, so they curve naturally to give a smooth outline.

Smooth-edged circles. From bottom to top:
a) white circle, knitted in intarsia, uses stitches to outline the circle round the sides to give a smoother edge.
b) green circle at the top with the stitches outlining the edge all round, combining increases and decreases and braid techniques (see Chapter 4).

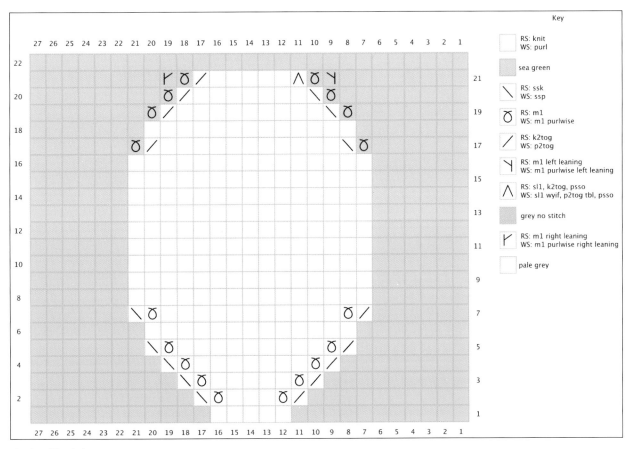

Chart for the white circle.

a) White circle

Cast on 27 sts.

Note: in intarsia knitting, make sure you cross the yarns over when you change colour, so they link and don't leave gaps.

In this piece, it's sometimes tricky to make a neat 'M1' new stitch. Here they are picked up from the strand of yarn between stitches in the previous row.

Row 1: col A, K11: col B, K5: col A, K11.

Row 2: col A, P10: col B, P2togb, M1, P3, M1, P2tog: col A, P10.

Row 3: col A, K9: col B, K2tog, M1, K5, M1, SSK: col A, K9.

Row 4: col A, P8: col B, P2togb, M1, P7, M1, P2tog: col A, P8.

Row 5: col A, K7: col B, K2tog, M1, K9, M1, SSK: col A, K7.

Row 6: col A, P7: col B, P13: col A, P7.

Row 7: col A, K6: col B, K2tog, M1, K11, M1, SSK: col A, K6.

Row 8: col A, P6: col B, P15: col A, P6.

Row 9: col A, K6: col B, K15: col A, K6.

Row 10: as row 8.

Rows 11 & 12: as rows 9 & 10.

Rows 13 & 14: as rows 9 & 10.

Rows 15 & 16: as rows 9 & 10.

Row 17: col A, K6, M1: col B, SSK, K11, K2tog: col A, M1, K6.

Row 18: col A, P7: col B, P13: col A, P7.

Row 19: col A, K7, M1: col B, SSK, K9, K2tog: col A, M1, K7.

Row 20: col A, P8, M1: col B, P2tog, P7, P2togb: col A, M1, P8.

Row 21: col A, K8, K into f&b of next st, M1: col B, S1, SSK, psso, K3, S1, SSK, psso: col A, M1, make another by picking up and knitting the st from the row below, K8.

Row 22: col A, P across the row.

b) Green circle

Taking this idea further, the top circle is outlined by stitches creating a curve all the way round, with a braid stitch at the top and bottom to tilt the stitches into a horizontal line which connects with the side increases and decreases, continuing the line round the sides. Where there is no shaping at the sides of the circle, the outline stitch is slipped to raise it slightly from the background and continue the line.

As in the previous circle, the 'M1' has to be done neatly, if necessary twisting the stitch so it doesn't leave a hole.

Cast on 27 sts and knit a plain edging in col A.

Row 1: K12, *return the last st to LH needle, YO, SSK* x 4, K11.

Row 2: P10, P2togb, M1, P4, turn work and pick up loop, checking that it will make a smooth line on the front of work, turn and purl it tog with next st, P10.

Row 3: K9, K2tog, M1, K5, M1, SSK, K9.

Row 4: P.

Row 5: K8, K2tog, M1, K7, M1, SSK, K8.

Row 6: P.

Row 7: K7, K2tog, M1, K9, M1, SSK, K7.

Row 8: P.

Row 9: K7, S1, K11, S1, K7.

Row 10: P6, P2togb, M1, P11, M1, P2tog, P6.

Row 11: K6, S1, K13, S1, K6.

Row 12: P.

Row 13: as row 11.

Row 14: P.

Row 15: K6, M1, SSK, K11, K2tog, M1, K6.

Row 16: P.

Row 17: K7, S1, K11, S1, K7.

Row 18: P7, M1, P2tog, P9, P2togb, M1, P7.

Row 19: K.

Row 20: P8, M1, P2tog, P7, P2togb, M1, P8.

Row 21: K9, M1, SSK, K5, K2tog, M1, K9.

Row 22: P10, M1, P2tog, P3, P2togb, M1, P10.

Row 23: K11, *YO, SSK, return st to LH needle* x 3, return st to LH, YO, S1, K2tog, psso, K10.

Row 24: P.

The hardest part of this last exercise was creating a horizontal stitch that blended seamlessly with the side edges, as the knitted stitch naturally wants to point upwards, not sideways. The only time a stitch travels horizontally in knitting is when it's being cast off, or in certain braids (*see* Chapter 4) which, in effect, lay the stitches along like a cast-off edge while creating new stitches at the same time. This was the method used here, and it could be explored and expanded to make a thicker, bolder edge using an i-cord: the same principle but with more stitches.

Curves in repeated patterns

The following pieces go on to explore vertical and horizontal curves in repeated patterns. The difficulty is in combining the two to make circles while moving in one direction.

Lucy Hague has come up with an intriguing and satisfying way of knitting circular textures, using a combination of short rows and knit and purl stitches, with the direction of the knitting making perfect circles.[3]

Curves travelling upwards

Vertical curves are easy, travelling with the knitting in an upward direction, moving from side to side but always following the growth of the knitting. They can move or wander either in a regular or in a more organic, freestyle pattern with separate columns moving to the right or left independently. The movement is made either by crossing a group of stitches over another stitch or group, or by increasing and decreasing next to the travelling stitches, which has the effect of pushing them to left or right. The number of rows there are between either the crossovers or the increases and decreases will determine how steeply they curve: making a movement every row will force the stitches to travel nearer to the horizontal, whereas having plain rows between will cause a more gradual, vertical movement.

a) Vertical curves (made with incs and decs)
Cast on a multiple of 20 sts.
Row 1: *P7, K2, P2, K2, P7*, rep from * to *.
Row 2: *K7, P2, K2, P2, K7*, rep from * to *.
Row 3: as row 1.
Row 4: as row 2.
Row 5: as row 1.
Row 6: as row 2.

Lucy Hague has found a way of creating intricate circle patterns outlined with a group of stitches travelling smoothly all round.

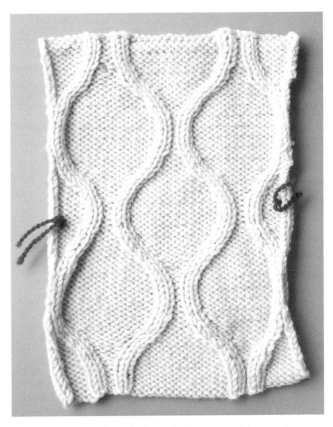

Bottom half (a): smooth curving lines using increases and decreases to move the stitches.
Top half (b): smooth curving lines using cables and crossovers to move the stitches.

Row 7: *P6, K2tog, K into f&b of next st, P1, P into f&b of next st, K1, SSK, P6*, rep.

Row 8: *K6, P2, K4, P2, K6*, rep.

Row 9: *P6, K2, P4, K2, P6*, rep.

Row 10: *K5, P2togb, P into f&b of next st, K3, K into f&b of next st, P1, P2tog, K5*, rep.

Row 11: *P4, K2tog, K into f&b of next st, P5, P into f&b of next st, K1, SSK, P4*, rep.

Row 12: *K3, P2togb, P into f&b of next st, K7, K into f&b of next st, P1, P2tog, K3*, rep.

Row 13: *P2, K2tog, K into f&b of next st, P9, P into f&b of next st, K1, SSK, P2*, rep.

Row 14: *K2, P2, K12, P2, K2*, rep.

Row 15: *P2, K2, P12, K2, P2*, rep.

Row 16: *K1, P2togb, P into f&b of next st, K11, K into f&b of next st, P1, P2tog, K1*, rep.

Row 17: *P1, K2, P14, K2, P1*, rep.

Row 18: *K1, P2, K14, P2, K1*, rep.

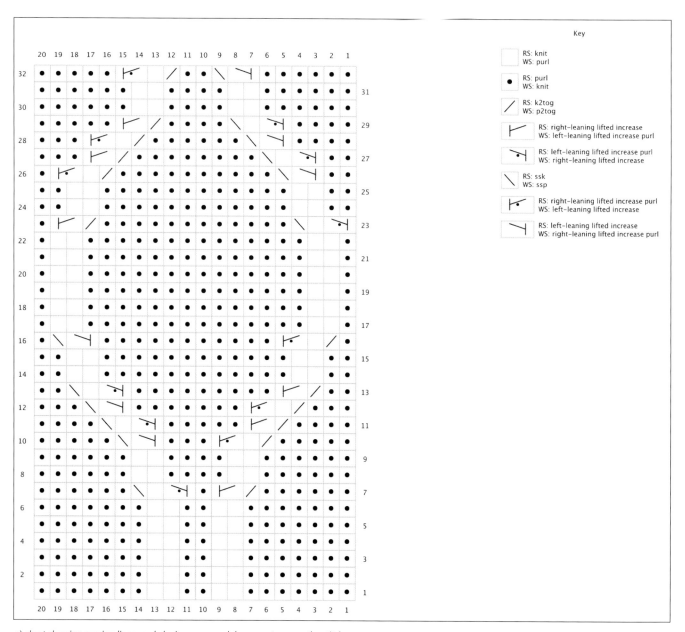

a) chart showing curving lines made by increases and decreases to move the stitches.

Row 19: as row 17.

Row 20: as row 18.

Row 21: as row 17.

Row 22: as row 18.

Row 23: *P into f&b of st, K1, SSK, P12, K2tog, K into f&b of next st, P1*, rep.

Row 24: *K2, P2, K12, P2, K2*, rep.

Row 25: *P2, K2, P12, K2, P2*, rep.

Row 26: *K1, K into f&b of next st, P1, P2tog, K10, P2togb, P into f&b of next st, K2*, rep.

Row 27: *P2, P into f&b of next st, K1, SSK, P8, K2tog, K into f&b of next st, P3*, rep.

Row 28: *K3, K into f&b of next st, P1, P2tog, K6, P2togb, P into f&b of next st, K4*, rep.

Row 29: *P4, P into f&b of next st, K1, SSK, P4, K2tog, K into f&b of next st, P5*, rep.

Row 30: *K6, P2, K4, P2, K6*, rep.

Row 31: *P6, K2, K4, K2, P6*, rep.

Row 32: *K5, K into f&b of next st, P1, P2tog, K2, P2togb, P into f&b of next st, K6*, rep.

Repeat from row 1.

b) Vertical curves (made with cabling)

Cast on a multiple of 20 sts.

Row 1: *P7, K2, P2, K2, P7* rep from * to *.

Row 2: *K7, P2, K2, P2, K7* rep from * to *.

Row 3: as row 1.

Row 4: as row 2.

Row 5: as row 1.

Row 6: as row 2.

Row 7: *P6, C1b, K2, P1C, P2, C2f, P1, K2C, P6*, rep.

Row 8: *K6, P2, K4, P2, K6*, rep.

Row 9: *P6, K2, P4, K2, P6*, rep.

Row 10: *K5, C1fF, P2, K1C, K4, C2b, K1, P2C, K5*, rep.

Row 11: *P4, C1b, K2, P1C, P6, C2f, P1, K2C, P4*, rep.

Row 12: *K3, C1f, P2, K1C, K8, C2b, K1, P2C, K3*, rep.

Row 13: *P2, C1b, K2, P1C, P10, C2f, P1, K2C, P2*, rep.

Row 14: *K2, P2, K12, P2, K2* rep.

Row 15: *P2, K2, P12, K2, P2* rep.

Row 16: *K1, C1f, P2, K1C, K12, C2b, K1, P2C, K1* rep.

Row 17: *P1, K2, P14, K2, P1* rep.

Row 18: *K1, P2, K14, P2, K1* rep.

Row 19: as row 17.

Row 20: as row 18.

Row 21: as row 17.

Row 22: as row 18.

Row 23: *P1, C2f, P1, K2C, P12, C1b, K2, P1C, P1* rep.

Row 24: *K2, P2, K12, P2, K2* rep.

Row 25: *P2, K2, P12, K2, P2* rep.

Row 26: *K2, C2b, K1, P2C, K10, C1f, P2, K1C, K2* rep.

Row 27: *P3, C2f, P1, K2C, P8, C1b, K2, P1C, P3* rep.

Row 28: *K4, C2b, K1, P2C, K6, C1f, P2, K1C, K4* rep.

Row 29: *P5, C2f, P1, K2C, P4, C1b, K2, P1C, P5* rep.

Row 30: *K6, P2, K4, P2, K6* rep.

Row 31: *P6, K2, P4, K2, P6* rep.

Row 32: * K6, C2b, K1, P2C, K2, C1f, P2, K1C, K6* rep.

Rep from row 1.

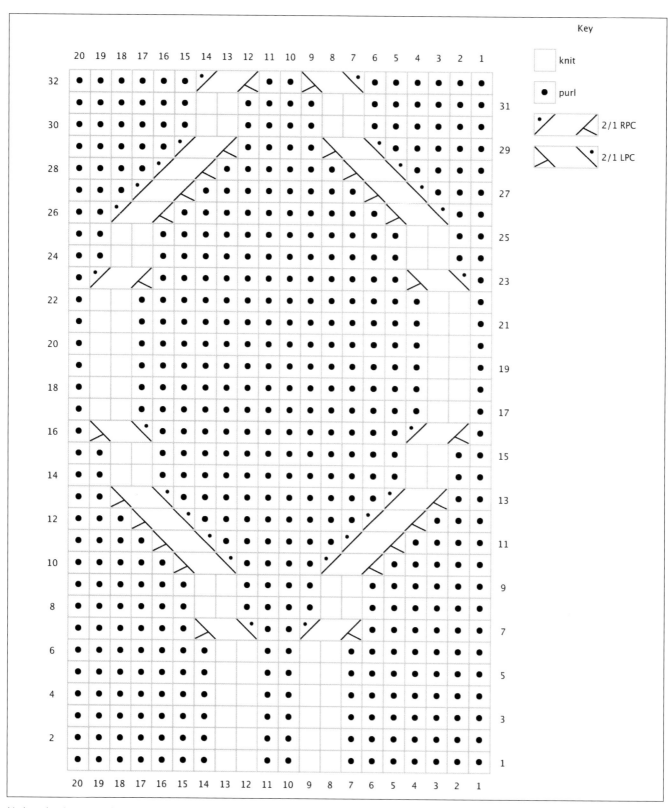

b) chart showing curving lines made by cables and crossovers to move the stitches.

Vertical curves (made with incs and decs) in parallel waves

Cast on a multiple of 12 sts + 10 edge sts (the chart shows the repeat only).

Row 1: P7, *K2, P10,* rep to last 3 sts, K2, P1.

Row 2: K1, P2, *K10, P2*, rep ending K7.

Row 3: as row 1.

Row 4: as row 2.

Row 5: as row 1.

Row 6: as row 2.

Row 7: P6, *K2tog, K into f&b, P9*, rep, ending P1 (not 9).

Row 8: K2, P2, *K10, P2*, rep ending K6.

Row 9: P6, *K2, P10*, rep ending P2 (not 10).

Row 10: K1, *K into f&b, P1, P2tog, K8*, rep ending K5 (not 8).

Row 11: P4, *K2tog, K into f&b, P9*, rep ending P3 (not 9).

Row 12: K3, *K into f&b, P1, P2tog, K8*, rep ending K3 (not 8).

Row 13: P2, *K2tog, K into f&b, P9*, rep ending P5 (not 9).

Row 14: K6, *P2, K10*, rep ending K2 (not 10).

Row 15: P2, *K2, P10*, rep ending P6 (not 10).

Row 16: K5, *K into f&b, P1, P2tog, K8*, rep ending K1 (not 8).

Row 17: P1, *K2, P10*, rep ending P7 (not 10).

Row 18: K7, *P2, K10*, rep ending K1, (not 10).

Row 19: as row 17.

Row 20: as row 18.

Row 21: as row 17.

Row 22: as row 18.

Row 23: *P into f&b, K1, SSK, P8*, rep ending P6 (not 8).

Row 24: K6, *P2, K10*, rep ending K2 (not 10).

Row 25: P2, *K2, P10*, rep ending P6 (not 10).

Row 26: K5, *P2togb, P into f&b, K9*, rep ending K2 (not 9).

Row 27: P2, *P into f&b, K1, SSK, P8*, rep ending P4 (not 8).

Row 28: K3, *P2togb, P into f&b, K9*, rep ending K4 (not 9).

Row 29: P4, *P into f&b, K1, SSK, P8*, rep ending P2 (not 8).

Row 30: K2, P2, *K10, P2*, rep ending K6.

Row 31: P6, *K2, P10*, rep ending P2 (not 10).

Row 32: K1, *P2togb, P into f&b, K9*, rep ending K6 (not 9).

Rep from row 1.

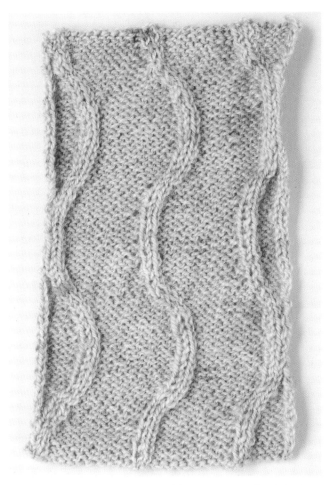

Smooth curving lines using increases and decreases to move the stitches in parallel waves.

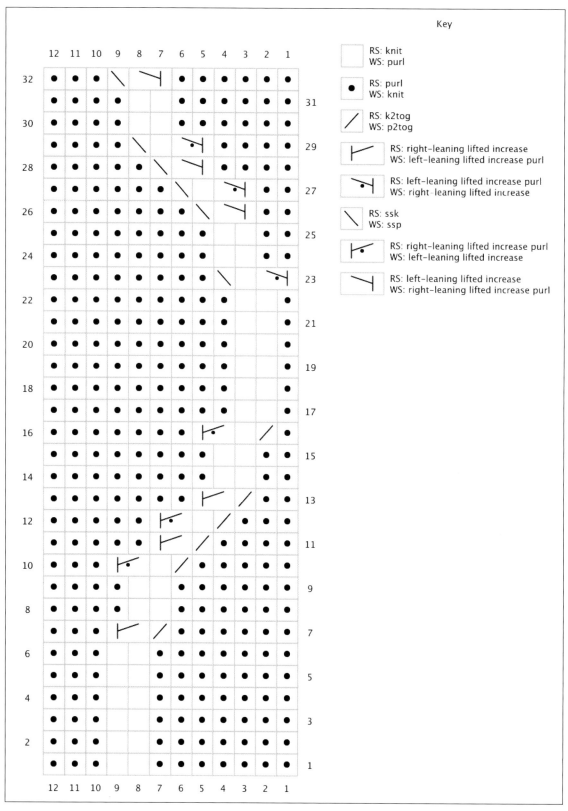

Chart showing one repeat of the parallel wavy lines.

Curves travelling sideways

Horizontal curves are different. Increasing and decreasing all along a row causes the whole row to tilt, similar to the effect of creating zigzags shown in Chapter 3. Zigzags used pairs of increases and decreases, causing sharp, pointed dips and troughs. Grouping several increases followed by several decreases produces a gentler movement and can therefore create curves, with the movement again reinforced by repeating this in later rows with the increases and decreases placed exactly above the previous ones, so the rows are pushed up by increases and dip down where stitches are decreased. If you are knitting on a plain background in stocking stitch, a few rows in reverse stocking stitch with the purl side on the front to make curves will stand forward and show up beautifully. However, this method of moving stitches up and down affects the whole fabric, so to achieve an even fabric, the same movement has to repeat in parallel rather than wandering freely, or the whole piece will buckle. This does not have to be a negative; *in order* to create a puckered, textured, uneven fabric, use this method to make the surface buckle and undulate, and experiment with moving rows randomly and not in a repeating pattern. Understanding what's happening enables creativity, and allows you to be in control and get the effect you want.

Horizontal wavy lines
Inspired by Britt-Marie Christoffersson.[2]

The curves here are made by knitting into stitches several rows below to hitch or tuck the rows, so although the background stitches are not influenced into curves themselves, they are a little distorted by the tucking to give a slightly textured ground.

Cast on a multiple of 18 sts.
Row 1 (RS): col A: K.
Row 2: col A: P.
Repeat these 2 rows until you have done 6 rows of st st, finishing on a K row.
Row 7: col B: K.
Row 8: col B: *(pick up 1 st 7 rows below and place it on LH needle. K that st tog with next st) twice, K13*, (pick up 1 st 7 rows below and place it on LH needle, K that st tog with next st) x 3, rep from *.
Row 9: col B: P.
Row 10: col B: K.
Rows 11–17: col A: cont in st st, starting with a K row.

Horizontal wavy lines inspired by Britt-Marie Christoffersson, made by tucking the fabric to pull the lines up and down.

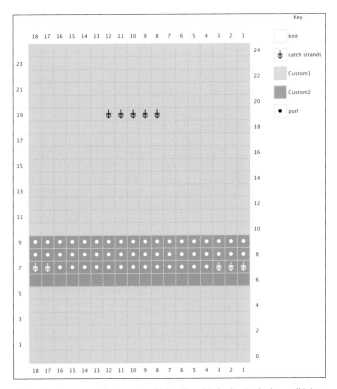

Chart showing one stripe in purl, which is then hitched or tucked to pull it into the waving motion.

Row 18: col A: *P6 (pick up 1 st 7 rows below and place it on LH needle. P this st tog with next st) x 5, P7, rep from *.

Rows 19–24: using col A, work in st st, beginning with a P row.

Rep rows 1–24.

Undulating wavy lines, incs and decs

In this piece, the movement is made by increasing and decreasing in groups of stitches, with the increases and decreases bunched together so that the stitches move gently, down towards the decreases, and are pushed up by the increases.

Cast on a multiple of 28 sts plus 2 edge sts.

P one row.

Row 1: *(K2, K into f&b of next st) x 2, (K2, K2tog) x 4, (K2, K into f&b of next st) x 2*, rep to end, K2.

Row 2: P.

Row 3: K.

Row 4: P.

Rep these 4 rows.

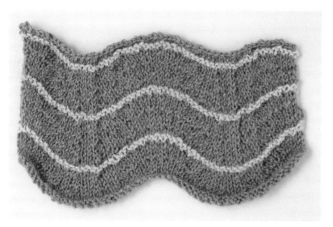

Parallel undulating wavy lines made with increases and decreases, so the whole fabric moves, not just the stripes of colour (stripes made by knitting 2 rows).

To put in a contrast wavy stripe as illustrated, work to the end of the repeat twice, then work row 1 in contrast colour, and knit row 2 instead of purling, and continue in main colour.

Shaping with increases and decreases every 4 rows gives a strong wave pattern. To make it steeper and more pronounced, repeat rows 1 and 2 throughout. To make it shallower, do more rows of plain stocking stitch between the shapings.

To make the waves shorter, bunch the increases and decreases closer together: here there are 2 knit stitches between each shaping, but one stitch or no stitches will create smaller waves. Adding more stitches makes for longer waves.

More horizontal wavy lines

Wavy i-cords

There is another approach to making a wavy or curved line of stitches lie sideways and travel horizontally up and down the row, which is slightly more difficult. An i-cord or braid is the best example of stitches travelling across at right angles to the background knitting (*see* Chapter 4). It can begin horizontally and then move gradually upwards, but obviously while you are knitting upwards, it cannot move down again. If you begin an i-cord at the beginning of the (right side) row and let it travel straight across the row for a while, you can abandon it mid-row and pick it up again on the next right-side row and continue a bit further, by which time it will have sloped up a little at a gentle slant, by two rows. To make a steeper slope, you could treat the group of stitches as a cable and cross them over background stitches, but you can't force them to move downwards! In all these cases, the background stays static: the i-cord travels across it.

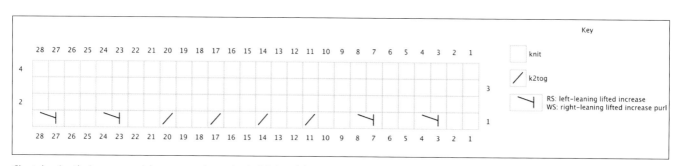

Chart showing the increases and decreases used to make the fabric undulate.

Following this thought, if the background rows travel up and down – for instance making groupings of short rows which will then raise the stitches in these areas so the rows are no longer horizontal – then the i-cord will follow their movement, up and down in a wavy line. In stocking stitch, these areas of short-row shaping will incline to bulge up from the surface, but using garter stitch as the background will create a less energetic grounding for the cord.

On a stocking-stitch ground, it's possible to make an i-cord beginning at each edge, each rising slightly, then meeting in the middle, where they can be grafted together invisibly. To do this, you begin one i-cord at the right-hand edge, leave it in the middle, knit normally to the end of the row, then begin another from the purl edge at the beginning of the next row, working in purl. Each can move gradually upwards towards each other until they meet: break the yarn and join them invisibly by grafting, rejoin a new yarn and continue knitting. This works as a one-off within the knitting but would be complicated to put into a repeating pattern.

The next samples show these ideas in practice.

Short-row i-cord wavy lines
The circle shown in sample 187 shows a curving i-cord, where the movement is caused by increases and decreases, and by crossing the i-cord over other stitches. In this example, the i-cord is made to move in a different way: it is pushed into a wavy line by the bulges created by short rows. Garter stitch is used as the background as it is rigid enough to keep the fabric flat. In this piece, the wavy i-cord lines undulate not in parallel but in alternating waves: to make them parallel, the short-row segments would need to be rearranged.

You could explore different scales of this idea, and experiment with different steepness of short-row knitting by leaving more or fewer stitches behind at each turn. In this piece, the rows move by 2 stitches each row from short to long rows, then back again. The numbers of stitches are staggered so the wrap-and-turn does not always come in the same place.

Cast on a multiple of 15 sts in col A.

Main short-row section
Row 1(RS): K15, w&t.
Row 2: K14, w&t.
Row 3: K11, w&t.

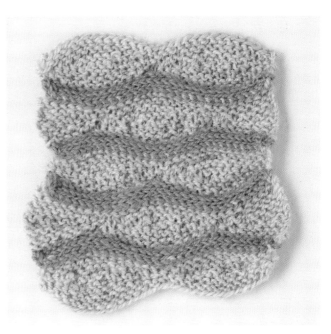

The i-cords are pushed up and down by areas of short-row knitting in garter stitch between them. i-cords are quite rigid and unwilling to be pushed around.

Row 4: K9, w&t.
Row 5: K7, w&t.
Row 6: K5, w&t.
Row 7: K3, w&t.
Row 8: K4, w&t.
Row 9: K5, w&t.
Row 10: K7, w&t.
Row 11: K9, w&t.
Row 12: K11, w&t.
Row 13: K13, w&t .
Row 14: K14, w&t.
Row 15: K15.
Rep from row 1, working on each group of 15 sts individually until you reach the end of the row.
Knit a complete row on the wrong side.

Make an i-cord:
Col B: cast on 3, K2, SSK, put 3 sts back on LH needle, *YO, K2, SSK, put 3 sts back on LH needle*, rep until the last SSK.
Put 3 sts back on LH needle, K1, K2tog.
Put 2 sts back on LH needle, K2tog, break off yarn *(check you have the correct no of sts at this point)*.
Slide sts back to begin again in col A on RS.
Now you need to make a side 'wedge' at each edge.

Row 1: K8, w&t.
Row 2: K8.
Row 3: K6, w&t.
Row 4: K6.
Row 5: K4, w&t.
Row 6: K4.
Row 7: K2, w&t.
Row 8: K2.
Row 9: K3, w&t.
Row 10: K3.
Row 11: K5, w&t.
Row 12: K5.
Row 13: K7, w&t.
Row 14: K7.
Row 15: K8, then work from main section until you reach the left edge.

Short-row section for left edge:

Row 1: K7.
Row 2: K7, w&t.
Row 3: K7.
Row 4: K5, w&t.
Row 5: K5.
Row 6: K3, w&t.
Row 7: K3.
Row 8: K1, w&t.
Row 9: K1.
Row 10: K2, w&t.
Row 11: K2.
Row 12: K4, w&t.
Row 13: K4.
Row 14: K6, w&t.
Row 15: K6.
Row 16(WS): K the whole row.

Make another i-cord, then repeat bands of main section i-cords, using the side sections every other band to produce wavy i-cord lines.

Smaller all-over curving patterns

Many lace stitch patterns create curves. The increases and decreases move groups of stitches away from the increases and towards the decreases in elegant, swirling patterns. They show beautifully in fine yarns, with the increases often made with a 'yarn over', creating holes which add to the lightness and delicacy of the fabric. However, these stitches can be used equally well in more solid fabrics, playing with texture and colour. If groups of stitches are treated as knit-surface and purl-surface areas, they immediately push and pull into a 3D texture, adding a new dimension. This is illustrated in 'bubble stitch', below.

If you look at how increases and decreases in lacy patterns outline an area of stitches, you could use different colours to highlight the different areas, as shown in 'scroll stitch' below, worked in a Fair Isle way in two colours.

Patterns of this kind are full of movement, made by the way increases and decreases manipulate groups of stitches.

Bubble stitch, also known as 'embossed' leaves
Here is a stitch with a smaller repeat, using increases and decreases to cause the stitches to curve constantly back and forth, creating a raised textured stitch.

This pattern is not new. Sometimes called 'falling leaves' or 'embossed leaves' in old knitting books, it's a great example of how increases and decreases can move the stitches into

Bubble stitch: increases and decreases in a repeating pattern to make leaf-shapes; they are similar to the reversing zigzags in Chapter 3, but with alternate surfaces pushed forward and back by knit- and purl-faced stocking stitch.

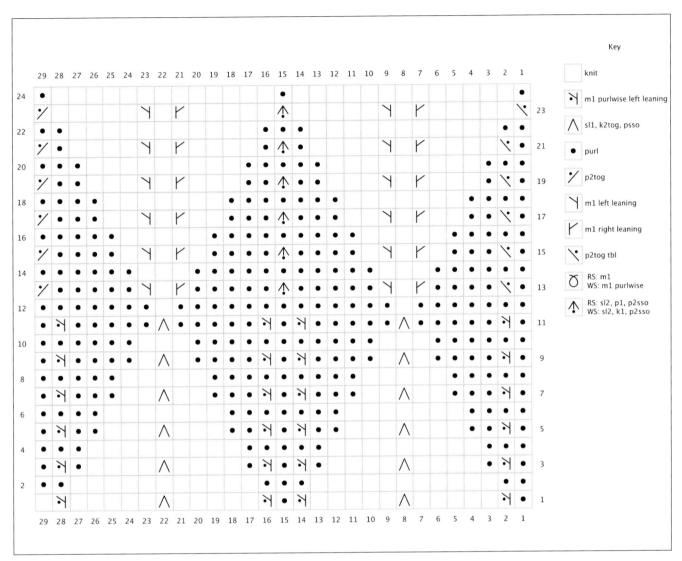

Key

	knit
⅄	m1 purlwise left leaning
∧	sl1, k2tog, psso
•	purl
∕	p2tog
⅂	m1 left leaning
Γ	m1 right leaning
⟍	p2tog tbl
ϑ	RS: m1 WS: m1 purlwise
⬙	RS: sl2, p1, p2sso WS: sl2, k1, p2sso

Chart for bubble stitch.

natural curves. It may be written in stocking stitch, with knit as the right side, or the leaf shapes can be put into higher relief by placing a couple of purl stitches between the leaves, raising them forwards.

The natural tendency of the pushing and pulling of knit-side against purl-side encourages exploring this further. The knit stitches want to push forward next to the purls at the edges of the leaf, but in the centre, they are inclined to push the other way, making the centre of the leaf concave on the knit side, bubbling up on the purl side, reversing knit and purl sides. So in this example, alternate leaves are in knit face and

purl face, inviting even more texture, and making a reversible fabric, mirroring on each side.

The leaf shape could be any size; in this sample it is 13 sts at the widest point, increasing out from one st, and its reverse neighbouring leaf fits snuggly in between, with no plain or spacing stitches between the leaves.

Cast on a multiple of 14 sts, + 1 edge st.
Row 1: P1, *M1 purlwise, K5, S1, K2tog, psso, K5, M1 purlwise, P1*, rep from * to * ending P1.
Row 2: K2, *P11, K3*, rep ending K2.

Row 3: P1, *M1 purlwise, P1, K4, S1, K2tog, psso, K4, P1, M1 purlwise, P1*, rep from * to *, ending P2.

Row 4: K3, *P9, K5*, rep ending K3.

Row 5: P1, *M1 purlwise, P2, K3, S1, K2tog, psso, K3, P2, M1 purlwise, P1*, rep.

Row 6: *K4, P7, K3*, rep ending K4.

Row 7: P1, *M1 purlwise, P3, K2, S1, K2tog, psso, K2, P3, M1 purlwise, P1*, rep.

Row 8: *K5, P5, K4*, rep ending K1.

Row 9: P1, *M1 purlwise, P4, K1, S1, K2tog, psso, K1, P4, M1 purlwise, P1*, rep from * to *.

Row 10: *K6, P3, K5*, rep, ending K1.

Row 11: P1, *M1 purlwise, P5, S1, K2tog, psso, P5, M1 purlwise, P1*, rep.

Row 12: *K7, P1, K6*, rep, ending K1.

Now the shapes change direction:

Row 13: P1, P2tog, P4, *M1 (in this section M1 knitwise), K1, M1, P5, S1, P2tog, psso, P5*, rep from * to *, ending M1, K1, M1, P5, P2tog.

Row 14: as row 10.

Row 15: P1, *P1, P2tog, P3*, K1, M1, K1, M1, K1, P4, S1, P2tog, psso, P4*, rep from * to * ending P2tog.

Row 16: as row 8.

Row 17: P1, P2tog, P2, *K2, M1, K1, M1, K2, P3, S1, P2tog, psso, P3*, rep from * to * ending P2tog.

Row 18: as row 6.

Row 19: P1, P2tog, P1, *K3, M1, K1, M1, K3, P2, S1, P2tog, psso, P2*, rep from * to * ending P2tog.

Row 20: as row 4.

Row 21: P1, P2tog, *K4, M1, K1, M1, K4, P1, S1, P2tog, psso, P1* rep from * to * ending P2tog.

Row 22: as row 2.

Row 23: P2tog, *K5, M1, K1, M1, K5, S1, P2tog, psso, K5*, rep from * to * ending P2tog.

Row 24: K1, *P13, K1*, rep from * to *.

These 24 rows form the pattern.

Scroll stitch (also known as travelling vine)

This is another stitch made by balancing increases and decreases so that whole groups of stitches move to right or left creating a natural energy of movement, almost dance-like in the patterns formed. Any traditional lace pattern containing increases and decreases that make the stitches move and

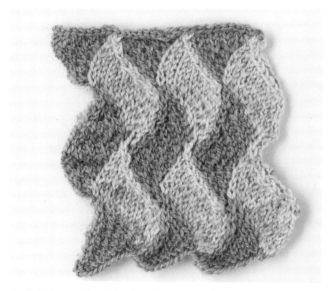

Scroll stitch, sometimes knitted as a lacy pattern; this creates curves with increases and decreases when knitted in two colours.

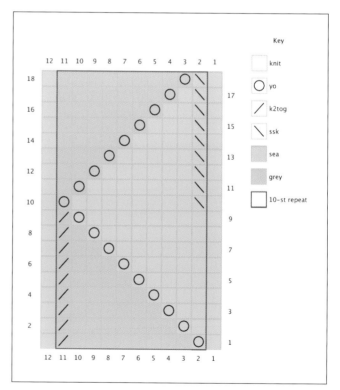

Chart for scroll stitch, looking more rigid than the flowing pattern created by knitting.

swirl could be interpreted in this way, using different colours to highlight the different directions of the moving areas of stitches. This piece uses two colours in a Fair Isle technique, both travelling across the row.

Cast on a multiple of 10 sts plus 2 edge sts.
Row 1: col A K1, *col A YO; col B K8, K2tog*, rep, ending col A K1.
Row 2: col A P1, *col B P2tog, P7; col A YO, P1*, rep to end, col A P1.
Row 3: col A K1, *col A K2, YO; col B K6, K2tog*, rep, ending col A K1.
Row 4: col A P1, *col B P2tog, P5; col A YO, P3*, rep to end, col A P1.
Row 5: col A K1, *col A K4, YO; col B K4, K2tog*, rep ending col A K1.
Row 6: col A P1, *col B P2tog, P3; col A YO, P5*, rep to end, col A P1.
Row 7: col A K1, *col A K6, YO; col B K2, K2tog*, rep ending col A K1.
Row 8: col A P1, *col B P2tog, P1; col A YO, P7*, rep to end, col A P1.
Row 9: col A K1, *col A K8, YO, col B K2tog*, rep, ending col A K1.
Now the shapes change directions:
Row 10: col A P1, *col B YO; col A P8, P2togb*, rep to end, col A P1.

Row 11: col A K1, *SSK, K7; col B YO, K1*, rep ending col A K1.
Row 12: col A P1, *col B P2, YO; col A P6, P2togb*, rep to end, col A P1.
Row 13: col A K1, *SSK, K5; col B YO, K3*, rep ending col A K1.
Row 14: col A P1, *col B P4, YO; col A P4, P2togb*, rep to end, col A P1.
Row 15: col A K1, *SSK, K3; col B YO, K5*, rep ending col A K1.
Row 16: col A P1, *col B P6, YO; col A P2, P2togb*, rep to end, col A P1.
Row 17: col A K1, *SSK, K1; col B YO, K7*, rep ending col A K1.
Row 18: col A P1, *col B P8, YO; col A P2togb*, rep to end, col A P1.

Summary

This chapter has looked at a few ways of creating curves either within or travelling over the fabric. More ways of creating curves and movement in a knitted design can be found in the chapter on modular knitting.

CHAPTER 7

BUILDING BLOCKS

Knitting in modules or building blocks is quite different from knitting across the width of the fabric, both in the method and in the design possibilities, breaking away from the horizontal structure of knitting and enabling a freedom to think in all directions, including three-dimensionally.

The blocks or modules are joined as you knit, and can start from any point, working sideways, downwards or upwards. There are two basic methods of knitting in building blocks of short-rows, but to be clear, both are different from the term 'short-row knitting' where shaping is made by knitting back and forth on a few stitches *within* the full width of the knitting, pushing the rows out of horizontal. In short-row knitting, it all happens within the complete width: in modular knitting, the actual rows are short and are used to create small (or large) building blocks which then create the total width of the finished piece.

Firstly, modular or 'domino' knitting is built from blocks (often square) which contain regular decreases which shape the block so that the rows either curve or turn a mitred corner, working until all the stitches are decreased and the block is finished, at which point you begin again by picking up the stitches from the previous block to make the next. These modules can be any size, large or small; they are made and joined in individually. They can be positioned either with the decrease travelling diagonally or vertically up the finished fabric.[1]

Secondly, the very different method of entrelac knitting is also made of repeated blocks of any size, but in this case, the stitches are not decreased but the same number retained on the knitting needle, with rows of blocks travelling diagonally, first one way then the other, again joined by picking up stitches from the previous block but at the same time, working it together with the neighbouring block so it is joined on two sides. Subsequent blocks join with the remaining two sides to make a complete knitted fabric on the bias. This stitch is easier to knit than to describe in words!

Both these forms of knitting with building blocks are covered in great detail in other books (*see* Further Resources). In this chapter, we are looking at how you can develop these techniques to change the shape of the building blocks and therefore influence the complete fabric, and so shape designs for garments and other items by using different stitches. We will explore beyond the usual way of knitting both entrelac and domino/modular knitting, looking at other aspects covered in this book for normal or straight knitting in relation to modular knitting: coloured patterning, cables, creating curves, working on the bias, and working in different directions.

Modular or domino knitting

In its simplest form, the modular block is cast on, decreased by two stitches on alternate rows in the centre, and worked in garter stitch. This method results in the same number of rows to stitches: begin with 40 stitches to make a 20-stitch-wide square, decrease 2 stitches on alternate rows, and all stitches have gone after 40 rows. Garter stitch acts as a brake to keep the fabric firm and flat, resulting in (as near as possible) a square, which then fits together in a satisfying regular flat fabric. In order for it to join at every side, the decreases all travel in the same direction (as usual, these are the basic 'rules' which, when understood, can of course be bent or broken).

As you decrease, the fabric draws in, turning a corner at the decrease point, so the cast-on edge ends up as two sides of the square, with every row forming an 'L'. If you change colour or work a stripe across the module, it will also turn the corner, so any stripe becomes an L-shape: great for designing!

If you change colour for the last few rows, a small square or dot is produced. This is also a useful design tool as it's much easier than putting a dot into a larger area of knitting. Here the structure does it for you; when there are few stitches left, a change of colour naturally forms this dot or spot.

This basic square structure can be developed into rectangles with two lines of decrease or L-shaped modules with three sets. In fact, any shape that will tessellate or fit together will work (*see* below for more on knitting different shapes).

The decreases link visually across the squares to make diagonal textured lines through the fabric, so are an enormously important part of the finished design: even in a plain yarn the textures will catch the light and show the decrease and change of direction of the garter stitch, which can be enough interest in itself in a design. However, this decrease line is a very strong element, and can be made more prominent by certain methods of decreasing, or made

Detail of modular knitted squares jacket with a stripe and dot pattern.

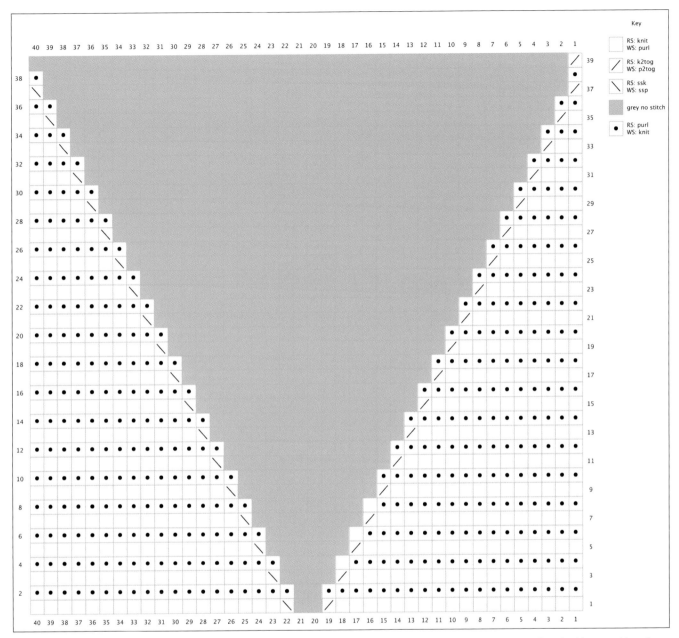

Chart showing a 40-stitch block with a double decrease in the centre. The decrease stays joined together all the way to the top, pulling the sides up and in to form a diamond or square shape.

more blurred with other methods. For example, if you work on an odd number of stitches, decreasing three stitches into one in a particular way gives a sharper point or corner to the square, and this can be highlighted to give a clear knit stitch travelling up the decrease by purling the centre stitch on the wrong side.

The follow sections provide instructions for knitting a square module, looking at different decreases.

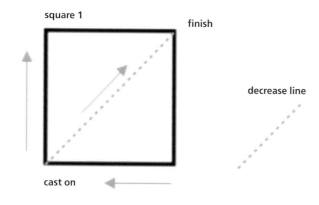

square 1

finish

decrease line

cast on

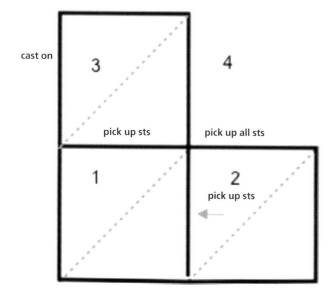

cast on

3

4

pick up sts

pick up all sts

1

2

pick up sts

cast on

The basic construction of the square modules, with decrease diagonally along the centre. To join them:
Square 2: cast on half the stitches, pick up the second half from square 1.
Square 3 is picked up from square 1 for half the stitches, and cast on for the second half.
For square 4, all stitches are picked up: half from square 2, half from square 3.

Decreasing on an even number of stitches

The first sample shows garter-stitch blocks of 40 sts.

a) bottom left

Cast on 40 sts.
Row 1: K18, K2tog (centre of row), SSK, K18.

Row 2: K.
Row 3: K17, K2tog (centre), SSK, K17.
Row 4: K.
Row 5: K16, K2tog (centre), SSK, K16.
Row 6: K.
Row 7: K15, K2tog (centre), SSK, K15.
Row 8: K.
Row 9: K14, K2tog (centre), SSK, K14.
Row 10: K.
Row 11: K13, K2tog (centre), SSK, K13.
Row 12: K.
Row 13: K12, K2tog (centre), SSK, K12.
Row 14: K.
Row 15: K11, K2tog (centre), SSK, K11.
Row 16: K.
Row 17: K10, K2tog (centre), SSK, K10.
Row 18: K.
Row 19: K9, K2tog (centre), SSK, K9.
Row 20: K.

Here we have four squares on an even number of stitches with different double decreases at the centre.
a) bottom left square with two decreases at the centre: K2tog, SSK.
b) bottom right square, with two decreases at the centre: SSK, K2 tog.
c) top left square, two decreases at the centre: K2tog, SSK, purling the 2 centre stitches on the reverse row.
d) top right square, with two decreases at the centre: SSK, K2 tog, purling the 2 centre sts on the reverse row.

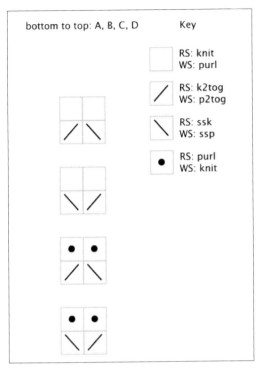

bottom to top: A, B, C, D

Key

RS: knit
WS: purl

RS: k2tog
WS: p2tog

RS: ssk
WS: ssp

RS: purl
WS: knit

A chart showing the four different decreases on even numbers of stitches from bottom to top: a, b, c, d.

Row 21: K8, K2tog (centre), SSK, K8.
Row 22: K.
Row 23: K7, K2tog (centre), SSK, K7.
Row 24: K.
Row 25: K6, K2tog (centre), SSK, K6.
Row 26: K.
Row 27: K5, K2tog (centre), SSK, K5.
Row 28: K.
Row 29: K4, K2tog (centre), SSK, K4.
Row 30: K.
Row 31: K3, K2tog (centre), SSK, K3.
Row 32: K.
Row 33: K2, K2tog (centre), SSK, K2.
Row 34: K.
Row 35: K1, K2tog (centre), SSK, K1.
Row 36: K.
Row 37: K2tog (centre), SSK.
Row 38: K.
Row 39: K2tog and fasten off.

b) bottom right

Cast on 40 sts.
Row 1: K18, SSK, (centre of row), K2tog, K18.
Row 2: K.
Continue decreasing in this way on the 2 sts either side of the centre and knitting on even rows (as for A, with the different decrease arrangement) until you have 2 sts left, K2tog and fasten off.

The difference between A and B is subtle: the decrease in A is slightly raised.

c) top left

Cast on 40 sts.
Row 1: K18, K2tog (centre of row), SSK, K18.
Row 2: K, but always P the centre 2 sts.
Continue decreasing in this way on the 2 sts either side of the centre and knitting on even rows with 2 purls at the decrease, until you have 2 sts left. K2tog and fasten off.

d) top right

Cast on 40 sts.
Row 1: K18, SSK, (centre of row), K2tog, K18.
Row 2: K, but always P the centre 2 sts.
Continue decreasing in this way on the 2 sts either side of the centre and knitting on even rows with 2 purls at the decrease, until you have 2 sts left. K2tog and fasten off.
Comparing C and D, both are strongly raised.

Decreases c) (2 decreases at centre) showing how this strong line encourages the fabric to fold.

If you purl the two centre stitches on reverse rows, this becomes extremely prominent in two ways: the centre stitches become stocking stitch which pushes further lengthways than garter stitch, so stretching the centre diagonal until it almost pulls the module out of true square. At the same time the action of the two knit stitches raises the decrease line up above the garter-stitch ground, (as knit raises above purl in ribbing), therefore creating a concave diagonal line on the reverse, making the module want to fold in half, as shown in this illustration. What a great design tool, either for creating strong diagonals within a design, or to use in a 3D shape to create folds and corners. Decrease C is obviously the cleanest, strongest diagonal line as the stitches lie right over left (K2tog), then left over right (SSK), following the line, whereas in D the stitches cross the opposite ways, interrupting the smooth diagonal.

Decreasing on an odd number of stitches

On these four variations, the decrease works on the centre three stitches, decreasing from three to one, creating a sharper angle and pointed corner. These blocks are all worked on 39 stitches. It's worth marking the centre stitch to keep the decrease in line. Also check by counting that there is always the same number of stitches on either side of the centre.

a) bottom left

Cast on 39 sts.
Row 1: K18, S1, K2tog, psso, K18.
Row 2: K.
Continue decreasing in this way on the 3 sts at the centre of the row, and knitting on even rows until you have 3 sts left, S1, K2tog, psso and fasten off.

b) bottom right

Cast on 39 sts.
Row 1: K18, S2 as if knitting them tog, K1, p2sso, K18.
Row 2: K.
Continue decreasing in this way on the 3 sts at the centre of the row, and knitting on even rows until you have 3 sts left, S2 as if knitting them tog, K1, p2sso and fasten off.

Four squares on an odd number of stitches with different decreases at the centre:
a) bottom left square with 3 stitches decreasing to one at centre: S1, K2 tog, psso.
b) bottom right: square with 3 stitches decreasing to one at centre: S2 as if knitting them together, K1, p2sso.
c) top left: square with 3 stitches decreasing to one at centre: S2 (knitwise), K1, p2sso.
d) top right: square with 3 stitches decreasing to one at centre: S2 as if knitting them tog, K1, p2sso, and on the reverse row, purl the centre decrease stitch.

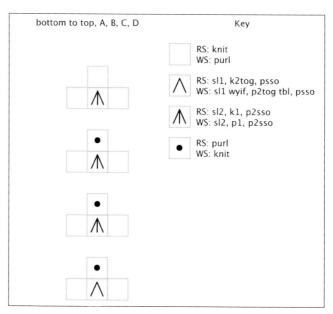

Chart showing the four different decreases used on an odd number of stitches from bottom to top: a, b, c, d. Note the written instructions for different ways of slipping stitches.

c) top left

Cast on 39 sts.
Row 1: K18, S1 (knitwise), S1 more, K1, p2sso, K18.
Row 2: K.
Continue decreasing in this way on the 2 sts either side of the centre and knitting on even rows with 2 purls at the decrease, until you have 3 sts left, S1 (knitwise), S1 more, K1, p2sso, and fasten off.

The difference between A, B and C is subtle, the decrease in A being slightly flatter than the other two.

d) top right

Cast on 39 sts.
Row 1: K18, S2 as if knitting them tog, K1, p2sso, K18.
Row 2: K, purling the centre decrease stitch.
Continue decreasing in this way on the 3 sts at the centre of the row, and knitting on even rows with purl in the centre until you have 3 sts left, S2 as if knitting them tog, K1, p2sso and fasten off.

This decrease is transformed by such a small difference, purling the centre stitch on the reverse, to give a clean knit stitch travelling across diagonally. Again, it raises up from the garter stitch, and would make a strong fold line if you wanted to make a 3D shape from these modules.

Now to question the rules: what happens if:
a) you don't always join with decreases in the same direction?
b) you don't work in garter stitch?

Different directions

Modular squares changing direction on alternate rows, leaving a pattern of natural gaps between.

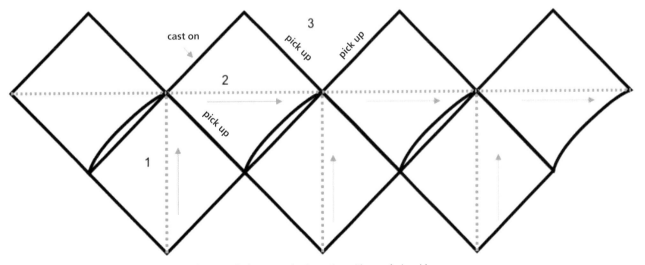

Diagram showing the way the modules are knitted, in rows facing upwards alternating with rows facing sideways.

A simple way of making the blocks change direction and leave gaps is done by picking up half the stitches from a different side of the block to the 'usual' one, then casting on the second half of the stitches to make it decrease at right angles. This will cause gaps to form.

Different stitches

We've seen that garter stitch draws up the length, resulting in a square. Stocking stitch produces a longer module, which doesn't lie flat and inert such as garter stitch but wants to do its usual trick: curl up at the cast-on edge and curl under at the sides. When these modules are joined, adjusting the longer side length against the shorter cast-on edge combined with the tendency to curl up results in an undulating wavy textured surface, making lots of possibilities for creating interesting surfaces.

Welting stitch, made from two or more rows of knit-face and purl-face stocking stitch, works like a horizontal ribbing and draws up the length so you have longer cast-on edges, and shorter side edges. To make this stitch, work the usual modular structure with decreases in the centre of the row, and for the main stitch either:

K2 rows, P2 rows, (a smaller ridged effect)

Or:

Work a 3-row welting (for a larger ridged pattern):

Row 1: K.

Row 2: P.

Row 3: K.

Rep these 3 rows.

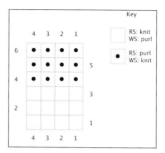

Chart for welting stitch.

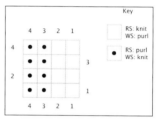

Chart for ribbing stitch.

Design with rib and welt modules fitting together; see another version of this design in Chapter 8, pattern 6. (Photo: Ann Richards)

What about ribbing? This will pull in widthways to give a narrow cast-on edge, but the side edges remain long like stocking stitch. Here, joining the short edge to the long edge of the neighbouring block creates huge tension, pushing and pulling so the modules almost buckle up in their efforts to settle into the fabric.

The yarn plays a very important part in this energy or movement. Any inert yarn with no stretch or bounce such as cotton, linen or alpaca, for example, will let the ribbing settle into a flat fabric, whereas a strong energetic wool will want to let the ribbing pull in and will retain its spring. Even without a bouncy yarn, the texture of the different directions of ribbing alone makes for a strong design with contrasting directions, although without the elasticity.

So another possibility occurs – to alternate blocks of different stitches. A 3-row welting pattern fits in a satisfying way between blocks of K2, P2 rib, short base edge to short side edge, and the same with the long edges. This makes a flat ribbed fabric with an attractive zigzag rhythm; the ribs have different textures: knit stitches showing in the vertical rib, purl in the welting stitch, creating differently angled 'joins': shallow zigzags for the shorter edges, steeper zigzags where the longer sides join. These can be emphasized with a change in colour or a stripe, as shown in the cardigan design with rib and welt modules fitting together, and in the pattern in Chapter 8.

Modular blocks, whether in garter stitch or other stiches, can be positioned to create either a straight edge with decreases forming diagonals, or placed to make a zigzag edge and vertical decreases. (If you want this alignment with vertical decreases but retaining a straight edge, the zigzag edge can be filled in with half modules or triangles.) Ribbing and welting have more movement than garter stitch, so if these are placed as if to make a 'straight' edge, it will in fact be slightly scalloped or wavy.

The very different shapes of a 'square' module in ribbing, left, which has a short cast-on edge and long side edges; and the welting module, right, with a long cast-on edge and shorter side edges.

To join the modules and make a straight edge, pick up half the stitches from a neighbouring block and cast on the second half (as shown in the diagram here) with the decrease travelling diagonally. For a zigzag edge, work two individual blocks, place them in position with the decreases vertical, and to make a third, pick up half the stitches from the edge of one block, half from the other.

These are the 'rules' for joining and arranging modular knitting to make a solid fabric. They could be arranged in different directions, but changing direction leaves a gap; it might involve sewing up some of these seams at the end, unless the gaps become part of the design. The mixed blues sample shown earlier shows modules in rows of upward-facing blocks alternating with sideways-pointing blocks. This construction creates gaps or slits which become part of the design, giving scope in a garment to play with different colours worn underneath and to highlight the gaps. The different directions also create energy and movement in the design, as the decrease line keeps changing rather than producing a continuous line.

Changing stitches within modules

We've looked at different stitches used to create a block or module, but what happens if you use a different stitch on each half of the module? It can pull in on one half and pull up on the other, making an asymmetric shape as illustrated below. Placed as squares with a straight edge, this 'crooked' module becomes another tool for shaping the overall fabric. The distorted shape can then be joined to create a bias fabric, leaning in one direction: and reversed to create the other direction.

There is a second effect here: as well as the means to a way of shaping each block and therefore the whole fabric, the textures of different stitches make a visual pattern across the fabric, especially if knitted in a smooth, untextured yarn: a cotton or a smooth, soft wool.

Here are some examples of different stitches for textured patterns.

Garter and moss stitch

Cast on 39 sts. The decrease makes a sharp delineation between the stitches.
Row 1: K18, S2 (as if to knit them together), K1, P2sso, (K1, P1), rep to end.

Row 2: (P1, K1), rep to centre, P centre st, K to end.

Row 3: K to centre 3 sts, S2 (as if to knit them together), K1, P2sso, (P1, K1) to end, finishing P1.

Row 4: (P1, K1), rep to centre, P1, P centre st, K to end.

Rep rows 3 and 4 until all the stitches have been decreased, break yarn and finish off.

There isn't much difference in the shaping power between these two stitches: garter stitch pulls up lengthways, and so does moss stitch. Moss stitch does also push out sideways, making it slightly wider than garter stitch.

Comparing garter and moss stitches in one module, divided by a clear decreasing line.

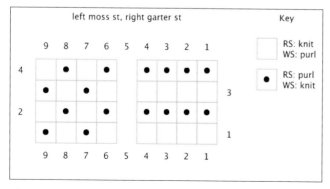

Chart showing moss stitch on the left, garter stitch on the right.

Asymmetric modules for shaping

Single rib, 2-row welting

Comparing 2-row welting and K1, P1 rib in one module, divided by a clear decreasing line: the shape begins to pull into a rectangle.

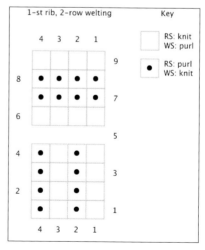

Chart showing K1, P1 rib at the bottom, 2-row welting stitch at the top.

Cast on 39 sts and mark the centre stitch.

Row 1: K to 1 st before centre, S2 (as if to knit them together), K1, P2sso, (K1, P1) to end.

Row 2: (K1, P1) to centre, P centre st, K to end.

Row 3: P to centre, S2 (as if to knit them together), K1, P2sso, (P1, K1) to end, ending P1.

Row 4: (K1, P1) to centre ending K1, P centre st, P to end. Rep these 4 rows until all stitches are decreased, fasten off.

This combination gives texture and shaping, with the ribbing pulling in the width and the welting pulling up the length.

Double rib, 3-row welting

This block is half in K2, P2 rib, half in 'welting' stitch, which has a repeat of 6 rows: K, P, K; K, P, K.
Cast on 40 sts.

Row 1: *K2, P2* for 16 sts, K2, K2tog. This is the halfway point, mark it with a tag of yarn or stitch marker; P2tog, P to end.

Row 2: K to centre, P1, work in K2, P2 rib to end (matching stitches in the rib).

Row 3: rib to 2 sts before centre, K2tog, K2tog, K to end.

Row 4: P to centre, P1, rib second half to end.

Row 5: rib to 2 sts before centre, K2tog, K2tog, K to end.

Row 6: K to centre, P1, rib to end.

Row 7: rib to 2 sts before centre, K2tog, P2tog, P to end.

Row 8: K to centre, P1, rib to end.

Row 9: as row 3.

Row 10: as row 4.

Row 11: as row 5.

Row 12: as row 6.

Row 13: as row 7.

Row 14: as row 8.

Row 15: as row 3.

Row 16: as row 4.

Row 17: as row 5.

Row 18: as row 6.

Row 19: as row 7.

Row 20: as row 8.

Row 21: as row 3.

Row 22: as row 4.

Row 23: as row 5.

Row 24: as row 6.

Modular knitting using different stitches to shape the fabric: with garter-stitch squares at the bottom, and tall, narrow modules at the top knitted half in K2, P2 rib and half in 3-row welting — a useful way of shaping modular knitting.

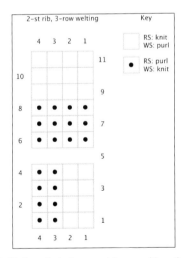

Chart shows K2, P2 rib at the bottom, and 3-row welting stitch at the top.

Row 25: as row 7.
Row 26: as row 8.
Row 27: as row 3.
Row 28: as row 4.
Row 29: as row 5.
Row 30: as row 6.
Row 31: as row 7.
Row 32: as row 8.
Row 33: K2, K2tog, K2tog, K2.
Row 34: P3, P3.
Row 35: K1, K2tog, K2tog, K1.
Row 36: P4.
Row 37: K2tog, K2tog.
Row 38: P2.
Row 39: K2tog, and fasten off.

These blocks need a definite, strong decrease pattern to keep the two stitches visually separate in the centre and avoid confusion, and the change in stitch would get lost on very small blocks: you need a size large enough to show the design clearly. When these modules are joined, those combining a rib with a welting stitch lean heavily in one direction. Reversing the stitches creates the opposite lean, so combinations could be tried for shaping in different ways. They would work very well in shaping a garment, for example, drawing in a fabric which begins with 'normal' garter-stitch squares then progresses to other stitches or these asymmetric blocks.

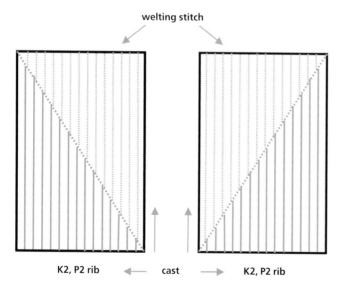

A 'square' module using half ribbing and half welting pulls into a rectangle.

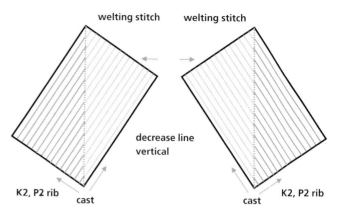

If these rectangles are tipped on end so the decrease runs up vertically, asymmetric shapes can be built.

Stocking stitch used both sides

A 'square' module in stocking stitch, half knit-face and half purl-face, creating tension and movement in the fabric, and a very strong pleat along the decrease line. This idea was used in the design shown at the opening for this chapter.

This will shape the module and create pleating. Because stocking stitch wants to curl at the edges, if it's used alternating knit- and purl-side within one building block, the push and pull creates movement and texture. In a simple knitted module with decrease at the centre, this is very noticeable along the decrease line, and when the blocks are joined together this line creates a strong pleating throughout the knitted fabric. However, at the sides of the blocks, where the top edge of the knit surface joins to the side edge of the purl, and vice versa, they cancel each other and make a flat join: all the movement is in the centre at the decrease.

Cast on 40 sts (this counts as row 1: when the blocks are joined, row 1 will be the picking-up row).
Row 2(WS): K20, P20.
Row 3: K19, P19.
Row 4: K to 2 sts before centre, SSK, P2tog, P to end.
Row 5: K to centre, P to end.
Rep these last 2 rows until 2 sts left, K2tog and fasten off.

Cables in modular knitting

There's a lot going on with knitting a square module. Both the change of direction in the knitting at the decrease point and the fact that the rows decrease rapidly so the surface space becomes smaller, do not invite an elaborate, complicated stitch pattern which might confuse the eye (not to mention the hand of the knitter), so unless you are working in large modules, it works better to keep the design of each block simple.

The decrease is a strong element in making a square, but there is clear space running up the side edges of the block, which would seem a logical place to add embellishment. It's also possible to run a cable up the centre, decreasing on either side to create a strong, decorative diagonal. Visually, these will all join together when used en masse, standing out from the garter-stitch background in a bold line. They would work well placed either diagonally or vertically, with the added structural element which might be useful: they have the added effect of stiffening the fabric as well.

How do you make these design decisions? Knitting samples takes time, and any short cuts are welcome to visualizing the finished piece. One way of working out designs for modular knitting would be to cut out paper or card squares, sketch out the design in a simple way, such as a strong diagonal or a cable up the sides of the square, then play with the cards in different arrangements to see which you like. Another way is to photograph one square and put it into repeat on a screen, then play with the arrangement. Any method to help make decisions before you begin the slow process of knitting is a help!

In this next example, to help the cable stand out clearly, there is a purl stitch either side. This is also where the decrease happens, and as it's easier to make the decreases match either side of the centre by working in knit, the decreases are made on the wrong-side rows.

A simple cable twist

A simple cable twist of 2 over 2 stitches travelling along the centre, with the decreases on either side.

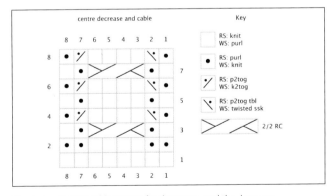

Chart showing the cable pattern for the centre, and the decreases.

This is knitted on an even number of stitches.

Cast on 40 sts. This counts as row one, as on subsequent modules this will be the row of picking up the stitches, so instructions run from row 2.

Row 2: K18, P4, K18.
Row 3: K17, P1, cable 2*, P1, K17.
Row 4: K16, K2tog, P4, SSK, K16.
Row 5: K16, P1, K4, P1, K16.
Row 6: K15, K2tog, P4, SSK, K15.
Row 7: K15, P1, cable 2*, P1, K15.
Row 8: K14, K2tog, P4, SSK, K14.
Row 9: K14, P1, K4, P1, K14.
Row 10: K13, K2tog, P4, SSK, K13.
Row 11: K13, P1, cable 2*, P1, K13.
Row 12: K12, K2tog, P4, SSK, K12.
Row 13: K12, P1, K4, P1, K12.
Row 14: K11, K2tog, P4, SSK, K11.
Row 15: K11, P1, cable 2*, P1, K11.
Row 16: K10, K2tog, P4, SSK, K10.
Row 17: K10, P1, K4, P1, K10.
Row 18: K9, K2tog, P4, SSK, K9.
Row 19: K9, P1, cable 2*, P1, K9.
Row 20: K8, K2tog, P4, SSK, K8.
Row 21: K8, P1, K4, P1, K8.
Row 22: K7, K2tog, P4, SSK, K7.
Row 23: K7, P1, cable 2*, P1, K7.
Row 24: K6, K2tog, P4, SSK, K6.
Row 25: K6, P1, K4, P1, K6.
Row 26: K5, K2tog, P4, SSK, K5.
Row 27: K5, P1, cable 2*, P1, K5.
Row 28: K4, K2tog, P4, SSK, K4.
Row 29: K4, P1, K4, P1, K4.
Row 30: K3, K2tog, P4, SSK, K3.
Row 31: K3, P1, cable 2*, P1, K3.
Row 32: K2, K2tog, P4, SSK, K2.
Row 33: K2, P1, K4, P1, K2.
Row 34: K1, K2tog, P4, SSK, K1.
Row 35: K1, P1, cable 2*, P1, K1.
Row 36: K2tog, P4, SSK.
Row 37: P1, K4, P1.
Row 38: P2tog, P2, P2tog.
Row 39: SSK, K2tog.
Row 40: P2.
Row 41: K2tog and fasten off.

*cable 2: *either* cable 2b, K2, K2C *or* K the 3rd and 4th sts without taking off the needle, then K 1st and 2nd sts and take all off. Both these methods cross the left pair of stitches over the right.

A 3-fold twist

A 3-fold cable along the centre of the module with the decreases on either side. This wider cable creates a flatter corner, which will cause the cable to stand up more when several modules in this pattern are joined.

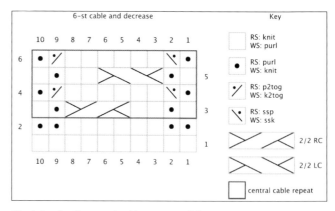

Chart showing the central cable pattern and decreases.

This is knitted on an even number of stitches, cabling on the centre 6 stitches.

Cast on 40 sts (again, this counts as row 1).
Row 2: K17, P6, K17.
Row 3: K16, P1, K2, C2f, K2, K2C, P1, K16.
Row 4: K15, K2tog, P6, SSK, K15.
Row 5: K15, P1, C2b, K2, K2C, K2, P1, K15.
Row 6: K14, K2tog, P6, SSK, K14.
Row 7: K14, P1, K2, C2f, K2, K2C, P1, K14.
Row 8: K13, K2tog, P6, SSK, K13.
Row 9: K13, P1, C2b, K2, K2C, K2, P1, K13.
Row 10: K12, K2tog, P6, SSK, K12.
Row 11: K12, P1, K2, C2f, K2, K2C, P1, K12.
Row 12: K11, K2tog, P6, SSK, K11.
Row 13: K11, P1, C2b, K2, K2C, K2, P1, K11.
Row 14: K10, K2tog, P6, SSK, K10.
Row 15: K10, P1, K2, C2f, K2, K2C, P1, K10.
Row 16: K9, K2tog, P6, SSK, K9.
Row 17: K9, P1, C2b, K2, K2C, K2, P1, K9.
Row 18: K8, K2tog, P6, SSK, K8.
Row 19: K8, P1, K2, C2f, K2, K2C, P1, K8.
Row 20: K7, K2tog, P6, SSK, K7.
Row 21: K7, P1, C2b, K2, K2C, K2, P1, K7.
Row 22: K6, K2tog, P6, SSK, K6.
Row 23: K6, P1, K2, C2f, K2, K2C, P1, K6.
Row 24: K5, K2tog, P6, SSK, K5
Row 25: K5, P1, C2b, K2, K2C, K2, P1, K5
Row 26: K4, K2tog, P6, SSK, K4
Row 27: K4, P1, K2, C2f, K2, K2C, P1, K4
Row 28: K3, K2tog, P6, SSK, K3.
Row 29: K3, P1, C2b, K2, K2C, K2, P1, K3.
Row 30: K2, K2tog, P6, SSK, K2.
Row 31: K2, P1, K2, C2f, K2, K2C, P1, K2.
Row 32: K1, K2tog, P6, SSK, K1.
Row 33: K1, P1, C2b, K2, K2C, K2, P1, K1.
Row 34: K2tog, P6, SSK.
Row 35: P1, K2, C2f, K2, K2C, P1.
Row 36: P2tog, P2, P2tog.
Row 37: K4.
Row 38: P2tog, P2tog.
Row 39: K2tog, fasten off.

Bias fabric in modular knitting

As we have seen, in each module the knitting changes direction. In the simple square module this happens at right angles, so the grain or drape of the knitting is a mixture of vertical (less stretchy) and horizontal (more stretchy) fabric. This combination, together with the picked-up stitches at the edges and the decrease give the overall fabric a strength so that it holds its shape well. This depends on the yarn used, but altogether, it is a strong structure.

If you use it with the decreases travelling vertically, all the stitches will be on the diagonal and you have a bias fabric with its characteristic drape, although this is somewhat curtailed by the picked-up edges in blocks of garter stitch as compared with larger area of plain knitting, so there is not such a noticeable difference in drape on the bias in this form of construction.

Modular knitting and slip stitches

Using a simple square to build the blocks in modular knitting, if you are working on a reasonably small scale (perhaps with blocks of 45 stitches or fewer), it's tricky to fit in any complicated stitches or pattern repeats. Truthfully, simple ideas work best in modular knitting, like small stripes or blocks of colour. The units don't have to be small; you can build in large blocks as well, then there is more room for intricacy and extra stitch patterns. With slip stitches and colour patterns, it's worth a look at what happens to the shape of the module, which can be distorted by the stitches. As discussed in Chapter 5, because not every stitch is knitted in slip-stitch patterning, the fabric pulls in slightly and the length is shortened as well, so although slip-stitch patterns can be used decoratively, they can also create shaping. This will be exaggerated if you are working on bigger modules and will show up less on small ones. Any slight pull-up in the length or restriction in the width will be more obvious over a larger area. You could play with alternating blocks of slip-stitch patterns and blocks of garter stitch, as shown here, then the following examples consider some simple ideas using slip stitch within the modules *combined with* straight garter stitch in half of each block. All of these could be scaled up for working larger building blocks. The simplest of dot patterns have been chosen rather than large motifs, as they read clearly within a rapidly decreasing space.

In all these examples, after the first square is knitted, the subsequent squares are joined by picking up stitches. Some have half the stitches cast on then the other half picked up, and some the other way round. When you have three modules joined in an L-shape, the fourth has all stitches picked up from the two neighbouring squares.

Dotty modules compared with stripes

Dotty slip stitch
(The chart shows the sl st repeat from row 3.)
Cast on 40 sts in colour A (this counts as row 1).

Garter-stitch squares alternating with a dot slip-stitch pattern: all are worked in 2-row stripes of each colour. The slip-stitch squares pull in and up to make them smaller than the plain garter stitch.

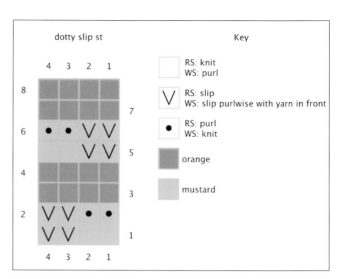

Chart showing slip-stitch pattern.

Row 2: col A: P, and mark the centre.
Row 3: col B: (K2, S2), rep to 2 sts before centre, ending K2, SSK, K2tog, (K2, S2), rep to the end, ending K2.
Row 4: col B: (K2, yf, S2, yb), rep to centre, ending K2: P the 2 centre sts, (K2, yf, S2, yb), rep ending K2.
Row 5: col A: K to 2 sts before centre, SSK, K2tog, K to end.
Row 6: col A: P.
Row 7: col B: (S2, K2) rep to 2 before centre, SSK, K2tog, (K2, S2) rep to end.
Row 8: (S2, yb, K2, yf) rep to centre 2 sts, P these 2, (yb, K2, yf, S2) rep to end.
Row 9: col A: as row 5.
Row 10: col A: as row 6.
Rep rows 3–10 until 2 sts remain, K2tog and finish off.

Striped square
Cast on 40 sts in colour A (this counts as row 1).
Row 2: col A: K, and mark the centre.
Row 3: col B: K to 2 sts before centre, SSK, K2tog, K to the end.
Row 4: col B: K.
Row 5: col A: K to 2 sts before centre, SSK, K2tog, K to end.
Row 6: col A: K.
Repeat rows 3–6 until 2 sts remain, K2tog and finish off.

2-pattern modules

A simple dot in slip stitch with stripes
This is used as shaping and patterning.
Slip all stitches purlwise.
Cast on 40 sts in colour A (this counts as row 1).
Row 2: col A: K, and mark the centre.
Row 3: col B: K18, SSK, K2tog, (S1, K1) (=18 sts) to the end.
Row 4: col B: (K1, yf, S1, yb) to centre, K to end.
Row 5: col A: K to 2 sts before centre, SSK, K2tog, K to end.
Row 6: col A: K.
Row 7: col B: K to 2 sts before centre, SSK, K2tog, (S1, K1) to the end.
Row 8: col B: (K1, yf, S1, yb) to centre, K to end.
Repeat rows 5–8 until you have 2 sts left, K2tog and fasten off.

The decrease in this example makes the stripes 'kick' at the corner. A different decrease could be used, perhaps 3 stitches decreasing to 1, for a sharper corner.

Here the slip-stitch half of the block is shorter and narrower than the striped areas, creating quite a firm fabric and making the surface buckle slightly. This would be more pronounced in larger modules, and could be almost ignored at this scale.

Each module is half garter stitch, half a small dot slip-stitch pattern, and both patterns are worked in 2-row stripes of each colour.

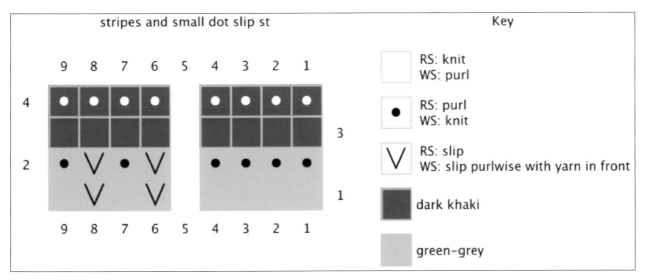

Chart showing the slip stitch on the left and the striped pattern on the right.

A larger dot stitch with stripes

Dots on left, stripes on right
Slip all sts purlwise.
Cast on 40 sts in colour A (this counts as row 1).

Row 2: col A: P to centre, mark the centre, K to end.
Row 3: col B: K to 2 sts before the centre, SSK, K2tog, (S2, K2) to the end, ending S2.
Row 4: col B: (S2, yb K2, yf) to centre, (ending K1), K to end.
Row 5: col A: K to 2 sts before centre, SSK, K2tog, K to end.

Each square is half garter stitch and half a larger dot-slip-stitch pattern, but the patterns swap sides to create a strong diagonal pattern through the fabric.

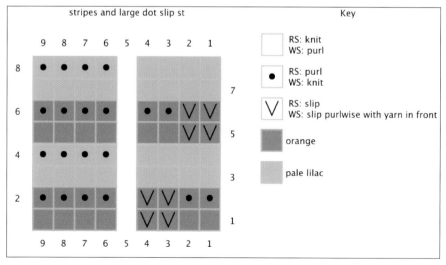

Chart showing the striped pattern, left, and slip-stitch dots, right.

Row 6: col A: P to centre, K to end.
Row 7: col B: K to 2 sts before centre, SSK, K2tog, (S2, K2) to the end.
Row 8: col B: (K2, yf, S2, yb) to centre, (ending K1), K to end.
Row 9: col A: K to 2 sts before centre, SSK, K2tog, K to end.
Row 10: col A: P to centre, K to end.
Rep rows 3–10 until 2 sts left, K2tog and fasten off.

If this is joined to a square with the patterns reversed, the dots join to neighbouring dots make diagonal bands across the fabric, and the stripes do the same, although with a change of angle in the striping. Reverse pattern:

Dots on right, stripes on left
Slip all sts purlwise.
Cast on 40 sts in colour A (this counts as row 1).
Row 2: col A: K to centre, mark the centre, P to end.
Row 3: col B: (K2, S2) 2 sts before the centre (ending K2), SSK, K2tog, K to end.
Row 4: col B: K to centre, K1, (K2, yf S2, yb) to end, ending K2.
Row 5: col A: K to 2 sts before centre, SSK, K2tog, K to end.
Row 6: col A: K to centre, P to end.
Row 7: col B: (S2, K2) to 2 sts before centre, SSK, K2tog, K to end.
Row 8: col B: K to centre, K1, (K2, yf, S2, yb) to end.
Row 9: col A: K to 2 sts before centre, SSK, K2tog, K to end.
Row 10: col A: K to centre, P to end.
Rep rows 3–10 until 2 sts left, K2tog and fasten off.
In these examples, the slip stitches draw up the length of the knitting, but then so does garter stitch so they pretty much match in length. In the larger dot pattern, the 2-row stripe of colour A between the slip-stitch rows is in stocking stitch to help it spread out to match the length of

the stripes. The width of the dot stitch is narrower. More contrasts could be used to create a fabric that undulates rather than lying flat.

Different scales

As we have seen, modular blocks of any shape need to fit together, but can be of different sizes. For example, larger blocks could be placed next to two, three, or more small blocks, using half the number of stitches to fit two against a larger block, or a third of the stitches to fit three, and so on. They don't have to be square: rectangular shapes work, on their own or mixed with squares or other shapes.

Three ways of knitting a rectangle

1.) a double square
Simply cast on double the number of stitches and follow the instructions for the square, repeating each row. So, with a 40-st square, cast on 80 sts.

Row 1: *K18, K2tog (centre of row), SSK, K18*, rep.
Row 2: K.
And continue, repeating each row to make two decrease points.

2.) short-row rectangles
This method is described by Sonya Hammond.[2]

Here, there is one decrease travelling diagonally but placed between a short edge and a longer edge, with the long

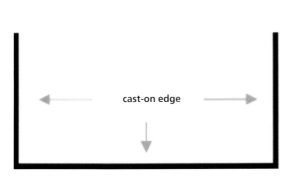

One way of knitting a rectangular module is to knit a double square.

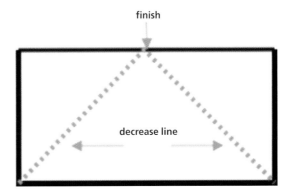

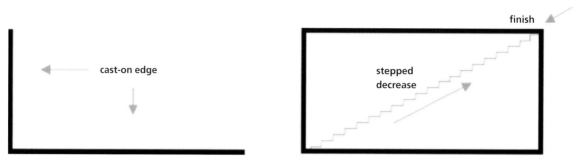

Another way of knitting a rectangular module, casting on a short and a long side, and shaping with short rows so both sides finish at the same time.

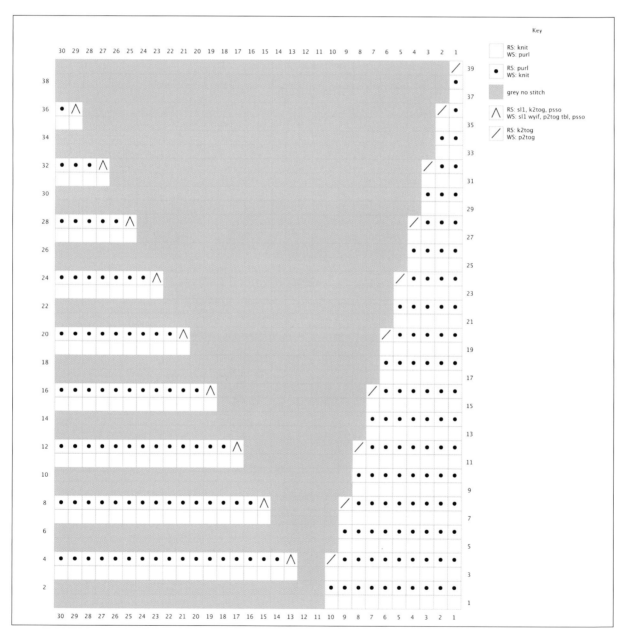

Chart for short-row rectangular module.

edge twice as long as the short edge. To make it fit with the 20-st square, cast on 30 sts (20 for the long side, 10 for the short side).

K20, insert marker, K10.

Row 1: K to marker, w&t.

Row 2: K.

Row 3: K whole row.

Row 4: K to 3 sts before marker, S1, K2tog, psso, (marker), K2tog, K to end.

Rep these 4 rows to the end, and fasten off.

The long side decreases 2 sts on alternate rows, the short side 1 st, but the short side has twice as many rows.

3.) a rectangle shaped by different stitches

See the 'single rib, 2-row welting' and 'double rib, 3-row welting' methods described earlier in the chapter.

Other shapes

Other shapes can be built to fit together, such as L- or T-shapes.

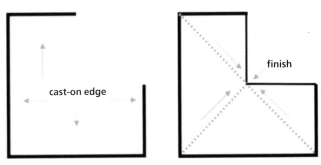

L-shaped module made by knitting with three decreases. Follow the directions for knitting a square, repeating each row three times.

Curves

Shell modules

Another very different shape that works well in modular knitting is the scallop or shell shape. These have a curved base and side edges, so will also fit together in various ways to make energetic patterns full of movement. This shape is a well-known pattern from early Islamic tiling. Its great advan-

Curves in modular knitting: these scallop shapes fit together in several ways, and can also fit in with a double-sized module.

tage is that it not only fits together with the modules all travelling in the same direction, but also fits equally well sideways, at right angles, creating fascinating geometric patterns with flowing curves. To create this shape in knitting, rather than having one point of decrease, there are several decreases along the row (still in pairs to keep the shape regular), made every fourth or even sixth row, decreasing to a point where all the stitches are gone. The decreases have the effect of pulling the cast-on edge up into a curve: think of 'old shale' and other traditional Shetland patterns where undulating waves are caused by increases and decreases. In curved modules, the sides are also curved inwards. Different stitches will alter the length of the module: stocking stitch works well, or a few garter-stitch rows or stripes can be inserted to prevent it from growing too long to fit together comfortably.

In the scalloped jacket design in Chapter 8, inspired by shapes in nature such as the layers in a wasps' nest or clusters of mushrooms, larger modules are used to make a curved hemline, with smaller ones fitting in to build the shape of the jacket.

Entrelac – another form of modular knitting

In a way, even though difficult to describe in words how it works, this stitch has a simpler structure than the modular knitting described above where each block is worked independently. Although it is built of blocks, each is a clear, flat piece of knitting: there is no decrease in the middle, so depending on the size you choose to work, there is room to play with decoration as well as using different stitches for shaping.

As described earlier, it is constructed on the diagonal, and therefore has the advantage of a good bias drape and fit, with the added firmness of the picked-up and joined-in edges to hold it in shape.

How did these interesting stitches evolve? Possibly they occurred independently in different areas, but evidently entrelac was used as a decorative stocking-top pattern in the earlier twentieth century, as described by Veronica Gainsford in 1978,[3] where she calls the stitch 'basket plait'. It's a fascinating structure which does look plaited, reminiscent of birch baskets from northern Scandinavia and Russia.

It is usually worked in stocking stitch, and this time the maths works out so that there are twice as many rows as stitches, because the edge stitch is joined by working it together with the stitches from the neighbouring group on alternate rows, creating two rows to each join or link. Each block is therefore a rectangle, although pushed into a square or diamond format by the fact that each long side is joined to a shorter edge. As it's usually knitted in stocking stitch, it has the typical stocking stitch tendency to curl under at the sides, and forwards at top and bottom which, when added to the fact that picking up the stitches for each

Entrelac stitch worked in blocks of 4 stitches, with triangles to fill in at the edges and form straight sides.

block along the side of the previous block gathers these sides into a shorter row, makes it puff or bubble up (one stitch is picked up for each two rows). This three-dimensional look is partly what gives the illusion that it's made of woven strips, often highlighted by working alternate rows of blocks in two different colours to suggest a weave effect; but this woven look is another characteristic that can be questioned, explored and developed.

Blocks can be of any size, although it's fiddly to work on a very small scale. For example, 4-stitch blocks look almost like cabling where the stitches really are woven over and under each other, but this is harder to knit: the awkward part in entrelac is turning the work every row to work back and forth, which becomes more laborious when the rows are short. There is a huge advantage here if you can 'knit back backwards' as Elizabeth Zimmerman describes in her book *Knitting without Tears*[4]. In other words, knitting in complete mirror image; a way of knitting often learnt by a left-handed knitter sitting opposite the right-handed teacher and imitating knitting in reverse. Zimmerman says, 'I argued – rightly, I think – that with two-needle knitting, working across in knit and back in looking-glass knit, one could achieve stocking stitch without the nuisance of purling': and one could add, for entrelac, without the nuisance of constantly turning.

The directions below are written for a 6-stitch repeat of three blocks: not very big blocks, but large enough to get to grips with how the stitch works. It also produces a gratifyingly wide piece of knitting, even on 18 stitches, as entrelac (because it's knitted on the diagonal) produces a much greater width than straight knitting.

Completing this exercise gives you all the tools you need to create a piece of knitting with straight edges, so as well as the blocks, you learn how to make base, side and top triangles to fill in the gaps created by diagonal blocks.

Basic entrelac, 6-st repeat

In these instructions, the main **building blocks** are printed in **bold**, all triangles (bottom edge, sides and top edge) are in plain print.

They are knitted in stocking stitch, with the blocks worked first in one direction (starting on the knit side), then the next blocks in the opposite direction, starting on the purl

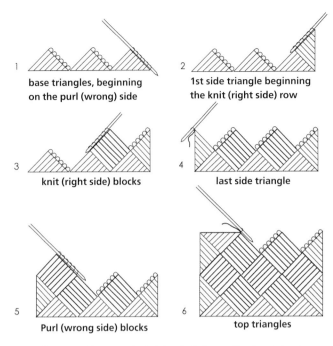

1. base triangles, beginning on the purl (wrong) side
2. 1st side triangle beginning the knit (right side) row
3. knit (right side) blocks
4. last side triangle
5. Purl (wrong side) blocks
6. top triangles

A step-by-step guide to entrelac knitting, including making base triangles, and side and top triangles to create straight edges.

side. This way of beginning makes a more flexible edge than casting on all stitches first.

Base triangles
1] These are worked on the purl side. Cast on 2 sts.
Row 1: *K2, turn.
Row 2: S1, increase into next st (by knitting into front and back of st *or purling into f&b: this does not make much difference*), turn.
Row 3: S1, K2, turn.
Row 4: S1, P1, increase into next st [=the last st], turn.
Row 5: S1, K3, turn.
Row 6: S1, P2, increase into last st, turn.
Row 7: S1, K4, turn.
Row 8: S1, P3, increase into last st, turn.
Row 9: S1, K5, turn. [**]
Row 10: S1, P4, increase into last st. *This completes a triangle of 6 sts* plus 1st st of next triangle. Turn.
K1 (leaving the complete triangle alone now), turn.
Increase into st (to make 2), turn.

Rep from * to make three base triangles.
On the 3rd, work to **, turn, S1, P5.

Turn the work round so the K side is facing.

1st row of blocks (including side triangles)
2] **first**: Side triangle (this begins the new row of blocks on the knit side).
Row 1: K2, turn.
Row 2: P2, turn.
Row 3: inc in 1st st (by knitting into front and back of st), S1, K1 (this is 1st st of next group), psso; turn.
Row 4: P3 turn.
Row 5: inc in 1st st, K1, S1, K1, psso, turn.
Row 6: P4, turn.
Row 7: inc in first st, K2, S1, K1 psso, turn.
Row 8: P5, turn.
Row 9: inc in 1st st, K3, S1, K1,psso.
Edge triangle is complete.

3] **Knit blocks:** *continue with K side facing to make the main blocks.*
*Pick up and K6 sts evenly along edge of next triangle, (on subsequent knit blocks, you'll be picking up from previous blocks, not triangles).
[turn and S1, P5, turn and S1, K4, S1, K1, psso] 6 times =
1 block complete; rep from * to edge of last triangle.

4] Last side triangle, still on the K side.
Pick up and K6 evenly along edge of last base triangle, turn.
Row 2: P2tog, P4, turn.
Row 3: S1, K4, turn.
Row 4: P2tog, P3, turn.
Row 5: S1, K3, turn.
Row 6: P2tog, P2, turn.
Row 7: S1, K2, turn.
Row 8: P2tog, P1, turn.
Row 9: S1, K1, turn.
Row 10: P2tog, 1 st remains on RH needle, and *edge triangle is complete.*
Turn the work.

5] **Purl blocks: this is the next row of blocks, with P side facing.**
Using st on RH needle as stitch 1, pick up and P 5 sts evenly along edge of triangle just finished [turn and S1, K5, turn and S1, P4, P2tog] 6 times, then cont as follows:

*pick up and P6 sts evenly along side of next block, turn and S1, K5, turn and S1, P4, P2tog 6 times, rep from * to end.
Turn the work
Another row of knit blocks is now worked as before, but picking up from edges of purl blocks. Alternate the knit and purl blocks, with side triangles on the knit rows.
[So, to continue, rep 2, 3, and 4, then 5, for as long as you want.]
Finishing with *knit blocks*, then to make a straight top, make 'top triangles'.
[NB: it's easier to finish the top triangles on the purl row as there are no side bits to worry about]:

6] Top triangles
Using st left on RH needle as the 1st st, *pick up and P5 sts evenly along edge of block or triangle just worked, turn.
Row 1: S1, K5, turn .
Row 2: P 2 tog, P3, P2 tog, turn.
Row 3: S1, K4 turn.
Row 4: P 2 tog, P2, P2 tog, turn.
Row 5: S1, K3, turn.
Row 6: P 2 tog, P1, P2 tog, turn.
Row 7: S1, K2.
Row 8: P2tog, P2tog, turn.
Row 9: S1, K1, turn.
Row 10: P2tog, P2tog, turn.
Row 11: S1, K1, turn.
Row 12: P2tog rep from * until you have filled the gaps in the top row, breaking off the thread at the end.

There are many ways of developing this intriguing stitch to make it look and behave quite differently from the usual basket-woven bubbly fabric. For example, even in stocking stitch, the blocks can be flattened by shortening the rectangle. If you join the last stitch to its neighbour in the very first pick-up-stitches row rather than picking up and knitting back, you eliminate 2 rows, shortening each block.

What happens if you use different stitches? Some work better than others: some textured stitches flatten the fabric completely, but also confuse the surface and lose the clarity of the construction. This needs exploring patiently, as too much texture can detract from the dynamic back-and-forth movement of the blocks, therefore losing something of the energy of the stitch.

Detail of entrelac stitch in K2, P2 ribbing creating a very different effect full of tension and movement.

Here, 8-stitch blocks of entrelac are worked in 2-row stripes, which highlight the zigzag movement of this stitch.

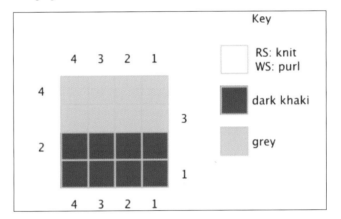

Chart showing 2-row stripes pattern.

If you use stitches that alter the shape of each block enough, then you can play with shaping the whole fabric or garment. Ribbing provides an extreme example. Knit 2, Purl 2 rib retains the length of the block, but instead of wanting to puff up, it pulls inwards, creating a long, narrow strip. The side edges are then pulled in the opposite direction by the picked-up stitches of the next block pulling it the other way, and the energy here then creates curves, fighting first one way then the other, and almost dancing back and forth. This stitch can make a wonderfully fitted garment, combining the stretchiness with the bias direction of the fabric.[5]

Stripes and colours

Any stripe of colour (or texture) will accentuate the diagonal movement of the blocks, whether a regular stripe or something as simple as a couple of rows of garter stitch.

Occasional stripes
Stripes could be used occasionally, as shown in this cushion, where the design plays with the alternating direction of the blocks by using stripes every 3 rows of blocks with plain colours between.

Entrelac cushion, playing with stripes and plain colours. (Photo: author)

Here 2 rows of a contrast colour (several shades are used to create more movement) at the beginning and end of each block form an outline or trellis pattern, especially if knitted in garter stitch.

Outlining each block

A contrast colour at the beginning or end of each block also has this effect, but then joins to create a zigzag travelling through the fabric. Taking this further, a coloured stripe at both ends results in an outline to each block, combining to form a trellis pattern all over.

Changing scale

It's also easy to break away from a repeated pattern with this stitch: it gives the chance to make each block individual with no need for regular colour changes. Regular patterns can be reassuring, calming, or even exciting, and in many ways easier to visualize than a spontaneous random approach, but entrelac opens doors to experimenting. If you prefer to plan a project rather than plunge straight in, an entrelac pattern could be sketched or painted on paper, or juggled with squares of paper or card, or even balls of yarn arranged in different ways to see how the colours work.

If the blocks are not too small, intarsia motifs and patterns are easy to insert, and on larger blocks, Fair Isle or slip-stitch patterns work well. Different stitches have the additional shaping tool of pulling the length up to make shorter blocks, not just to flatten the 'woven' look of the stitch, but to shape a garment.

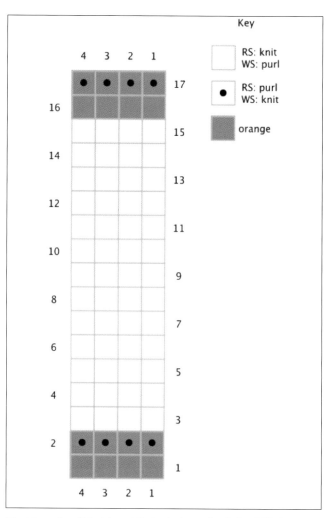

Key

□	RS: knit WS: purl
●	RS: purl WS: knit
▨	orange

Chart for garter-stitch stripes at the beginning and end of each block.

This stitch gives freedom to change colour and scale for each block, so colour patterns can either be planned, or created randomly. (Photo: author)

Intarsia motifs

Using the entrelac framework, in this piece, a motif has been knitted in intarsia with the simple vertical shape accentuating the zigzagging direction of the blocks. Subtly different shades have been used to enliven and soften the rigid structure.

Intarsia motifs knitted in the centre of each block, with a contrast stripe at the beginning and end to create a trellis effect. In this piece, the motifs are in silk, contrasting with natural black wool.

Space-dyed yarn

Using yarn dyed with a ready-made pattern (whether home-dyed or a commercial patterned sock yarn) will produce quite a different pattern according to the length of the rows, so entrelac gives an opportunity for experimenting with this effect. This is great to explore if you have access to dyeing your own yarns, but there are many retail suppliers of patterned yarn. Even a simple patch of colour that would create streaks across a wide piece of knitting will make a small stripe in entrelac. It can be a little unpredictable, but will make some kind of almost regular pattern in entrelac, changing according to the size of the block, keeping the eye moving over the geometric structure, which is then punctuated by the slightly irregular dye patterns.

Space-dyed yarn used for half of each block creates a strong zigzag design up the fabric.

Chart for intarsia motif in centre of each block.

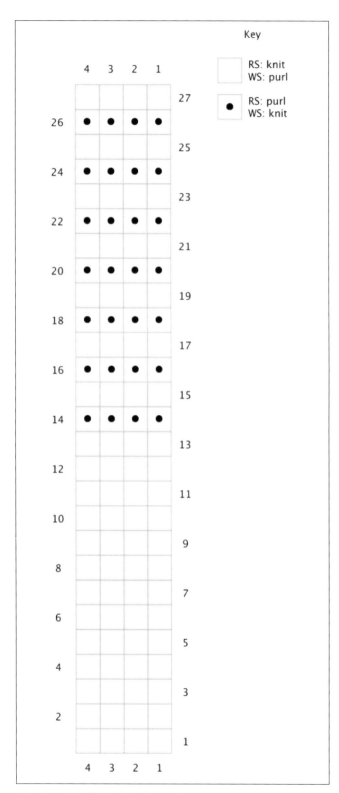

Key

☐	RS: knit WS: purl
●	RS: purl WS: knit

Chart showing half of each block in stocking stitch, half in garter stitch. The garter-stitch area will knit up shorter.

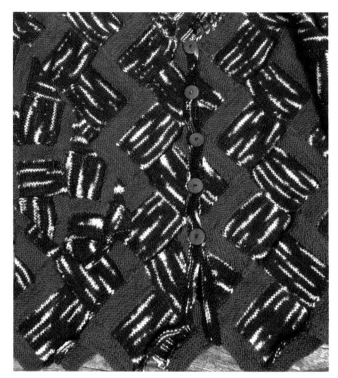

Detail of jacket knitted in space-dyed yarn in stocking stitch for part of each block, then a red garter-stitch band, creating a strong zigzag pattern. (Photo: author)

Short rows

These samples illustrate an insert in short-row knitting within each block, creating an 'eye' shape that can either sink back if worked in stocking stitch on a garter-stitch ground or if the stitches are used the other way round, the 'eye' rises up and the background falls back. Short rows could be used in all sorts of ways to distort the blocks further and create irregular textured surfaces.

Slip stitches

Any slip-stitch pattern can work well in entrelac, with the added effect of shortening each block, depending on how many stitches are slipped within the pattern. You could use all-over patterns as illustrated in Chapter 5, or design a motif to fill each block as shown here, similar to the diagonal pattern

in 'textured slip stitches' in Chapter 5, where the garter stitch stripe is also helping to draw up the length and keep the blocks flat.

Edging entrelac

The edge triangles described in the original small sample piece are useful for all sorts of projects. The side edge triangles create straight edges for a jacket front or for a cushion or bag, while the top triangle can be used in neck shaping or top edges for hats, cushions or bags. However, there's no obligation to have straight edges for everything: this stitch produces a natural decorative zigzag edge: simply miss out the bottom edge triangles and begin with plain blocks, and you have your zigzag.

On the jacket illustrated in Chapter 8 Pattern 2, side triangles give a straight front edge, but the bottom is left as a zigzag. These edge blocks are knitted in garter stitch so they lie flat and don't curl; stocking-stitch blocks follow to give maximum width, changing to ribbed blocks to draw in the shape at the waist. The single stripe at the beginning of each block makes the zigzag line that travels upwards.

Eye-shaped motifs knitted in short rows in space-dyed yarn within each block. In stocking stitch on a garter-stitch ground these sink back, but in garter stitch on a stocking-stitch ground they come forward.

Using cotton yarn, slip-stitch patterns help to hold the fabric firmly.

Chart for slip-stitch pattern making a diamond.

Detail of jacket (Pattern 2 in Chapter 8), showing how the stitches shape the design: garter stitch for the first blocks (to lie flat), then stocking stitch for fullness, moving into ribbing to draw in the shape.

Entrelac with random stripes, and a checkerboard of small blocks fitting within the large ones.

Different scales

Entrelac blocks can be of different sizes and still join together. This sample shows 8-stitch blocks with random garter-stitch stripes, some self-coloured and some contrasting, highlighting the alternating directions of the blocks. At the top, 4-stitch blocks have been worked by fitting four to each larger block. Small blocks can be fitted in anywhere, either singly or to create a panel within the larger blocks, although some of the joins will have to be sewn.

Leaving gaps

If you want gaps between the blocks, there are a few different ways to achieve this. A simple way is at the beginning of the block. Pick up one or two stitches only, cast on until you are a couple of stitches before the end, and pick up the last two stitches, then complete the block in the usual way.

Another way is to combine with other stitches, perhaps a row of entrelac alternated with modular knitting. Alternating rows of entrelac and diamond-modules automatically produces a gap, making a decorative design with regular openings.

Energized or overspun yarn

Energized yarn (described in Chapter 3) creates something extraordinary in entrelac stitch. The yarn causes the stocking-stitch fabric to lean in one direction, but as we have seen, the blocks of stocking stitch in entrelac already lean first one way then the other in alternating directions. This added energy of the overspun yarn pushes the blocks further, accumulating in a surge of energy where four corners meet and push upwards, creating a three-dimensional textured fabric. This happens at alternate meeting points of four blocks, with the energy moving away from the corners on one group and towards the next, shown very clearly in this 'energized entrelac' sample, which is knitted in 14 stitch blocks. The larger the blocks, the more pronounced this effect will be, as seen below in a sweater using blocks of 20 stitches.

Energized entrelac, pushed into peaks by overspun yarn, creating extraordinary swirling peaks of texture.

Sweater in energized yarn and entrelac stitch. (Photo: Ann Richards)

Here, the energized yarns are alternately S-spin and Z-spin, changing each row of blocks, neutralizing the bias lean so they can lie flat, although unusually long-shaped.

S and Z spin

This sample shows another idea, where blocks are knitted in S-spin energized yarn in one row of blocks, and Z-spin in the next, alternating the direction of the spin on alternate rows of blocks throughout. Here, the stitches are allowed to lean sideways within the block, and the opposite lean negates any extra movement, creating a flat fabric with elongated blocks.

CHAPTER 8

PROJECTS

'I cherish the hope that more and more people will be able to design their
knitted garments themselves. It is so rewarding not to be inhibited by a fixed pattern
but rather to acquire knowledge and to use one's potential creativity to enjoy
the process of knitting as much as the finished garments.'

Britt-Marie Christoffersson, Swedish Sweaters, Taunton Press 1990 (translated)

The designs in this chapter all relate to the ideas and techniques discussed in this book, using stitches to shape the garments and construction to achieve a particular drape or effect, and are knitted as much as possible without seams. Most of them keep to a basic, simple shape with any fitting created by the stitches, but some have pieces inserted (seamlessly) to give added flair and interest.

They can be varied, improvised, personalized, customized and improved using your own ideas and the sizing guide below. These pieces were all knitted in 4-ply wool, but can be adapted for other yarns if you do a tension swatch as described.

Working out sizing

Sizing can be daunting, especially if the design is very stretchy, such as the ribbed designs, which pull in and look much smaller than they are.

Here is a simple way to work out your sizing, whether you are knitting for yourself or for someone else.

To work out what size you want your garment to be, a good guide is to measure something you feel comfortable in. This will give the right amount of 'fit' rather than working from your body measurement and trying to estimate how much extra to allow, unless you are aiming for a figure-hugging fit. If you are knitting a one-off for someone else, use the same method.

1. Measure straight across a garment that is the correct fit, flat on a table ('**a**').
2. Now knit a sample or swatch in the stitch you want to use, and measure your tension in the chosen stitch over a few centimetres, preferably 10 or more ('**b**').
3. Count the number of stitches in this measurement ('**c**').

The measurement you want (a) is now divided by the size of your test piece (b) and multiplied by the number of stitches in this measurement. This gives you the number of stitches you need to cast on.

$$\frac{a}{b} \times c = \textbf{no. of stitches needed.}$$

If the chosen stitch is very stretchy, like ribbing, measure the tension with it slightly stretched if you want a fitted garment, or measure as it lies naturally without stretching for a looser fit.

For any stitch with a pattern repeat, go back to your stitch pattern and see if it will fit with the number of stitches needed, and adjust if it needs to be a little bigger or smaller.

If you can't make it fit easily, consider having some plain or different areas at the sides to accommodate the odd group of stitches that won't fit your pattern.

Depending on the chosen pattern, you may need to know how many rows long your sweater will be, and the same calculation can be done, dividing the length of the garment by the length of the sample, multiplying by the number of rows in the sample.

Sizing modular knitting

To work out sizing for all the modular knitted designs: this can be done using the same formula, but in a way it's easier, as once you achieve one square or diamond in the correct size, you know it will work (*see* below). It would also work if you wanted to use a different thickness of yarn and/or needle size: just aim for the correct module size for your garment and follow the chart to make the shape.

Size
- Follow the instructions above to decide the width of the garment you want.
- Look at the knitting pattern and see how many squares or modules it has across the width.

Measurement
If it is – for example – six modules wide, divide your measurement by six for the size of the module: if it's square, measure the width across; if it's sitting as a diamond, measure the width corner to corner, as it will lie. Be as accurate as possible, and don't worry if the size of each module is something fiddly like 11.75 or 8.33; a calculator will sort it out for you. If you are not accurate, it will show more when it is multiplied by 6 or 12, so it will change the overall size. There is a simple calculation below, to find how many stitches you need to cast on for each square*.

However, to change the size by a large amount, you could just as easily make more (or fewer) modules, so the scale of the design within each square is not changed but stays the same as in the illustrated design. Draw out a new diagram with more modules in the width or length as needed as your guide.

Tension
Try a square with the given number of stitches, but if the size comes out wrong, there are several ways of getting it right. The first two are 'guesstimates'.

1: Alter the needle size (this might need some experimenting).
2: Alter the number of stitches (again, some guesswork involved).
3: *The accurate way.*
  - First, be sure you are happy with the needle size: change to a smaller or larger size if your knitting seems too loose or too tight. This is worth trialling to get the feel you want.
  - Knit a square in the smallest size stated in the pattern, for example 39 stitches, and measure it from side to side, as it will sit in the garment (square or diamond). Measure it both ways and take the average measurement. Here, you are not measuring the number of stitches cast on, but the width of the square, which is actually half of the stitches.
  - Now go back to the size your square is supposed to be.

Formula for working out sizing
Using a calculator, work it out like this:
The measurement you want your square to be
Divided by the size your square has turned out x no of **cast-on** sts in your sample square.
(Note: although the width of the square across is half the number of cast-on stitches, this calculation still works to tell you the full number of stitches per module.)
So, for example, if you want a 7.5cm (3in) square and your sample turned out 8.5cm ($3\frac{3}{8}$in) having cast on 39 stitches, this is the calculation:

$$\frac{7.5}{8.5} \times 39 = 34.4$$, therefore cast on 34 or 35 stitches (depending whether you need an odd or even number of stitches) and it will produce a 7.5cm (3in) square.

If your knitting is tighter and your sample was only 7cm ($2\frac{3}{4}$in), the calculation would be:

$$\frac{7.5}{7} \times 39 = 41.7$$ sts, so you need to cast on 41 or 42 stitches to make it 7.5cm (3in).

This works for the scallop-shaped modules as well – just measure the width as it will sit in the garment.

Sizing entrelac

The same calculation will work, using the number of stitches in each block. Use the horizontal (diagonal) measurement across the block to give you the width, as it will sit diagonally in the garment; and note the number of stitches used in that block.

For example, a 12-stitch block may measure 4.5cm ($1\frac{3}{4}$in) across the row, but this is not relevant. You need the diagonal measurement, which may be 12 stitches = 7cm ($2\frac{3}{4}$in), then use the same calculation as before.

The patterns in this chapter can therefore be adapted to different sizes, but also to using different thicknesses of yarn, particular the modular designs. Whatever the yarn, if the module comes out the size you need, you can follow the diagram to make the shape.

The ribbed designs depend on using a fairly springy yarn that keeps its shape: smooth, heavy yarns would lie much flatter and drape more heavily, still giving a visual, textured pattern, but would not hold the shape of the garment in the same way as a strong wool.

Rib-welt shaped waistcoat

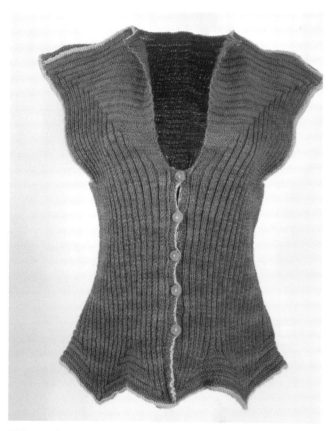

Waistcoat shaped by ribbing and welting.

Waistcoat, back view.

Yarn: MC 450g of 4-ply wool, 50g of CC
Knitting needles: 3¼mm [10]
Size: measuring without stretching across the ribbed body 66[72,78]cm, but over the hips where the design is wider, 92[100,108]cm.
These sizes would easily stretch to 10cm (4in) larger in the ribbing for a fitted shape. If you would like to customize your own size, follow the instructions in the introduction to this chapter, but for the ribs and welts to fit together it needs to be a number of stitches divisible by 24.

The pattern on this jacket is created by the change from ribbing to welting stitch: it has no other shaping. The welting gives the square shoulders and the wider hem, which has six 'points' around the bottom. It begins in welting stitch and changes gradually to K2, P2 ribbing, finished with a contrasting i-cord edging.

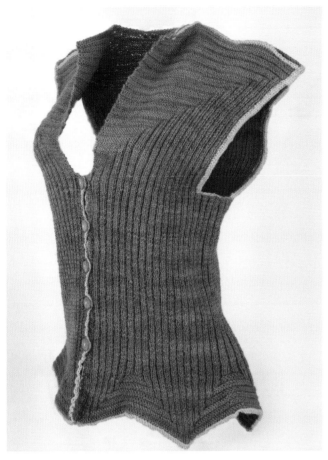

Waistcoat, side view.

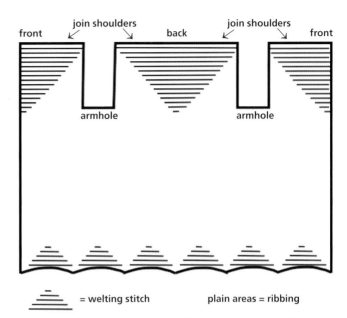

The shape of the whole waistcoat, knitted from the bottom in one piece, showing the welting stitch (plain areas are ribbed).

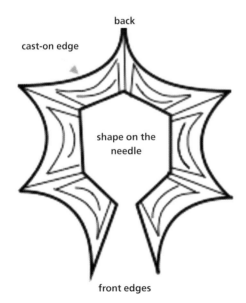

The peplum, beginning with welting stitch and gradually pulled in by the ribbing.

Chart shows smallest size

Using CC cast on 288[312,336] sts. Change to MC. This counts as row 1.

Row 2(WS): P.

Row 3: K.

Row 4: K.

Row 5: P.

Row 6: K.

Now while keeping the welting stitch going as from row 4 (knit, purl, knit: knit, purl, knit), start introducing the ribs like this:

Row 1: (this is right side, but with purl side towards you) *P1, K46[K50,54] sts, P1*, rep to end.

Row 2: *K1, P46[K50,54] K1*, rep to end.

Row 3: as row 1.

Row 4: *K1, P2, K42[46,50] P2, K1*, rep to end.

Row 5: *p1, K2, P42[46,50] K2, P1*, rep to end.

Row 6: as row 4.

Row 7: *P1, K2, P2, K38[42,46] P2, K2, P1*, rep to end.

Row 8: *K1, P2, K2, P38[42,46] P2, K2, K1*, rep to end.

Row 9: as row 7.

Row 10: *K1, P2, K2, P2, K34[38,42] P2, K2, P2, K1*, rep to end.

Row 11: *P1, K2, P2, K2, P34[38,42] K2, P2, K2, K1*, rep to end.

Row12: as row 10.

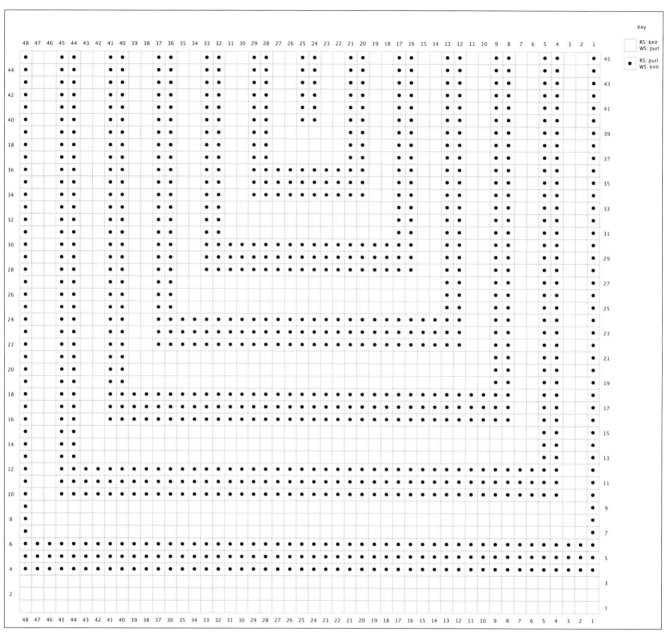

Chart showing one repeat of the peplum shaping in the smallest size.

Row 13: *P1, (K2, P2) x2, K30[34,38] (P2, K2) x 2, P1*, rep to end.

Row 14: *K1, (P2, K2) x2, P30[34,38] (K2, P2) x 2, K1*, rep to end.

Row 15: as row 13.

Row 16: *K1, (P2, K2) x 2, P2, K26[30,34] P2, (K2, P2) x 2, K1*, rep to end.

Row 17: *P1, (K2, P2) x 2, K2, P26[30,34] K2, (P2, K2) x 2, P1*, rep to end.

Row 18: as row 16.

Row 19: *P1, (K2, P2) x3, K22[26,30] (P2, K2) x 3, P1*, rep to end.

Row 20: *K1, (P2, K2) x3, P22[26,30] (K2, P2) x 3, K1*, rep to end.

Row 21: as row 19.

Row 22: *K1, (P2, K2) x 3, P2, K18[22,26] P2, (K2, P2) x 3, K1*, rep to end.

Row 23: *P1, (K2, P2) x 3, K2, P18[22,26] K2, (P2, K2) x 3, P1*, rep to end.

Row 24: as row 22.

Row 25: *P1, (K2, P2) x4, K14[18,22] (P2, K2) x 4, P1*, rep to end.

Row 26: *K1, (P2, K2) x4, P14[18,22] (K2, P2) x 4, K1*, rep to end.

Row 27: as row 25.

Row 28: *K1, (P2, K2) x 4, P2, K10[14,18] P2, (K2, P2) x 4, K1*, rep to end.

Row 29: *P1, (K2, P2) x 4, K2, P10[14,18] K2, (P2, K2) x 4, P1*, rep to end.

Row 30: as row 28.

Row 31: *P1, (K2, P2) x5, K6[10,14] (P2, K2) x 5, P1*, rep to end.

Row 32: *K1, (P2, K2) x5, P6[10,14] (K2, P2) x 5, K1*, rep to end.

Row 33: as row 31.

Row 34: *K1, (P2, K2) x 5, P2, K2 [6,10] P2, (K2, P2) x 5, K1*, rep to end.

Row 35: *P1, (K2, P2) x 5, K2, P2[6,10] K2, (P2, K2) x 5, P1*, rep to end.

Row 36: as row 34.

Row 37: *K1, (P2, K2) x 5, P2, K2 [2,6] P2, (K2, P2) x 5, K1*, rep to end.

Row 38: *P1, (K2, P2) x 5, K2, P2[2,6] K2, (P2, K2) x 5, P1*, rep to end.

Row 39: as row 37.

Row 40: *P1, (K2, P2) rep to last 3 sts, K2, P1.

Row 41: *K1, (P2, K2) rep to last 3 sts, P2, K1.

Row 42: as row 40.

Now carry on in K2, P2 rib until it measures 26cm (10¼in) in ribbing or adjust the length to suit.

Armholes and change of pattern

The right side has a clear line of 2 knit stitches coming up from the centre of each dip, so finish on a right-side row, and begin with the *wrong side facing*.

The welting stitch now begins in the middle of the back and at each front edge, and moves outwards to replace the ribbing.

Mark the centre back point following the rib up from the centre point of the dip at mid back, 156 stitches for each half.

At the same time, the armholes begin.
Put 72[78,84] sts at each end of the row on stitch holder for the fronts.

Back (144[156,168] sts)
row 1: cast off 11[15,19] sts, rib for 58[60,62] sts, K6, rib to end.

row 2: cast off 11[15,19] sts, rib for 58[60,62] sts, P6, rib to end.

row 3: rib for 58[60,62] sts, K6, rib to end.

row 4: rib for 56[58,60] sts, K10, rib 56[58,60].

row 5: rib for 56[58,60] sts, P10, rib 56[58,60].

row 6: as row 8.

row 7: rib for 54[56,58] sts, K14, rib 54[56,58].

row 8: rib for 54[56,58] sts, P14, rib 54[56,58].

row 9: as row 7.

row 10: rib for 52[54,56] sts, K18, rib 52[54,56].

row 11: rib for 52[54,56] sts, P18, rib 52[54,56].

row 12: as row 10.

Continue in this way until the welting stitch has replaced the ribbing, and work 12 more rows in welting st (or adjust length here), (K, P, K) x 4, put sts on a stitch holder.

Right front
Row 1: K3, rib 72[78,84].

Row 2: cast off 11[15,19] sts, rib to the last 3 sts, P3.

Row 3: K3, rib 58[60,62].

Row 4: rib 56[58,60], K5.

Row 5: P5, rib 56[58,60].

Row 6: as row 4.

Row 7: K7, rib 54[56,58].

Row 8: rib 54[56,58], P7.

Row 9: as row 7.

Row 10: rib 52[54,56] K9.

Row 11: P9, rib 52[54,56].

Row 12: as row 10.

Continue in this way until the welting stitch has replaced the ribbing, and work 12 more rows in welting st (K, P, K) x 4, put sts on a stitch holder.

Left front

Row 1: cast off 11[15,19] sts, rib to the last 3 sts, K3.

Row 2: P3, rib 60.

Row 3: rib 58[60,62], K3.

Row 4: K5, rib 56[58,60].

Row 5: rib 56[58,60], P5.

Row 6: as row 4.

Row 7: rib 54[56,58], K7.

Row 8: P7, rib 54[56,58].

Row 9: as row 7.

Row 10: K9, rib 52[54,56].

Row 11: rib 52[54,56], P9.

Row 12: as row 10.

Continue in this way until the welting stitch has replaced the ribbing, and work 12 more rows in welting st (K, P, K) x 4, put sts on a stitch holder.

Joining shoulders

Using CC, beginning at neck edge of right front, knit and cast off 16[20,24] sts. Continue knitting the rest of the front shoulder.

Without breaking the yarn, pick up the corresponding back, and knit 43 sts, then knit and cast off the next 40 sts, and knit the remaining 43 sts.

Without breaking the yarn, pick up the left front and knit 43 sts, then knit and cast off the remaining 16[20,24] sts.

Now put front and back shoulders parallel, wrong sides tog, and using CC, cast off each shoulder through back and front, joining as you go.

Armhole edge

Crochet an edge to the underarm ribbing of 20 sts in CC.

Now using CC, pick up and knit 70 sts from the base of the armhole to the shoulder, and 70 sts down the other side (adjust to your tension and chosen length to fit). Knit back one row.

i-cord

Make a 3-st i-cord to finish the armhole continuing in CC:

Pick up and K the 1st st, cast on 2 sts, then *K2, S1, K1, psso, and slip these 3 sts back onto LH needle*, rep from * to * until you have 3 sts left. K1, S1, K1, psso, pass 1st st over, and fasten off.

Sew in the loose ends.

Front bands

Using MC, pick up and knit about 94 sts along the front edge along the ribbing only, not along the front welting stitch. Check the number of stitches for your tension and length so it doesn't pull, adjusting to the length you have made.

Make a K2, P2 ribbed band for 4 rows and insert buttonholes if you wish (directions for buttonholes in pattern 3), casting off in CC.

Entrelac jacket, shaped by stitches

Entrelac jacket shaped by different stitches.

Yarn: MC 550[575]600g of 4-ply wool, CC 100g.
Needles: 3¼mm [10]
Size: actual measurement, 96[101,106]cm round the hips, with the ribbing drawing the shape in to make a closer fit at the top.
Tension: each block should measure 12[12.5,13.25]cm measure across the width (as it lies diagonally in the jacket, not on the needle).

If you would like to customize your own size, follow the instructions in the introduction to this chapter.

This jacket has 8 'squares' or 'blocks' all round, two for each front and four for the back.

The base blocks are worked in garter stitch, then there are 3 rounds of stocking stitch, then the remainder is worked in K2, P2 rib, with the first 2 rows of each block in CC in garter stitch.
More on entrelac knitting in Chapter 7.

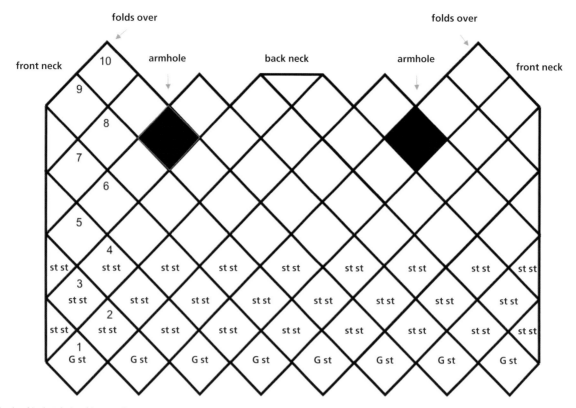

Layout for body of jacket, knitted in one piece.

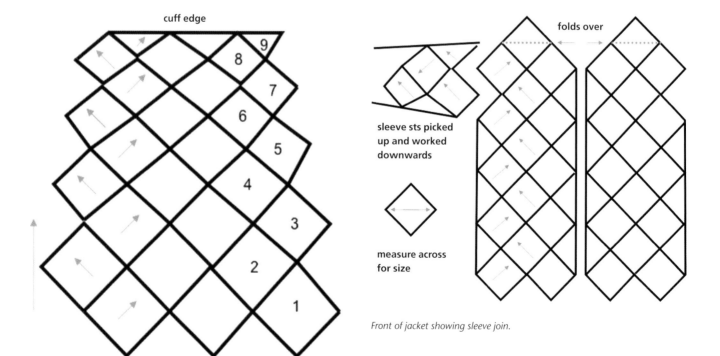

Front of jacket showing sleeve join.

sleeve, pick up sts from body and work in the round

Layout for sleeve, picked up from the body, and knitted down.

1st row of blocks [giving a zigzag edge]

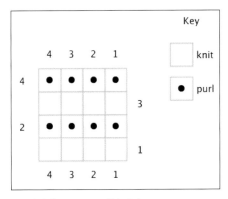

Chart for garter stitch (bottom row of blocks).

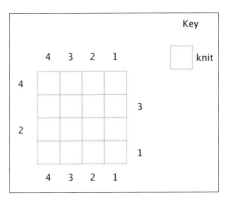

Chart for stocking stitch, the next 3 rows of blocks.

Stitch pattern

This begins at the right front of jacket.

Using CC, *cast on 20[21,22] sts. Knit 1 row, then change to MC. Work in garter st for 43[45,47] rows. Break off yarn. *(There are extra rows in these base blocks as garter st knits up shorter than stocking st.)*

Leaving this first block on the needle, and using CC, rep from * and work 2nd square exactly the same. Continue until you have 8 blocks, all held on the needle.

Depending whether you cast on to the right or the left-hand needle, you may need to put the needle in the other hand; just check that the right side of the blocks all face the same way.

Second and even-numbered rows of blocks

(All now worked in stocking st after the first 2 rows of garter st in CC.)

This row of blocks must start and finish with an 'edge triangle' to give the straight edges for the front.

Begin on the wrong side at left front edge.

1st edge triangle [centre front]

Using MC, with wrong side facing, P2, turn, K2, turn.

Row 3: K into f&b of first st, P2tog [joining with previous square], turn.

Row 4: S1, K2, turn.
Row 5: K into f&b of first st, K1, P2tog, turn.
Row 6: S1, K3, turn.

Cont in this way, increasing on the 1st st on odd-numbered rows, and joining with previous square with the P2tog on alt rows, working in stocking stitch throughout.

When this triangle is complete, continue 2nd row of blocks [there will be seven complete squares and an edge triangle at either end]:

Stocking st blocks (working from the wrong side)

Using CC, pick up and P 20[21,22] sts downside of next square, turn.

S1, **P** 19[20,21], turn. Change to MC and *work in st st: S1, P17[18,19], P2tog, turn.

S1, K19[20,21], turn*.

Rep from * to * until the last st of the next row is joined.

Carry on until you have seven whole blocks, then for the final front edge make another.

Last edge triangle

Pick up sts as usual in CC and purl back 1 row, then work in MC in stocking st:

now at the end of every right-side row K2tog. This decrease will make a triangle with a vertical edge.

3rd row of blocks (working on right side)

With RS facing: **using CC, pick up and **K** 20[21,22] sts downside of block. Turn, S1, knit 19[20,21], turn. Change to MC and work in st st.

S1, K17[18,19], K2tog [=last st + 1st st of next square], turn. P. rep these 2 rows * to * in st st, until all sts joined. Rep from ** to end.

4th row of blocks

Work as for 2nd row.

5th row of blocks

work as 3rd row **but now using K2, P2 rib, which continues for the rest of the jacket**, but keep the 2 rows garter st in CC at the beginning of each square.

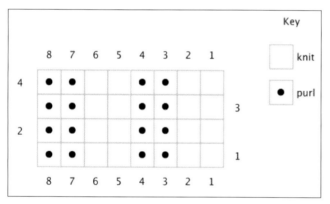

Chart for K2, P2 ribbing, used for the remainder of the jacket.

6th row of blocks

Work as for 4th row but in rib.

Divide for armholes

Back

7th row of blocks

Work across as row 5, then put the two blocks for each front onto stitch holders and work on the centre four for the back. With RS facing and using CC, cast on 20sts loosely.

Using MC, work in pattern as usual until four blocks are complete. Leave any stitches that will be picked up for the sleeve on a stitch holder, following the diagram.

8th and 9th rows of blocks

Follow the diagram, leaving the sides open for the sleeves (black on the diagram), casting on stitches where needed by the armhole. Begin each block as usual with CC, then using MC, work in pattern as usual until four blocks are complete. Leave any stitches that will be picked up for the sleeve on a stitch holder, following the diagram.

10th row of blocks

This has just triangle in the centre for the back of the neck.

Triangle for neck shaping

With WS facing and using CC, pick up and purl 20sts along side of the 'neck' block (*see* diagram).

Row 1 (RS): S1, pattern to last 2 sts, K2togb.

Row 2: change to MC, K1, pattern 18sts, P2tog.

Cont decreasing in this way at the end of even-side rows, and joining in the blocks as usual until 1 st remains, and fasten off.

Fronts

Slide sts for the fronts back onto needle and work rows of blocks as for rows 8 and 9 for the back, including front edge triangles where needed. The neck now slopes as shown on the diagram.

Row 10 blocks: there are just two blocks (ribbed) for the shoulders, which will fold over to join the shoulder: sew these into the gap at the back beside the neck triangle.

Sleeves

The sleeves are worked in rounds of three blocks, picked up from the body at the top and worked downwards in K2, P2 rib throughout, with the first 2 rows in CC as before.

1st round	2nd round	3rd round	4th round	5th round	6th round	7th round
20[21,22] sts	20[21,22] sts	20[21,22] sts	18[19,20] sts	18[19,20] sts	16[17,18] sts	14,15,16] sts

Slide 2 sets of sts from st holders at the armhole onto short circular needle and pick up 20[21,22] loops from cast-on sts from the remaining block to make the 3rd set of sts. Where necessary, pick up stitches from the armhole edge.

The blocks need to decrease in size after the first 2 rows of blocks, to shape the sleeve. This is done by decreasing evenly on the last row of every block to the number of sts needed for the next round, and picking up a smaller number of sts along the side of the blocks.

1st and alternate rows of blocks are begun with RS facing, using CC for the first 2 rows, then MC.

2nd and alternate rows are begun with WS facing.

The sizes of the blocks are different for each size, so are given separately.

Follow your size across for the number of stitches per block in each round.

If you need to add more for length, make the eighth round the same as the seventh. The sleeve could finish with a zigzag edge, or for a straight edge at the cuff, finish with three triangles. These can be made as for the triangle at back of neck.

Neck rib

Using CC, with RS facing, pick up and knit 24[26,28] sts along the neck edge, 40[40,44] along the back top triangle, and 24[26,28] along the second front neck edge (adjust to fit your tension but check the number is divisible by 4). Knit 1 row.

Pick up MC and work in reversible stretchy rib* in two colours:

Row 1(RS): *with both colours back, K1 MC, K1 MC weaving in CC. Bring both colours fwd, P1 CC, P1 CC weaving in MC. Repeat from *.

Row 2: *with both colours back, K1 CC, K1 CC weaving in MC. Bring both colours fwd, P1 MC, P1 MC weaving in CC. Repeat from *.

Rep rows 1 and 2, then on row 5, increase 1 st in MC by knitting into the front and back of the first of every pair of knit sts. From now on, the rib has 3 sts in MC and 2 in CC, making the neck band flare out slightly into a stand-up (or fold-down) collar.

When you have worked 14 rows (adjust length here), cast off in MC.

This jacket has no cuffs, but they could be knitted to match the collar.

Front bands

Using MC, pick up and knit 32[34[36] sts along the edge of each front triangle. There needs to be plenty of stitches so the bands don't pull in, so adjust for your tension.

Work in reversible stretchy rib** in two colours:

Row 1(RS): *with both colours back, K1 MC, K1 MC weaving in CC. Bring both colours fwd, P1 CC, P1 CC weaving in MC. Repeat from *.

Row 2: *with both colours back, K1 CC, K1 CC weaving in MC. Bring both colours fwd, P1 MC, P1 MC weaving in CC. Repeat from *.

To make buttonholes in row 4, follow the directions in pattern 3, adjusting the size to suit your buttons.

** reversible stretchy rib is described in Chapter 5. It gives a strong, stretchy edge with the reverse colour showing inside the collar.

Modular swing-back jacket

Modular jacket with longer swing-back on the bias.

Jacket, front view.

Jacket, side view.

Jacket, back view.

Yarn: MC 760[800,850]g of 4-ply wool, with 100g of col B, 50g of col C

Needles: 3 1/3mm

Size: Actual size 116[122,128] cm measured under arms (the narrowest part)

Tension: the squares measure 7.5[8,8.5]cm

Colours: MC col A, stripe col B, dot col C

To customize your own size, follow the instructions in the introduction to this chapter.

This is a loose jacket with slim sleeves: the upper part of the sleeve measures 30[32,34]cm. The modules sit as squares at the front, but hang diagonally as diamonds on the back, giving it a loose, longer swinging back.

It could be knitted in one piece with double-modules at the sides following the diagram, or as this is a large piece, you could knit separate fronts and a single piece for the back, sewing the side seam. The sleeves can be attached by working from the body and knitting downwards, or knitted separately and sewn on at the end.

See diagram for the layout of the squares, and where to place the colours for stripes and corners.

Basic square [garter st with stripe]

Cast on 39[41,43] sts in MC. The cast-on (and later pick-up) rows counts as row 1.

*Row 2: K.

Row 3 (RS): knit 18[19,20], S1, K2tog, psso, K 18[19,20]. Mark the centre with a tag of wool or stitch marker that can travel up the rows to remind you where to decrease and to keep the decreases in line: this sort of decrease makes a neat diagonal which is part of the design.

Row 4: K.

Row 5: K 17[18,19], S1, K2tog, psso, K 17[18,19].

Row 6: K.

Row 7: change to col B, K16[17,18], S1, K2tog, psso, K16[17,18].

Row 8: P col B.

Row 9: MC K 15[16,17], S1, K2tog, psso, K15[16,17].

Cont in this way, in garter st; every row knit, decreasing on RS rows, changing to col C when 9 sts are left:

K3, S1, K2tog, psso, K3.

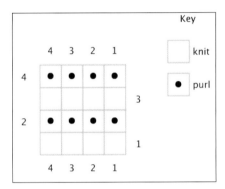

Garter-stitch chart.

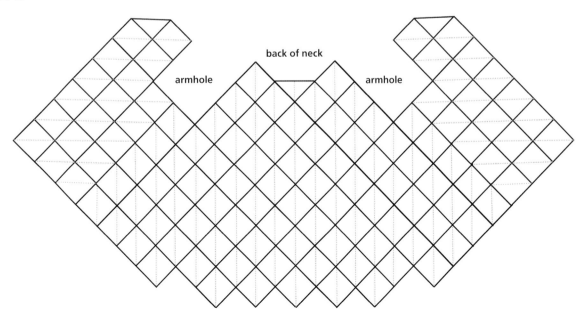

Layout for the body, fronts and back in one piece.

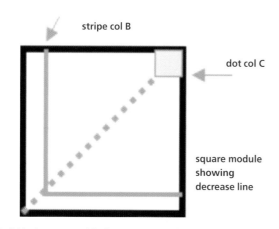

stripe col B

dot col C

square module
showing
decrease line

Individual square module showing stripe and corner dot.

Continuing col C, knit back.
Continue decreasing as before, until 3 sts left: S1, K2tog, psso.
Pull thread through*.
*Weave the end in when picking up the sts for the next square, or
sew in afterwards.*

Back

Begin at the bottom by knitting ten separate diamonds. Then
these are joined in the next row of diamonds by picking up
stitches from the base diamonds.
Follow the diagram, some will have stitches cast on as well as
picked up, as in square 2 and square 3.
To knit a seamless version, see note at the end.

Square 2
Using MC, cast on 20[21,22], then with RS facing, pick up
19[20,21] along the side of square 1 (*see* diagram). Follow
instructions * to *.

Square 3
Using MC, pick up 19[20,21] along side of square 1
(*see* diagram), then cast on 20[21,22]. Follow * to *.
Now follow the diagram, and where the squares are between
others, pick up all the sts from the previous edges. Otherwise,
cast on edges where needed.
There are eleven diamonds across at the widest point.

Back neck shaping

Make a half 'top' diamond to fit at centre back for the neck
shaping by picking up the sts as usual, then on every RS row,
K2tog at the beginning of the row, do the usual decrease in
the centre, and SSK at the end of the row, until all the sts
are gone.

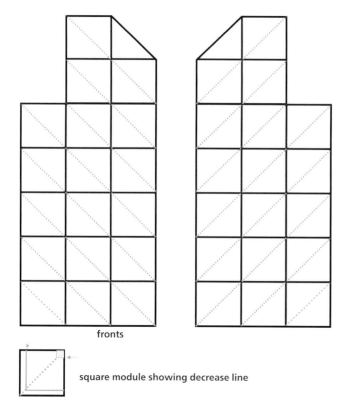

fronts

square module showing decrease line

*Diagram of the fronts, which could be knitted separately or joined to the back
at the sides with double squares.*

Fronts

Make a separate piece for each front (or *see* note below for seamless version), seven squares total length of fronts. The diagonals go in opposite directions on each front (*see* diagram).

Front neck shaping

Work a triangle or half-square for front of neck by picking up 20(21,22) sts from side of one previous square, working in the usual pattern, and decreasing 1 st at neck edge corner on alt rows in place of the usual central decrease.

Sleeves

These are worked from the top down in squares. These start off the same size as the squares on the body, but then get smaller towards the cuff in order to shape the sleeve.

Join the shoulders of the jacket (*see* diagram). The sleeves can be picked up and knitted from the shoulder, or knitted separately and sewn in at the end.

Begin at top of sleeve with four squares, leaving the underarm open and sew the seam at the end. The decreases go the opposite way on each sleeve.

Work 2 rows of squares at the normal size, then each row after that, pick up 2 fewer sts per square (space them out evenly, so they still fit edge to edge with the square you are picking up from).

Work from the diagram, adjusting the length to fit.

Cuff

Pick up 60 sts in MC, 15 sts from each square, and work a cuff in K2, P2 rib for 3cm (1¼in), cast off loosely in rib.

Neck and bands

Neck
Using col B, pick up and K 26[27,28] sts along slope of front neck, 22[23,24] sts from each square at back of neck, and 26[27,28] more sts along last front neck. K 1 row, change to MC.
Work in K2, P2 rib for 8 rows, and cast off.

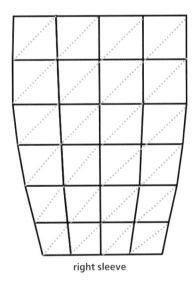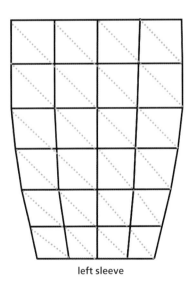

right sleeve   left sleeve

Diagram of sleeves, with decreases travelling in the opposite direction on each: they could be picked up from the body and knitted downwards.

Front bands

Using col B, pick up and K 22[23,24] sts from each square, all along each front edge. NB: the ribbing will pull in slightly, so 22[23,24] sts are needed rather than the usual 20[21,22]. K 1 row, change to MC and work in K2, P2 rib for 8 rows.

Buttonholes

(a strong buttonhole inspired by Elizabeth Zimmerman)
To make buttonholes in row 4, work 3 rows of ribbing and make them on the 4th row.

- *Work to the chosen position for buttonhole. These are 3 sts wide, so adjust for the size of your buttons.*
- *Bring yarn to the front of work, and drop it.*
- **slip another st from LH needle to RH needle, pass 1st sl st over 2nd to cast off 1st st. Rep from * until 3 sts are cast off.*
- *Slip last cast-off st back onto LH needle.* **Turn work.**

Pick up the hanging yarn and pass it between needles to the back. Using cable cast-on (i.e. placing needle between the sts to make new st), cast on 4 stitches, but don't place last st on LH needle yet. Bring yarn back through to the front between last 2 sts, put last st on needle.

- Turn work.

Slip end st from LH needle to RH needle, then cast off extra cast-on st over it. Work to next buttonhole position and repeat.

The seamless version

To knit the body in one piece you need double squares at the side 'seams': begin at the bottom of the back and build the diamonds upwards and outwards stopping one diamond before the side 'seam'. Make the fronts separately, again stopping one square before the side 'seam', then pick up for the *double square* under the armhole from both the back and the front, joining them together. *See* Chapter 7 for knitting a double square or rectangle.

The first one will be picked up at the sides and cast on at the base, but then the subsequent oblongs can be picked up all round (*see* diagram).

Ribbed jacket with inserts and 'slashed' sleeves

Fitted jacket with slashed sleeves.

Yarn: MC 400 [450,500]g of 4-ply wool with 100g of CC

Needles: size 3¼mm [10]

Tension: over stocking stitch: 27sts = 10cm (difficult to measure over ribbing: stretch very slightly)

Size: this is a close-fitting jacket with ribbed body and sleeves with gaps made by 'giant buttonholes'. Stretched out slightly, it measures 95[100,105]cm

If you would like to customize your own size, follow the instructions in the introduction to this chapter.

Construction: Knitted in one piece with no side seams, the main part is in ribbing, beginning in strips, leaving gaps for 'inserts' to be knitted at the end.

MC = main colour

CC = contrast colour

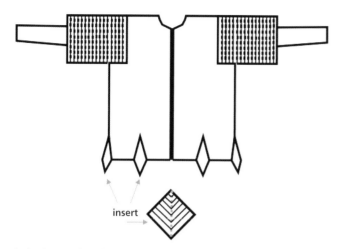

Jacket front, with modular inserts.

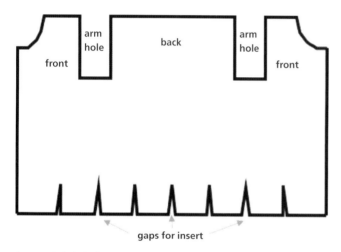

Layout of whole body with gaps for inserts.

Body

Ribbed panels for bottom of jacket

Using CC, cast on 36[36*,40] sts (the stitches need to be divisible by 4 so the ribbing fits together).

Break off yarn and change to MC. Knit the 1st row (right side) to give a clear colour-change, then work in K2, P2 rib, starting each piece 'K2, P2', so that the ribbing will fit when all are joined together. Work for 14cm (5½in). Break off yarn and put sts on a holder.

Make eight of these individual pieces (two for each front and four for the back).

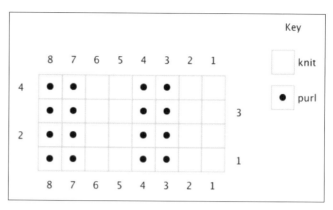

Chart for ribbing.

For the middle size, make strips in alternate sizes: 36 and 40 sts, to make the ribbing fit when joined together.
Now work in ribbing across all the eight pieces: 288[304,320] sts, working without shaping until it measures 30[34,38]cm from the bottom, or adjust the length here.

Armholes

Start shaping the armholes. Put 72 [76,80] sts for each front on stitch holders and work on 144[152,160] sts for the back.

Back

Working in ribbing, cast off 12 sts at beg of next 2 rows: 120[128,136] sts. Work straight in ribbing until it measures 25cm (9¾in) from armhole, put sts on a holder.

Fronts

Cast off 12 sts at armhole edge, 60[64,68] sts. Work straight in ribbing for 15cm (6in), then shape neck.

Neck

Cast off 12 sts at neck edge, then continue in ribbing, decreasing 1 st at the neck edge on alternate rows until you have 36[40,44]sts, then work straight until it measures the same as the back.

To shape the shoulder, work in ribbing, leaving 4 sts behind at shoulder edge on alternate rows, turning and ribbing back, until the last 4 sts have been worked. The shoulders can now be joined. Either leave the stitches on the needle and graft together in Kitchener stitch with the same number of sts from the back shoulder, or cast off and sew together.

Work two fronts.

Sleeves

Using CC, pick up and knit 148 sts from the base of the armhole, up over the shoulder, and down to the base of the armhole (not underarm). Knit 1 row.

Change to MC and begin sleeve pattern:

**RS facing, P4, *K14, P4*, rep to end.

WS rows: K4, * P14, K4*, rep to end.

Rep these 2 rows until you have done 12 rows altogether.

Change to CC and knit a whole row. Turn.

Now make the opening. This is made like a large, firm buttonhole in one row, by casting off without using the yarn, then picking up the yarn and casting on again. So each end of the slit is linked to make tidy edges:

K4, *bring yarn forward, S1, take yarn back, leave it hanging there, cast off 14 sts *without knitting them*. Slip the last st back onto LH needle.

Turn the work (RS facing) and pick up the yarn passing it to the back, and cast ON 14 sts using 'cable' cast-on, then cast *on 1 more stitch*, but do not place it on LH needle yet.

Cable cast-on

Make each stitch by placing the needle between the sts to make new st, then putting it on the LH needle.

Bring yarn back through to the front between last 2 sts, put the last st on the needle.

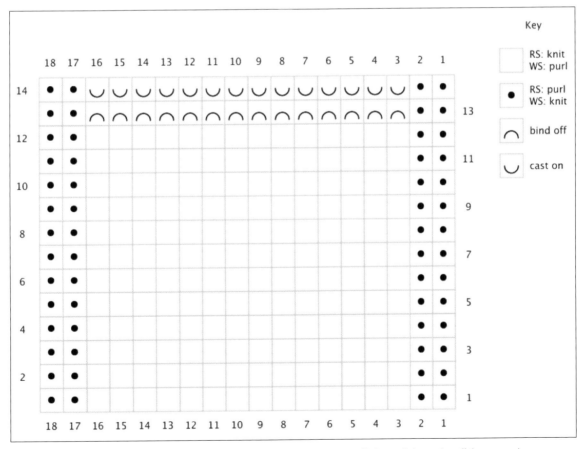

Chart showing one repeat of pattern for sleeve (picked up and knitted downwards) with pattern of holes made by casting off then on again.

Turn work (WS facing again).

Slip end st from LH needle to RH needle, then cast off the extra cast-on st over it.

K4, and repeat from * to make eight slits. Note: the chart shows the openings made by casting off in row 13 and on again in row 14. This would work as well, but the written description gives a slit in one row with firmer edges.

Change back to MC and rep from **, continuing in this pattern of 12 rows and then slits, until the sleeve measures 34cm (13½in), ending before the next slit, so you finish with the plain 12 rows, then begin the long ribbed cuff.

Cuff

Using CC K1 row, then on the wrong side (next row), knit and decrease evenly to 78 sts. This is a rapid decrease making quite a 'puffed' sleeve top, and you will need to K2tog most of the way along the row.

Change to MC and work 1 row K on right side, then in K2, P2 ribbing the same as the body, for 8cm ($3\frac{3}{8}$ in).

Now decrease 1 st at either end of every 8th row until you have 60 sts. The cuff should measure about 20cm (8in): adjust the length here.

Change to CC and cast off in ribbing, not too tightly.

Work two sleeves, and sew the sleeve seam, and the underarm.

Inserts

These squares are knitted into the gaps at the bottom of the jacket.

With RS facing using CC, pick up and knit 40 sts up one side of the slit, then 1 st at the top, and 40 down the other side to make 81 sts.

Knit 1 row CC.

Change to MC and work a module with centre decrease on every RS row:

Row 1: K39, S1, K2tog, psso, K39.

Row 2: P.

Row 3: K38, S1, K2tog, psso, K38.

Row 4: K.

Row 5: P37, P3 tog, P37.

Row 6: K.

Cont in this pattern (K, P, K, K, P, K) working 1 st less on either side of the decrease on RS rows and continuing in the welting

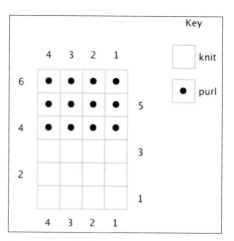

Chart for welting pattern on the inserts.

pattern until 3 sts are left. S1, K2tog, psso, break off yarn and pull through to fasten off.

Make seven of these inserts.

Neck

Using CC and with RS facing, pick up and knit 35 sts round the curve of the neck, the stitches from the back of the neck stitch holder, and 35 round the other side to the front. Knit 1 row CC.

Change to MC and work in garter st, K every row, for 8 rows. Cast off in CC.

Front bands

Using CC and with RS facing, pick up and knit about 140 sts along the front edge. This will depend on your tension: you can check the number from the guide in the introduction to this chapter.

Knit 1 row CC, change to MC and work in garter st, every row knit, for 8 rows. Cast off in CC.

If you want buttonholes, make as miniature version of the sleeve openings casting off 2 or 3 sts according to the size of your buttons, on the 5th row of the band.

Sew sleeve seams and finish off.

Waistcoat in modular knitting with shaped back

Modular waistcoat shaped by stitches.

Back view.

Yarn: MC 300[300,350]g (in the illustration, several shades of main colour are used), 100g of CC

Needles: 3¼mm [10] 3mm[11] for edgings

Tension: 39-st square = 7.5[8,8.5]cm

Size: actual measurement: 90[96,102]cm bust, 45[48,51]cm long

If you would like to customize your own size, follow the instructions in the introduction to this chapter.

This waistcoat is made up from squares which are linked as they are knitted. The squares are cast on [or picked up from previous squares] along two sides, and decrease in the centre of alternate rows to form the square shape, with the rows turning a right angle. There is a plain panel of welting picked up and knitted across at the back, leaving a slit for an inset piece at the bottom edge.

See diagram for order of knitting the squares. The whole waistcoat could be knitted without seams by making double-squares at the sides and over the shoulder: *see* Chapter 7 for making a rectangle.

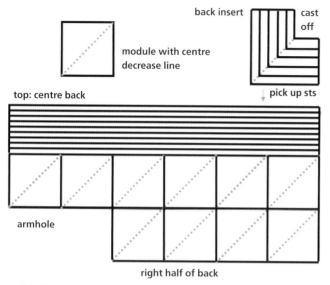

module with centre
decrease line

back insert

cast off

pick up sts

top: centre back

armhole

right half of back

Half the back, showing panel knitted across in welting stitch, and modular insert.

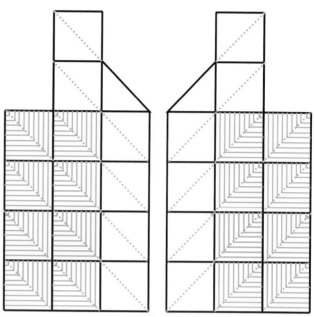

Waistcoat front
Plain squares = garter st,
striped squares = welting stitch

Waistcoat front, in garter stitch and welting stitch.

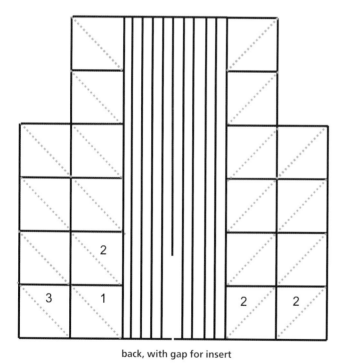

back, with gap for insert

Waistcoat back with gap left for insert.

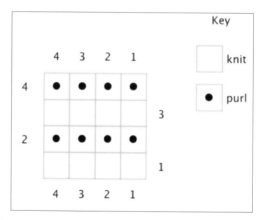

Chart for garter stitch.

Back

Begin with one half of the back (*see* diagram).

Square 1
Cast on 37[39,41] sts in MC (this counts as row 1).
*Row 2: K.
Row 3 (RS): K17[18,19] S2tog knitwise, [as if to knit], K1, p2sso, K17[18,19]. Mark the centre with a tag of wool or stitch marker that can travel up the rows with the knitting to remind you where to decrease and keep the decreases in line: this sort of decrease makes a neat diagonal, which is part of the design.
Row 4: K.
Row 5: K16[17,18], S2tog knitwise, K1, pass 2 sl st over, K 16[17, 18].
Row 6: K.
Row 7: change to CC, K15[16,17] slip 2 tog knitwise, K1, p2sso, K15[16,17].
Row 8: K.
Change back to MC, cont in this way knitting every row in garter st, decreasing on right side rows, changing to CC again when you have 9 sts left:
K3, slip 2 tog knitwise, K1, p2sso, K3.
Continuing in CC, knit back.
Continue decreasing as before, until 3 sts left: S2, K1, pass 2 sts over. Knit back, K2tog and pull thread through.*
Some squares will have half their stitches picked up and half cast on (*see* diagram).

Square 2
Cast on 19[20, 21] in MC, then with RS facing, pick up 18[19,20] along the side of square 1 (*see* diagram). Follow instructions * to *.

Square 3
Pick up 18[19,20] along side of square 2, *see* diagram, then cast on 19[20,21]. Follow * to *.
Now follow the diagram, and where the squares are between others, pick up all the sts from the previous edges. Otherwise, cast on edges where needed.
When you have made one back piece, make the back panel:

Back panel

Lay the back piece on its side (*see* diagram), and pick up and K 19[20,21] sts along the side of each square, six squares total length (114[120,126] sts altogether).
Work in welting stitch until there are five purl 'ridges'.
**Row 1: K.
Row 2: P.
Row 3: K.
Row 4: K.
Row 5: P.
Row 6: K.
Now put the bottom 38[40,42] sts on a holder to make the slit for the insert. Cast on 38[40,42] sts for the other side of the slit and continue in pattern until it is the same length as the first half, five purl ridges. Keep these stitches on a holder.
Now continue with the squares for the second half of the back, picking up the stitches from the back panel for half of each square, beginning at the bottom edge.

Front

Some of the squares on the fronts are made in 'welting' stitch. This makes the waistcoat more fitted. Each front can be made as a whole piece as usual by picking up the sts, but see the diagram for which st to use.

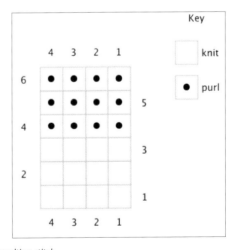

Chart for welting stitch.

*Welting st
*Row 1 (RS): in MC, K 17[18,19] S1, K2tog, psso, K17[18,19].
Row 2: P.
Row 3: K 16[17,18] S1, K2tog, p2sso, K16[17,18].
Row 4: K.
Row 5: P 15[16,17] sts, P3 tog, P15[16,17].
Row 6: K.

Cont in this 6-row pattern (knit, purl, knit; knit, purl, knit), decreasing on right side rows (1 fewer st either side of the decrease each time), changing to CC again when you have 9 sts left:

K3, S2tog knitwise, K1, p2sso, K3.

Continuing in CC, knit back and cont in garter st.

Continue decreasing as before, until 3 sts left: S2, K1, p2sso. Knit back, K2tog and pull thread through.*

Front neck

See the diagram for the position of this triangle or half-square for front of neck.

Using MC, pick up 19[20,21] sts from side of one previous square, working in the usual pattern, and decreasing 1 st at neck edge on alt rows in place of the usual central decrease.

Insert at centre back

This is made in welting stitch. With RS facing and using MC, pick up and K38[40,42] sts up one side of the gap at the base of the back panel, and 38[40,42] sts down the other side. Working in welting st**, work this module like the ones on the fronts until there are 49 sts left, and cast off.

Front bands

Using 3mm [11] needles and MC, pick up and K22[23,24] sts from each square, all along each front edge. NB: the ribbing will pull in slightly, so 22[23,24] sts are needed rather than the usual 19[20,21]. Work in K2, P2 rib for 8 rows, and cast off, making buttonholes if you wish (*see* directions for buttonholes in pattern 3).

Armhole edging

The armholes on this waistcoat are quite small, so either finish with a single line of crochet (the same as picking up stitches and casting off), or make a ribbed band to match the front bands.

Rib-and-welt modular jacket

Rib-and-welt modular jacket.

Yarn: MC 500[525,550,650]g 4-ply wool, 100g in CC
Needles: 3¼mm [10]. The ribbed stitches make a dense, heavy jacket.
Size: actual measurement across without stretching 45[48,50,52]cm
The stitch makes a very stretchy fabric, so these sizes are minimum measurements, it will stretch to much larger: if you want it to be fitted closely, aim for a smaller size.
If you would like to customize your own size, follow the instructions in the introduction to this chapter.

This jacket is made up from diamonds, which are linked as they are knitted. The diamonds are cast on (or picked up from previous diamonds) along two sides, and decrease in the centre of alternate rows to form the diamond shape, with the rows turning a right angle.
Alternate rows of diamonds are knitted in K2, P2 rib, alternating with 'welting stitch'.
Ribbing makes a long module with a short cast-on edge, welting produces a shorter cast-on edge and long sides, so the two fit together and create varying zigzags between.
MC = main colour
CC = contrast colour

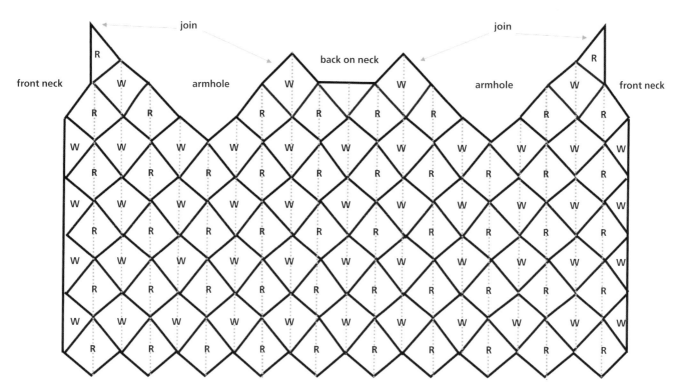

Layout for whole body knitted as one piece.

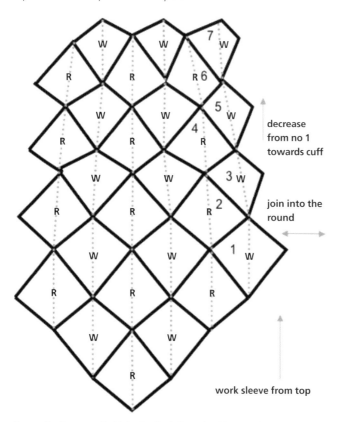

decrease
from no 1
towards cuff

join into the
round

work sleeve from top

Layout for sleeve, worked joined to body from shoulder to cuff.

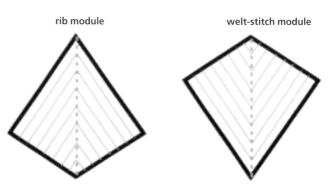

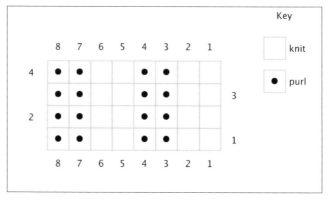

Left, ribbing module: right, welting module, showing the differing shapes which then fit together.

Chart for ribbing.

First row of diamonds, ribbing

Cast on 39[41,43,45] sts in CC, and knit back 1 row, change to MC (pick up or cast on counts as row 1).

Row 3 (RS): in MC, K2, P2 for 18[19,20,21] sts, (NB: it doesn't matter whether you end on K1, 2, or P1 or 2), S2tog knitwise, [putting the needle through the stitches *as if to knit them tog*] K1, p2sso, rib 18[19,20,21] sts matching the ribbing on either side of the decrease. For example, if you finished on 'P2, K2, P1', begin again with 'P1, K2, P2'. Mark the centre with a tag of wool or stitch marker that can travel up the rows with the knitting to remind you where to decrease and keep the decreases in line: this sort of decrease makes a neat diagonal, which is part of the design.

Row 4: work in rib, *purling* the centre st, so that the decrease is always knitted on the RS, purled on the WS, making a neat line (*see* note below **).

Row 5: rib 17[18,19,20] sts, S2tog knitwise, K1, p2sso, rib17 [18,19,20] sts.

Row 6: rib, purling centre st.

Row 7: rib 16[17,18,19] sts, S2tog knitwise, K1, p2sso, rib16 [17,18,19] sts.

Cont in this way in ribbing, decreasing on RS rows, keeping the knits and purls in line beside the decrease, while ribbing and purling the centre stitch on WS rows, until there are 3 sts left: S2, K1, p2sso. Pull thread through*.

(**If you are not getting the clear 'line' of the decrease, you may not be slipping the stitches in the way described; slip the 2 sts as if to knit them tog.)

Make 10 individual diamonds.

Second row of modules, welting stitch

Weave the ends in when picking up the sts for the next square, or sew in afterwards.

These are picked up from the sides of the ribbed diamonds and joined together.

Using CC, pick up and K19[20,21,22] sts along one edge, and 20[21,22,23] from the other edge, to make 39[41,43,45] sts (or pick up the central stitch in the middle if possible).

Row 2: K, change to MC.

Row 3 (RS): K18[19,20,21] sts, S1, K2tog, psso, K18[19,20,21] sts.

Mark the centre with a tag of wool or stitch marker that can travel up the rows with the knitting to remind you where to decrease and keep the decreases in line: the decrease makes a neat diagonal, which is part of the design, but is less pronounced than the decrease on the ribbed modules.

Row 4: P.

Row 5: K 17[18,19,20] sts, S1, K2tog, psso, psso, K17[18,19,20] sts.

Row 4: K.

Row 7: P16[17,18,19], P3tog, P16[17,18,19].

Row 8: K.

Cont in this 6-row pattern, decreasing on RS rows in the same way, but working in the pattern knit, purl, knit; knit, purl, knit. When there are 3 sts left, S1, K2tog, psso, pull thread through*.

From now on, these diamonds are knitted by picking up sts from previous diamonds, picking up 19[20,21,22] sts along one slope, and 20[21,22,23] sts up the other side, then cont as before from row 2 above. Rows of ribbing blocks alternate across the jacket with rows of welting blocks.

Follow the diagram to make the body of the jacket, all in one piece, making half-diamonds at front edges:

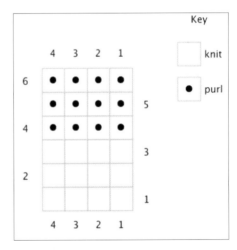

Chart for welting stitch.

Half-diamonds

Right front edge

Pick up 19[20,21,22] sts and work in welting st as before: K2tog at beg of each RS row, and knit WS, working till all sts have gone.

Left front edge

Pick up 19[20,21,22] sts and work in welting st as usual, knitting 2 tog at end of each RS row, until all sts have gone.

   See the diagram for the half-diamonds in rib on front shoulders; these will fold over and be sewn to join the shoulders.

Back of neck

You need to make a half-diamond to give a flat top edge to the back of the neck. These are made differently:
Pick up sts as usual, and as well as the usual decreases in the middle of the row, also decrease at beg and end of row. So on RS rows, working in welting st:
Work 2 tog, work to one st before centre, S1, work 2 tog, psso, work to last 2 sts, work 2 tog.
Cont until all sts are used up.

Sleeves

These are worked from the top down by picking up stitches (or knit separately and sew to join).
Pick up the sts for the sleeve diamonds as shown on the diagram, beginning with one at the top of the shoulder. To begin, pick up 19[20,21,22] sts again for each half, and one in the middle [39,41,43,45] sts.
Work in rows of modules following the sleeve diagram, and when you have three diamonds across, you can join the sleeve into the round (there are no half-diamonds).
To make the sleeve *decrease*, the diamonds must become smaller as it goes down. Begin decreasing from the armhole, when the sleeve is worked in the round.
At '1' on diagram, pick up 18[19,20,21] sts each half and one in the centre making 37[39,41,43] sts.
2] 17[18,19,20] and one in the centre making 35[37,39,41].
3] 16[17,18,19] and one in the centre making 33[35,37,39].
4] 15[16,17,18] and one in the centre making 31[33,35,37].
5] 14[15,16,17] and one in the centre making 29[31,33,35].
6] 13[14,15,16] and one in the centre making 27[29,31,33].

7] 12[13,14,15] and one in the centre making 25[27,29,31]. Cont like this until it measures the right length for you. If you finish on a round of welting stitch, the sleeve will have a gentle zigzag edge; if you finish on ribbing, the zigzag will be more pronounced.

Neck

Using CC, pick up 22[24,26,28] sts along diamond at front neck edge, 28[30,32,24] sts along each side and neck triangles, and 22[24,26,28] sts along last diamond. Knit back one row. Change to MC and work in K2, P2 rib for 10 rows.
Cast off in CC.

Front bands

Using CC, pick up and knit about 34–38 sts along the edge of each triangle on the front edge. Pick up the right number for your tension; it must lie flat and not pull in.
Knit back 1 row, then change to MC and work 8 rows in K2, P2 rib, cast off in CC.

Buttonholes

(a strong buttonhole inspired by Elizabeth Zimmerman)
To make buttonholes, work 3 rows of ribbing and make them on the fourth row.

- *Work to the chosen position for buttonhole. These are 3 sts wide, so adjust for the size of your buttons.*
- Bring yarn to the front of work, and drop it.
- *slip another st from LH needle to RH needle, pass 1st slip st over 2nd to cast off 1st st. Rep from * until 3 sts are cast off.
- Slip last cast-off st back onto LH needle. **Turn work.**

Pick up the hanging yarn and pass it between needles to the back. Using cable cast on (i.e. placing needle between the sts to make new st), cast on 4 stitches, but do not place last st on LH needle yet. Bring yarn back through to the front between last 2 sts, put last st on needle.

- *Turn work.*
Slip end st from LH needle to RH needle, then cast off extra cast-on st over it. Work to next buttonhole position and repeat.

Modular jacket, scallop shapes

Scallop-patterned jacket.

Yarn: MC 580[600,625]g of 4-ply wool, 100g of CC (the jacket illustrated uses random-dyed yarn)
Needles: size 3¼m [10] and 3mm [11] for cuffs and bands
Size: actual measurement 96[104,112]cm bust, and very slightly wider over the hips. The small modules measure 12[13,14]cm across.
Tension: try knitting a small module and check the measurement. If you would like to customize your own size, follow the instructions in the introduction to this chapter.

Structure: this jacket is made from scallop-shaped modules, linked as they are knitted. The shapes are cast on (or picked up from previous modules), and decrease every few rows in five places, making the curved shape.
There are two sizes of scallop module, with larger ones at the bottom of the jacket.
The chart shows a small module in the smallest size.
See diagram for the layout of the shapes, and begin at the bottom.

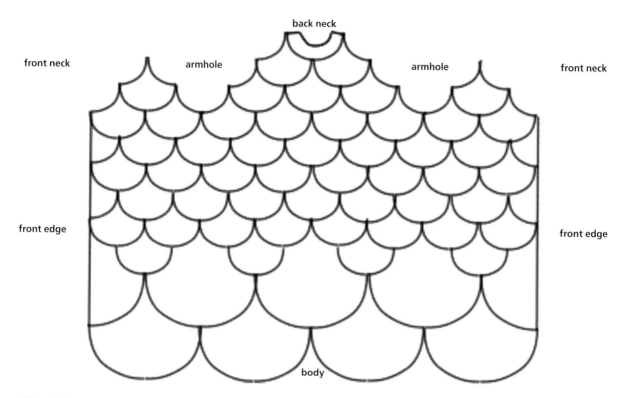

Layout of the whole body, with double-sized modules at the bottom.

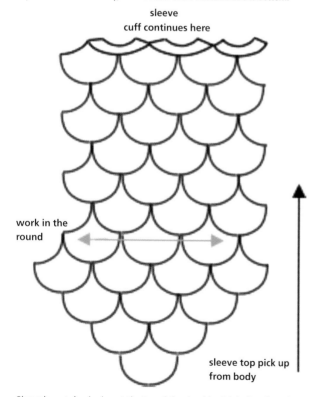

Sleeve layout, beginning at the top of the shoulder (picked up from the body) and working down.

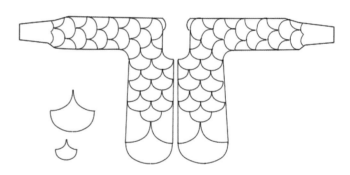

The front of the body showing how the sleeves join.

Large module

Cast on 76[79,82] sts in CC (cast-on or pick-up row = row 1).
Row 2: K.
Row 3 (RS): change to MC, K.
Row 4: P
Row 5: K2tog, *K22[23,24] S1, K2tog, psso*, rep from * to *, K22[23,24], S1, K1, psso (=70[73,76] sts).

Row 6: P.
Row 7: K.
Row 8: P.
Row 9: K.
Row 10: P.
row 11: K2tog, *K20[21,22], S1, K2tog, psso*, rep from * to *, K20[21,22], S1, k1, psso (=66[69,72] sts)..
§ **Row 12:** K (this makes a ridge on RS).
Row 13: K.
Row 14: P.
Row 15: K.
Row 16: P§.
Row 17: K2tog, *K18[19,20], S1, K2tog, psso*, rep from * to *, K18[19,20], S1, k1, psso (=60[63,66] sts).
Rep from § to §.
Row 23: K2tog, *K16[17,18], S1, K2tog, psso*, rep from * to *, K16[17,18], S1, k1, psso (=52[55,58] sts).
Rep from § to §.
Row 29: K2tog, *K14[15,16], S1, K2tog, psso*, rep from * to *, K14[15,16], S1, k1, psso (=46[49,52] sts).
Rep from § to §.
Row 35: K2tog, *K12[13,14], S1, K2tog, psso*, rep from * to *, K12[13,14], S1, k1, psso (=40[43,46] sts).
Rep from § to §.
Row 41: K2tog, *K10[11,12], S1, K2tog, psso,*, rep from * to *, K10[11,12], S1, k1, psso (=34[37,40] sts).
Rep from § to §.
Row 47: K2tog, *K8[9,10], S1, K2tog, psso* rep from * to *, K8[9,10], S1, K1, psso (=28[31,34] sts).
Rep from § to §.
Row 53: K2tog, *K6[7,8], S1, K2tog, psso* rep from * to *, K6[7,8], S1, K1, psso (=22[25,28] sts).
Rep from § to § .
Row 59: K2tog, *K4[5,6], S1, K2tog, psso* rep from * to *, K4[5,6], S1, K1, psso (=16[19,22] sts).
Rep from § to §.
Row 65: K2tog, *K2[3,4] S1, K2tog, psso* rep from * to *, K2[3,4], S1, K1, psso (=10[13,16] sts).
Rep from § to §.
Row 71: K.
Row 72: P.
Now follow instructions for each size separately:
Smallest size: K2tog, *S1, K2tog, psso* rep from * to *, S1, K1, psso.
P these 4 sts, then K2tog, S1, K1, psso: P these 2 sts, K2tog and break off yarn and fasten off.

Middle and large sizes: K2tog, *K1[2] S1, K2tog, psso* rep from * to *, K1[2] S1, K1, psso (=7,10 sts).
Middle size: K2tog, (S1, K1, psso) x 2, K1.
P these 4 sts, then (S1, K1, psso) x 2, K2tog, and break off yarn and fasten off.
Largest size: K2tog twice, S1, K2tog, psso twice.
P these 4 sts, then (S1, K1, psso) x 2.
P these 2 sts, then K2tog, break off yarn and fasten off.

Make four of these modules, one for each front, two for the back. They will join together in one piece with the next row of modules.

Second row of modules

These fit in between and join the first four, with half modules at each front edge.
Half module for **right-front** of jacket is picked up from bottom of the curve of the previous scallop to tip (*see diagram*).
Using CC, pick up and knit 38[40,41] sts.
Row 2: K.
Row 3 (RS): change to MC, K.
Row 4: P.
Row 5: K11[12,12] S1, K2tog, psso, K22[23,24] S1, k1, psso (=35[37,38] sts).
§**Row 6:** K, making a ridge on RS.
Row 7: K.
Row 8: P.
Row 9: K.
Row 10: P§.
Row 11: K10[11,11], S1, K2tog, psso, K20[21,22], S1, k1, psso (=32[34,35] sts).
Rep from § to §.
Row 17: K9[10,10], S1, K2tog, psso, K18[19,20], S1, k1, psso (=29[31,32] sts).
Rep from § to §.
Row 23: K 8[9,9], S1, K2tog, psso, K16[17,18], S1, k1, psso (=26[28,29] sts).
Rep from § to §.
Row 29: K 7[8,8], S1, K2tog, psso, K14[15,16], S1, k1, psso (=23[25,26] sts).
Rep from § to §.
Row 35: K 6[7,7], S1, K2tog, psso, K12[13,14], S1, k1, psso (=20[22,23] sts).

Rep from § to §.

Row 41: K 5[6,6], S1, K2tog, psso, K10[11,12], S1, k1, psso (=17[19,20] sts).

Rep from § to §.

Row 47: K 4[5,5], S1, K2tog, psso, K8[9,10], S1, k1, psso (=14[16,17] sts).

Rep from § to §.

Row 53: K 3[4,4], S1, K2tog, psso, K6[7,8], S1, k1, psso (=11[13,14] sts).

Rep from § to §.

Row 59: K 2[3,3], S1, K2tog, psso, K4[5,6], S1, k1, psso (=8[10,11] sts).

Rep from § to §.

Row 65: K 1[2,2], S1, K2tog, psso, K2[3,4], S1, k1, psso (=5[7,9] sts).

Rep from § to §.

Now follow instructions for separate sizes:

Smallest size: S1, K2tog, psso, S1, k1, psso.

K 1 row, P 1 row.

K2tog, P 1 row.

K2tog and break off thread, fasten off.

Medium size: K1, (S1, K2tog, psso) twice.

P3, then S1, K2tog, psso and fasten off.

Large size: K2tog, (S1, K2tog, psso) twice, K1.

P4, then K2tog, S1, k1, psso.

K2tog and fasten off.

Make the **next 3 modules** by picking up the stitches to fit in with first modules:

Using CC, pick up 38[39,41] sts from one side and 38[40,41] for the other side, *see* diagram.

Knit back one row, change to MC and work as for first module.

Half module for left front

Using CC, pick up 38[40,41] sts from the tip of the base module down to the side edge at left front:

Row 2: K.

Row 3: change to MC, K.

Row 4: P.

Row 5: K2tog, K22[23,24], S1, K2tog, psso, K11[12,12] (=35[37,38] sts).

§**Row 6:** K, making a ridge on the RS.

Row 7: K.

Row 8: P.

Row 9: K.

Row 10: P§.

Row 11: K2tog, K20[21,22], S1, K2tog, psso, K10[11,11] (=32[34,35] sts).

Rep from § to §

Row 17: K2tog, K18[19,20], S1, K2tog, psso, K9[10,10], S1, k1, psso.

(=29[31,32] sts).

Rep from § to §.

Row 23: K2tog, K16[17,18], S1, K2tog, psso, K8[9,9] (=26[28,29] sts).

Rep from § to §.

Row 29: K2tog, K14[15,16], S1, K2tog, psso, K7[8,8] (=23[25,26] sts).

Rep from § to §.

Row 35: K2tog, K12[13,14], S1, K2tog, psso, K6[7,7] (=20[22,23] sts).

Rep from § to §.

Row 41: K2tog, K10[11,12], S1, K2tog, psso, K5[6,6] (=17[19,20] sts).

Rep from § to §.

Row 47: K2tog, K8[8,10], S1, K2tog, psso, K4[5,5] (=14[16,17] sts).

Rep from § to §.

Row 53: K2tog, K6[7,8], S1, K2tog, psso, K3[4,4] (=11[13,14] sts).

Rep from § to §.

Row 59: K2tog, K4[5,6], S1, K2tog, psso, K2[3,3] (=8[10,11] sts).

Rep from § to §.

Row 65: K2tog, K2[3,4], S1, K2tog, psso, K1[2,2] (=5[7,9] sts).

Rep from § to §.

Now follow instructions for separate sizes:

Smallest size: K2tog, S1, K2tog, psso.

P 1 row.

K2tog, K1.

P 1 row.

K2tog and break off thread, fasten off.

Medium size: K1, (S1, K2tog, psso) twice.

P3, then S1, K2tog, psso and fasten off.

Large size: K2tog, (S1, K2tog, psso) twice, K1.

P4, then K2tog, S1, k1, psso.

K2tog and fasten off.

Small modules

These small modules will fit between the large ones and continue for the rest of the jacket. They are slightly less than half-size, to pull the shape in a little.

First, you need to fill the gaps between the large modules with four centre modules. Each is placed directly above the base module, with the centre at the point of the base module (*see* diagram).

Each module will have 34 [37,40] sts, so mark the centre point halfway along the slope of the large module.

Row 1: using CC, pick up 17[18,20] sts to the centre (the tip of the base module), and 17[19,20] sts to the mid-point the other side.

Row 2: K, change to MC.

Row 3: K.

Row 4: P.

With RS facing, make the decreases in the next row:

Row 5: K2tog, *K8[9,10], S1, K2tog, psso* rep from * to *, K8[9,10], SSK (=28[31,34] sts).

Row 6: P.

Row 7: K.

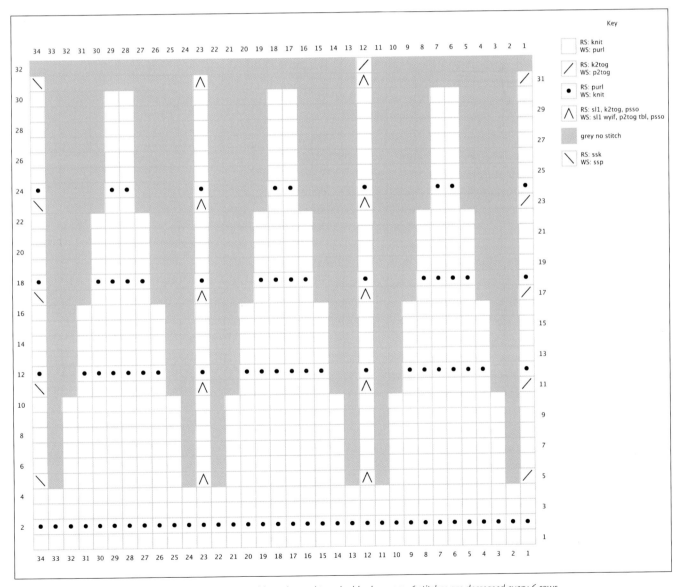

Chart for the small module, showing the single increase at either edge and two double-decreases: 6 stitches are decreased every 6 rows.

Row 8: P.

Row 9: K.

Row 10: P.

Row 11: K2tog, *K6[7,8], S1, K2tog, psso* rep from * to *, K6[7,8], SSK (=22[25,28] sts).

§**Row 12:** K (this makes a 'ridge').

Row 13: K.

Row 14: P.

Row 15: K.

Row 16: P§.

Next dec row:

Row 17: K2tog, *K4[5,6], S1, K2tog, psso*, rep from * to *, K4[5,6], SSK (=16[19,22] sts).

Rep from § to §.

Next dec row:

Row 23: K2tog, *K2[3,4] S1, K2tog, psso*, rep from * to *, K2[3,4], SSK (=10[13,16] sts).

Rep from § to §.

Row 29: K.

Row 30: P.

Now follow instructions for each size separately:

Smallest size: K2tog, *S1, K2tog, psso*, rep from * to *, SSK.

P these 4 sts, then K2tog, S1, K1, psso: P these 2 sts, K2tog, break off yarn and fasten off.

Middle and large sizes: K2tog, *K1[2], S1, K2tog, psso*, rep from * to *, K1[2] SSK.

Middle size: K2tog, K1, S1, K1, psso.

P these 3 sts, then *S1, K2tog, psso*, and break off yarn and fasten off.

Largest size: K2tog twice, S1, K2tog, psso twice.

P these 5 sts, then S1, K2tog, psso, K1.

Purl these 2 sts, K2tog, break off yarn and fasten off.

Make one scallop in the base of each gap in the large modules (= 4 altogether). From now on, the next row of modules will be picked up in the gaps between the large and the small, with half the stitches from the remaining edge of the large module, and half from the small one, eight modules all the way round.

Small modules fit together exactly. Using CC, begin at the cast-off tip, pick up and knit 17 sts along the edge to the bottom (*see* diagram) and 17 sts beginning at the bottom of the next scallop, finishing at the cast-off tip [34 sts].

Knit back 1 row, then change to MC and K 1 row, P 1 row.

Work as for the first scallop from §.

Half-scallops

Again, there need to be half-scallops to make the front edge of the jacket.

These are picked up as before; for **right-front** of jacket they are picked up from bottom of previous scallop to tip, 17[18,21] sts using CC.

Row 2: K.

Change to MC.

Row 3: K.

Row 4: P.

Row 5: K4[4,6], S1, K2tog, psso, K8[9,10], S1, K1, psso (=14[15,18] sts).

Row 6: P.

Row 7: K.

Row 8: P.

Row 9: K.

Row 10: P.

Row 11: K 3[3,5], S1, K2tog, psso, K6[7,8], S1, K1, psso (=11[12,15] sts).

§**Row 12: K** (this makes a 'ridge').

Row 13: K.

Row 14: P.

Row 15: K.

Row 16: P§.

Row 17: K2[2,4], S1, K2tog, psso, K4[5,6], S1, K1, psso (=8[9,12] sts).

Rep from § to §.

Row 23: K 1[1,3], S1, K2tog, psso, K2[3,4], S1, K1, psso (=5[6,9] sts).

Rep from § to §.

Row 29: K.

Row 30: P.

Now follow instructions for each size separately:

Smallest size: *S1, K2tog, psso*, rep from * to *, SSK.

Purl these 3 sts, then K2tog, K1, purl these 2 sts, K2tog, break off yarn and fasten off.

Middle size: K2tog, K1, S1, K2tog, psso.

P these 3 sts, then S1, K2tog, psso, break off yarn and fasten off.

Largest size: *S1, K2tog, psso* x 3.

P these 3 sts, then S1, K2tog, psso, K

break off yarn and fasten off.

Left front half scallops

Pick up 17[18,21] sts from tip to base of previous scallop.
Row 2: K.
Row 3: K.
Row 4: P.
Row 5: K2tog, K8[9,10], S1, K2tog, psso K4[4,6] (=14[15,18] sts).
Row 6: P.
Row 7: K.
Row 8: P.
Row 9: K.
Row 10: P.
Row 11: K2tog, K 6[7,8], S1, K2tog, psso, K3[3,5] (=11[12,15] sts).
§**Row 12: K** (this makes a 'ridge').
Row 13: K.
Row 14: P.
Row 15: K.
Row 16: P§.
Row 17: K2tog, K 4[5,6], S1, K2tog, psso, K2[2,4] (=8[9,12] sts). Rep from § to §.
Row 23: K2tog, K 2[3,4], S1, K2tog, psso, K1[1,3] (=5[6,9] sts). Rep from § to §.
Row 29: K.
Row 30: P.
Now follow instructions for each size separately:
Smallest size: *S1, K2tog, psso*, rep from * to *, SSK.
P these 3 sts, then K2tog, K1, P these 2 sts, K2tog, break off yarn and fasten off.
Middle size: K2tog, K1, S1, K2tog, psso.
P these 3 sts, then K2tog, K1, break off yarn and fasten off.
Largest size: *S1, K2tog, psso* x 3.
Purl these 3 sts, then K2tog, K1, K
break off yarn and fasten off.

Follow the diagram to make the body, with the shapes travelling up at a 'raglan-sleeve'-type angle at the armhole, and also leaving a gap for the neck.
Centre back neck scallop is shorter: cast off on row 6 instead of continuing to a point.

Sleeves

These begin at the top of the shoulder, joining with the body, starting from the neck and working downwards to the long cuff which gathers in the fullness of the sleeve. The sleeves can be worked in the round from the 4th row of modules onwards.

When it measures about 38–40cm (12–15¾in) under the arm (adjust length here), cast off the last round of scallops on row 6 (instead of going to a point).

Cuffs

Using CC and 3mm [11] needles, pick up and K28 from each of the cast-off scallops, spreading the stitches evenly so there are no gaps. If working in the round, P 1 round in CC.

Change to MC and work a K2, P2 cuff for the length you want, and cast off loosely.

Front bands

Using CC and 3mm [11] needles, pick up and K sts from each half module, all along each front edge, about 24[26,28] sts to each half module, and twice as many for the large ones. The ribbing will pull in slightly, so make sure you pick up enough sts. Work 1 row K, then change to MC and work in K2, P2 rib for 8 rows and cast off.

Buttonholes

Work to the chosen position for buttonhole on row 4 of the band.

Follow the instructions for pattern 3, which are for a buttonhole 3 sts wide, so adjust this to suit your buttons.

Neck

Using CC and 3mm [11] needles, pick up and K sts around the neck: the ribbing will pull in slightly, so this is a guide: 22 sts from first scallop at front neck edge, 24 from half scallop, 30 from shoulder scallop, 32 round back of neck, 30 from second shoulder, 24 from the half scallop, and 22 at the second front edge. Work 1 row K, then change to MC and work in K2, P2 rib for 8 rows and cast off.

ABBREVIATIONS AND GLOSSARY

Abbreviations

alt	alternate
b	back, or through the back
beg	beginning
C	cable
C2f	cable 2 forward
C2b	cable 2 back
CC	contrast colour
col	colour
cont	continue
dec	decrease
f	front
f&b	front and back (as in 'knit into front and back of st')
g st	garter st (every row knit)
inc	increase
K	knit
K1b	knit into back of stitch
K into f&b	knit into front and then back of st before taking off needle (making 1 new st)
K2tog	knit 2 stitches together
K2togb	knit 2 stitches together through backs of sts
LH	left-hand needle
MC	main colour
M1	make 1 extra stitch, according to instructions. Both 'K into f&b' and 'knit into bar before next st' make an extra stitch, with slightly different appearances.
P	purl

P1b	purl into back of stitch
psso	pass slipped stitch over
p2sso	pass 2 stitches over
P2tog	purl 2 stitches together
P2togb	purl 2 stitches together though back of stitch
rep	repeat
RH	right-hand needle
RS	right side
S	slip next stitch (purlwise unless stated differently)
sl st	slip stitch
SSK	slip next 2 sts knitwise one at a time onto RH needle. Slip them back to LH needle in their new orientation and knit together through backs.
	This instruction is the same decrease as S1, K1, PSSO, in that it decreases 2 stitches into 1 with the RH stitch lying on top. It may have a slightly neater result, as there is less chance of stretching the top stitch as it is passed over.
st	stitch
st st	stocking stitch (US stockinette stitch). Row 1 knit, row 2 purl, or in the round, knit.
S1, K1, psso	S1, Knit 1, pass slipped stitch over. This is the same as SSK, but SSK can have a neater finish.
thro	through
tog	together
WS	wrong side
w&t	wrap and turn. Used in short-row knitting, to prevent leaving a gap when you turn.
	Work to point of turning, bring yarn forward, slip next stitch, take yarn back, return slipped stitch to LH needle, turn.

yb	yarn back
yBb	yarn col B back
yBf	yarn col B forward

yf	yarn forward
YO	yarn over (take yarn over right-hand needle, creating a loop which becomes an extra stitch)

Glossary

Kitchener stitch, invisible grafting: a way of joining two pieces of knitting by using a sewing needle and thread to seamlessly join or graft the two together, linking the stitches as if knitted (*see* Further Resources).

Steeking is a way of reinforcing the stitches which although knitted in the round, are cut through to make an opening at the end, for inserting a sleeve or making an opening for a jacket.

Fair Isle or Jacquard knitting: the name Fair Isle comes from the Scottish island of that name, where there is a tradition of knitting colour patterns in two or more colours per row, with small groups of stitches in each colour, the unknitted yarn being woven or stranded behind. The term Jacquard is from a method of weaving used to create elaborate designs. Both terms are used to mean coloured knitted patterns.

Charts

The charts look at the right side or top of the fabric, so for example, if working back and forth and the stitch is indicated as 'knit', purl it on wrong side rows.

ACKNOWLEDGEMENTS AND THANKS

This book emerged from the lockdown of 2020/21 during the Covid pandemic. With normal life and work on hold, there was time and freedom to explore, experiment and play with knitting, with no pressure to produce finished items, but time to really investigate knitting for its own sake and to explore what stitches will do to alter the knitted fabric. This is something I have always encouraged through teaching, but is sometimes difficult to justify in normal life unless for a particular project or purpose, so it was a bonus to have this time to discover more and clarify thoughts: all helpful in designing.

Many people helped and encouraged me along the way. Meeting with textile friends Deirdre Wood, Julie Hedges and Ann Richards was great for discussing ideas, with help on organizing text and on photography from Ann. Emma Vining and Lorraine McClean advised on using knitting charts, something I've always thought essential as a back-up to written patterns (and for some people, a better alternative than text), which led to me using Stitchmastery for making the charts. Then Cathy and Hannah at Stitchmastery answered my questions patiently while I learnt the system.

Roger Mobsby of Diamond Fibres advised on the technicalities of spinning yarn and how the amount of twist affects the way it behaves, as did weaver, Ann Richards.

Thanks to Angharad Thomas who provided the photo of the Norwegian mittens (Chapter 5). Lucy Hague allowed me to illustrate her brilliant idea for knitting circular motifs (Chapter 6), also Sonya Hammond her solution for knitting modular rectangles (Chapter 7).

Crowood has been supportive throughout with clear-headed advice. I intended the book to be very visual, and this would not have been possible without Colin Mills' photography and imaginative way of bringing garments to life without using models.

Consistent help throughout my career has come from the following: firstly, my knitters, who have become 'remote' friends through phone and email contact – Joan Brown, Betty Cottle, Betty Dobson, Janet Hawkins, Barbara Jarman, Kneale Palmer and Clare Sampson; they have shown enthusiasm for knitting my designs and have done so with great skill. Secondly, thanks to customers who have tried and bought garments over the years and given most helpful feedback on designs. Lastly, thanks to Dan for patience and support through all the ups and downs.

REFERENCES

Introduction

1. Wool spun by Diamond Fibres from Romney Marsh sheep.

Chapter 1

1. *Journal of Mathematics and the Arts*, 3:2, 67–83, DOI: 10.1080/17513470902896561, 2009
2. Kitchener stitch, a way of invisibly grafting rows of knitting seamlessly; *see* Further Resources and search YouTube for a video demonstration.
3. AC knitwear tutorials (Arnall-Culliford Techniques): https://www.acknitwear.co.uk/tutorials-1
4. Norsk Folkemuseum, Boks 720 Skøyen, N-0214 Oslo https://norskfolkemuseum.no/en
5. Hoxbro, V., *Domino Knitting* (Interweave, 2002)
6. Pattern for mitred corner jacket, Ellen, A., *Knitting, Stitch-led Design* (The Crowood Press, 2015)

Chapter 2

1. Victoria and Albert Museum https://collections.vam.ac.uk/ search for knitted textiles
2. More designs using these stitches together can be found in Ellen, A., *Knitting, Stitch-led Design* (The Crowood Press, 2015)

Chapter 3

1. These knitters have experimented with energized yarn and can be searched on the internet: Kathryn Alexander with entrelac designs on pinterest.co.uk and ravelry.com.

2. Amy Tyler runs workshops on spinning and knitting: http://www.stonesockfibers.com
3. Jillian Eve, also a spinner, describes overspun yarn here: https://jillianeve.com/over-spun-yarn/
4. Richards, A., *Weaving Textiles That Shape Themselves* (The Crowood Press, 2012); Richards, A., *Weaving, Structure and Substance*, (The Crowood Press, 2021)
5. https://www.handweavers.co.uk/

Chapter 4

1. Bush, N., *Folk Knitting in Estonia* (Interweave Press, 1999)
2. Zimmerman, E., *Knitter's Almanac*, (Dover Publications, 1981)

Chapter 5

1. Methods of knitting Fair Isle and weaving in are shown in: Ellen, A., *Knitting, Colour, structure and design* (The Crowood Press, 2011) Ellen, A., *Knitting, Stitch-led Design* (The Crowood Press, 2015)
2. Lucy Neatby has a subscription YouTube channel with tutorials
3. These mittens were bought in 2013 at the Arctic Hotel, Sommaroy, outside Tromsø, Norway. They are labelled 'Hillesoy Husflidslag'; photo supplied by Angharad Thomas

Chapter 6

1. https://collections.vam.ac.uk/item/O10318/petticoat-unknown/
2. Christoffersson, B-M., *Pop Knitting* (Interweave Press, 2012)
3. Newgrange Shawl pattern by Lucy Hague; originally published in *Echoes of Heather and Stone*, Carol Feller, 2018 lucyhague.co.uk

Chapter 7

1. This method of knitting was written about by Virginia Woods Bellamy (1890–1976) who published a book on the technique in 1952 called *Number Knitting,* which went on to influence many knitters and designers through the twentieth century**.** *See* https://pieceworkmagazine.com
2. Sonya Hammond, *The Journal for Weavers, Spinners and Dyers* no 280, 2021
3. Gainford, V., *Designs for Knitting Kilt Hose and Knickerbocker Stockings* (Rannoch Press, 1978)
4. Zimmerman, E., *Knitting Without Tears* (Fireside, 1971)
5. Pattern project 8 in: Ellen, A., *Knitting: Colour, structure and design* (The Crowood Press, 2011)

Further resources

Books containing techniques referred to in this book:

Bush, N., *Folk Knitting in Estonia* (Interweave Press, 1999) – for knitted braid techniques

Drysdale, R., *Entrelac Knitting* (Sixth & Spring Books, 2017)

Collingwood, P., *The Maker's Hand: A Close Look at Textile Structures* (Bellew Publishing, 1987)

Christoffersson, B-M., *Pop Knitting* (Interweave Press, 2012)

Ellen, A., *Knitting: Colour, structure and design* (The Crowood Press 2011) – for joining seams, Kitchener stitch (grafting), picking up stitches, Fair Isle knitting methods

Ellen, A., *Knitting: Stitch-led design* (Crowood Press 2015) for knitting patterns using techniques in this book

The Harmony Guides to Knitting Stitches (Lyric Books, 1987) – for slip stitch, cable and many other patterns

Høxboro, V., *Knit to be Square* (Interweave Press LLC, 2008) – for modular/domino knitting

Richards, A., *Weaving Textiles That Shape Themselves,* (The Crowood Press, 2012) and *Weaving: Structure and Substance* (The Crowood Press, 2021) – for using high-twist yarn for different effects

Stanley, M., *The Handknitter's Handbook* (David and Charles, 1986) – for techniques, casting on and off, short rows, increases, decreases and so on

Mary Thomas's Knitting Book (Hodder and Stoughton, 1938) – for knitting techniques

Mary Thomas's Book of Knitting Patterns (Hodder and Stoughton, 1943) – for knitting stitches explained

Zimmerman, E., *Knitting Without Tears,* (Simon and Schuster, 1971) – for knitting tips, experimenting, knitting without patterns

Websites and references

Jillian Eve, also a spinner, describes overspun yarn here https://jillianeve.com/over-spun-yarn/

Lucy Hague: Newgrange Shawl pattern, by Lucy Hague (originally published in *Echoes of Heather and Stone*, Carol Feller, 2018), patterns with curves and spirals https://www.lucyhague.co.uk

Sonya Hammond, *The Journal for Weavers, Spinners and Dyers* no. 280, winter 2021 p.29, modular rectangles

Lucy Neatby: books and YouTube videos, double-cloth knitting and other techniques

Amy Tyler runs online workshops on spinning and knitting, http://www.stonesockfibers.com

Olga Buraya-Kefelian tutorials and patterns https://olgajazzy.com/techniques-tutorials/

Knitting charts

https://stitchmastery.com

Other techniques

Fair Isle knitting, weaving in the second yarn: there are various teaching videos on YouTube: look at several before choosing the most efficient.

Suppliers

https://www.handweavers.co.uk/ – overspun yarn

http://diamondfibres.co.uk – worsted spinning services

UK organizations

National organizations with regional groups, running lecture and workshop programmes:

Association of Guilds of Weavers, Spinners and Dyers, https://www.wsd.org.uk

The Knitting & Crochet Guild, which also has a collection intended to support the study and practice of knitting and crochet in the UK: https://kcguild.org.uk

INDEX